What people are sa~

Spiritual Beings or Economic Tools

Peter Strother's writing is powerful, challenging and yet deeply comforting, speaking to our time – a time when many lives are confused and uncertain. It has a real ring of truth about it and because of that relates to the situation many people find themselves in today. Globalisation and technology have brought the human race great possibilities but also increased our vulnerability, creating a restless generation which Peter addresses in his book with insight and tenderness. It is a book for those who believe in God and those who find any kind of belief almost impossible. Many will find in it a real sense of hope for their lives. Peter is a gifted writer with much to say and I hope this book is widely valued.

Dr. Peter Millar, author of several best-selling books on spirituality and global issues, including *A Time to Mend*, and a former Warden of Iona Abbey in Scotland

This is a perceptive, thought-provoking and timely book with real substance to it. Peter Strother's analysis of our current situation will resonate with many readers, who will be grateful for a literate description of inner and outer landscapes that is both accurate and original. His naming of a spiritual malaise and his commitment to finding a way out of it will elicit many unspoken or shouted amens.

Ron Ferguson, columnist, novelist, author of the best-selling biography of George MacLeod and former leader of Iona Community

Peter Strother has written a truly original and illuminating evocation of how we can change – not just by finding our true

Spiritual selves but by then going on to transform society through challenging the very economic and philosophical assumptions that underpin capitalism. Through a unique blend of analysis and dramatisation, Peter has brought alive our struggle for ultimate understanding and freedom that we all face today.

Stephen Richter, journalist, musician, BA (Hons) History and European Philosophy

Spiritual Beings or Economic Tools

Just who are we?

Spiritual Beings or Economic Tools

Just who are we?

Peter Strother

BOOKS

Winchester, UK
Washington, USA

First published by O-Books, 2018
O-Books is an imprint of John Hunt Publishing Ltd., Laurel House, Station Approach,
Alresford, Hants, SO24 9JH, UK
office1@jhpbooks.net
www.johnhuntpublishing.com

For distributor details and how to order please visit the 'Ordering' section on our website.
Text copyright: Peter Strother 2016

ISBN: 978 1 78279 844 6
978 1 78279 843 9 (ebook)
Library of Congress Control Number: 2016941210

A CIP catalogue record for this book is available from the British Library.

Design: Stuart Davies

Printed and bound by CPI Group (UK) Ltd, Croydon, CR0 4YY, UK

We operate a distinctive and ethical publishing philosophy in
all areas of our business, from our global network of authors to
production and worldwide distribution.

Contents

To the next generation – my daughter and son's.

Acknowledgments

To the family of my upbringing in the north of England and the people who cared for me early in my life.

To my wife, Anne, and my family in the Highlands and other parts of Scotland today.

Also to those who have been all along and still are close to me now. They all know who they are.

To Dominic James and the whole publishing team behind this book.

I thankfully acknowledge Darton, Longman & Todd and their kind permission to quote from Jean Vanier and Laurence Freeman.

Introduction

OK, I know that this may well sound extreme.

But I believe so many of us sense the truth of it in so many different ways in our daily lives.

So I will come straight out with it.

The reality that, for the most part, of what constitutes our existence on this earth, increasing numbers of us actually live at odds with who we really are.

"What?" I've no doubt some of you may ask.

So, I will repeat it again… for the majority of time, very many of us actually live cut off from a true awareness and critically an experience of who we actually are.

And it is our ultimate tragedy because, if we choose to, each and every one of us has the opportunity not only to surrender to a far higher force within ourselves, but through that to live fearlessly and to our absolute potential during our time on this earth for the good of all.

Nonsense, you may say to all this.

We know exactly who we are. And we do live to our full potential.

Others of you, however, may not be so certain at this particular stage in your life.

And perhaps because of what you are enduring in these turbulent times, you may well be asking, is this really possible?

Yes… believe it… it really is.

Because, and let's get to the crux of it straightaway, we are allowing ourselves, or feeling compelled by various controlling forces, to live apart from our original, spiritual and eternal selves.

At least many of us do that most of the time.

A realization of which begins to explain a lot to us when we look around and face up to what is really happening to us not just individually, but within our families, our communities, our country and across our world today.

Because inevitably, of course, there is a widespread and often destructive fallout to this schism in our increasingly agitated and perhaps dysfunctional lives. To this separation not necessarily from some form of religious allegiance, but more vitally from our actual relationship with and empowerment by the supreme loving force that is integral to our lives and all of life. That many personalize as God.

Just how traumatic was that always likely to be when you really think about it?

Indeed how even insane when you consider the full implications of so many of us actually living apart from the very Source of life, or at best content with a part-time relationship with it. In perhaps merely having faith in it rather than truly experiencing it. In merely having faith in a deeply compassionate God rather than experiencing His all-sustaining presence moment by moment in all we say and do.

For it must literally be – and years of struggle may teach us this, very often painfully – all or nothing if we truly want God's Spirit to take a reassuring and conclusive control of our lives. And if we truly want – once and for all – this Eternal Power to guide the affairs of our world to Divine effect.

So much so that our rejection of our 'disconnected' and therefore limited selves must, in the end, be total. However incomprehensible, even bizarre, this surrender may seem to the egotistical existence we may have built up to help us survive within the system that largely governs us today and which invades so many parts of our lives at this time.

A system that instills a sense of self-preservation and self-accumulation, and therefore of recurring need and competitive conditioning into us, and is therefore, predominantly, an expression of humankind's faithlessness and, as a result, its fear apart from the spiritual and eternal.

Something else we must face up to.

Hence its increasingly obsessive preoccupation with securing for itself and us some kind of illusory earthly 'salvation' through the monetary and materialistic, which will inevitably, of course, always fall short of answering deeper anxieties about our mortality. However much we may amass, very often at the expense of so many others in our world and our planet.

Highlighting the heart of the conflict between what the system offers to us and, at the same time, demands of us compared to what God does. And our consequent struggle to summon the time and energy to explore what our lives on this earth are really about. Until, in time – perhaps even a long time – our perspective is transformed absolutely and we begin to feel the liberating effects of turning in a whole new, bold and inspiring direction.

First of all though, we must begin to expose just why it is and what it is about our daily existences that increasingly seem to make this so difficult for so many of us.

Our lives which are dominated more and more by the pressurized, all-consuming nature of the governing order, so much so that many of us end up searching not just frantically but often desperately for this detached, personal salvation of our own. As we put our own personal economic and material wealth way ahead of the infinite sense of surety and contentment that ironically is already available to each and every one of us.

This is the calamitous deception about capitalism and its bigger brother globalization that this book will challenge and help lead us out of. Into no less than a full realization of just who we are as primarily spiritual beings united within our Universal God. Capable of experiencing His conscious, loving, outpouring presence, living dynamically through us, right now and every day, for the ultimate good of all, including ourselves.

For the apparently separate, yet relatively superficial and even automated lives very many of us have ended up living up to now have never and will never reflect who we are essentially.

They are merely a manifestation of who we are led to think we are, constructed on top of our original natures. Something, I have no doubt, that many of you may sense or even know already.

Now, I would like to say straightaway that this is not simply another attack on the capitalist system per se. Of course, very often, at least in some parts of our world, it can exhibit humankind's instincts to support and improve the human condition, particularly for example when helping to fund vast areas of healthcare, education and overseas aid.

But critically and to an increasingly greater extent this is now being compromised by its more blinkered, ruthless and tragic expression of man's frightened and, in the end, futile attempts to save himself amidst his illusory sense of an existence apart from the Divine. An existence which, of course, cannot possibly transform to any enduring effect our global community, never mind ourselves and our ultimate fate.

For how can it? If we ignore who we really are in God and don't let that supremely omnipotent Spiritual Force confront the full scale of what is actually happening. By expressing its loving, giving and unifying consciousness within and through each and every one of us, as inherently it must, first and foremost.

Even with the most humane of intentions, we will merely put off the radically selfless actions that need to be taken as we continue instead in putting the furthering of our anxious 'isolated' selves at the heart of much of what we think and do.

Now, for what it is worth, though in many ways it is important, I can assure you that any road to enlightenment I have been on has certainly not taken me across three continents on a converted rickshaw or into a tree-house retreat for two years in the Himalayas.

I don't for one moment doubt the potential worthiness of many such explorations for others. I have merely been led on a different path. The homeland path of personal striving, times of 'success' and 'failure,' and finally... finally absolute surrender to the spiritual, which – and this may be why it is so pertinent – is, in fact, well trodden by so very many of us, at whatever stage we are at.

It is also the central route to exposing our illusory images of ourselves as finally we see them for what they are.

Whatever our particular circumstances, the journey very often becomes one of desolate proportions, as, in the end, we are forced to tackle head-on the sheer senselessness of our attempts to control our own destiny, perhaps slouched down in some after-office bar somewhere. Or at the end of another shouting match with those who deep down we love so much. Or after yet one more desperate night rummaging around the Internet.

Ironically, it is precisely then, just when we may have given up hope and submitted utterly, that we are finally ripe to be filled by an extraordinary power in that very submission. A power that deep down and all along we may have sensed to be right at the center of who we are. And in the deafening silence of our despair find that the Life-force within that silence will not only reawaken but reassure us. In my case, almost about my right to a place in this world, such is the intense sense not just of dislocation I and many of us can feel within our competitive and often divisive society, but also the wider abandonment.

As our instinctive sense of communal belonging (reflecting our spiritual unity) is very often denied by this individualistic world that seems so alien, I believe, to so many of us.

Many of you, I am sure, can relate to these emotions, albeit, I repeat, in a multitude of different ways or through a multitude of different crises. And therefore I would like to go on to say to you that that is why, inevitably, we all share so much, because, in the end, we are all vulnerable. Vulnerable and ultimately in fear without a genuine and recurring awareness of God's presence within each of us. An experience of which will eventually lead us to rediscovering our true and, believe it or not, Divine identity.

But we can only rediscover it if we can summon the courage

to face up to our deluded state and sometimes blind insistence that our part in capitalism's relentless search for ever-increasing and therefore unsustainable growth is somehow our primary or even only hope of feeling ultimately secure at the end of the day. When inevitably it is so limited, so plainly unstable and so very often unsatisfying. At the same time sidetracking or even derailing us off our true quest.

Hardly surprisingly as it doesn't even begin to understand God as the origin of who we really are, of our eternal being, of all that He brings to us. As it focuses instead, however unintentionally, on squeezing us out of the time and space to explore our essential truth in the depth we need to. Beyond the, to a degree, rigid and even superficial dogmas that prevail within elements of institutional religion.

We must not let it do this.

We must not let this system overwhelm us with its incessant demands.

We must not let it manipulate us with its artificial sense of need.

We must not let it delude us with its ceaseless distractions.

We must not let it intoxicate us with its whole variety of excesses.

The scale and consequences of which our world does not fully comprehend, as what is deemed 'normal' is largely determined by those in power. So that we may not be fully aware of just how dysfunctional all our various individual and collective actions have become throughout our often chaotic existence, nor fully conscious of the overwhelming cynicism and negativity that have engulfed us as a result.

To counter all this, what we must do is summon, with God's help, the resolve to surrender to Him over and over and time and again. So that, as His enlightened consciousness reawakens within us, we can and indeed will, at long last, begin to see right through this increasingly indoctrinating system and to challenge it head-on.

To see it for what it truly is as no less than an anathema to who we really are.

To our genuinely empowering and loving spiritual nature in the Divine.

Feeling broken or a 'failure' in this world is not something that any of us should feel ashamed of. Nor is feeling poor, ostracized, oppressed or merely ground down. Indeed it can be our very saving, if, in our suffering, we do not run away but bravely face up to what we are experiencing. And then discover, in time, in our deeper searching, that the values of a compassionate, all-embracing God could never, in any case, have possibly been the same as this incessantly profit-driven and therefore often ruthless order.

Indeed, they couldn't be further removed from it. Something we recognize completely when we truly wake up, particularly on a global scale, to what it is committing more and more on a daily basis against so many billions of people in so many enslaving and life-depriving ways out of its insatiable greed.

Something that explains so much to us when we begin to see through it.

Something that clarifies so much for us when we become fully conscious of it.

Something that liberates each and every one of us when we can finally admit to it.

Admit the inescapable truth that fear, born out of not truly experiencing God, really is the very catalyst and driving force behind the extremes of capitalism. And that the present widespread level of chaos and despair reflects just how increasingly adrift so much of humankind actually is without a revitalized awareness of and access to the everlasting spring of life.

Our world has now reached the stage where it must choose either to believe and trust entirely in the supreme Spiritual Force behind our lives or not, and critically allow it to live through us or not, for the good of all, including ourselves.

We cannot continue to feign a surrender to God, or even practice a partial surrender, and then blindly or partially ignore Him. As we go on relying on ourselves while continuing to act ignorantly, indifferently or even callously over the fate of so many others and our planet to assure our own apparent 'salvation' as many of us are doing. However unaware we may be of the implications of our various financial and consumerist actions or inactions on a global scale. And however much, at the same time, we may contribute to charitable works.

For we simply cannot give our lives up to capitalism and to God.

To capitalism's primitive urges and God's inherently giving nature.

When they are so overwhelmingly contradictory.

So increasingly irreconcilable.

One becoming increasingly exclusive to the demands of an authoritarian, if lost, minority in our world, the other being so inclusive and integral to every single spiritual being.

A genuine recognition of our ultimate poverty without God, linked to a committed and, in time, liberating sense of surrender and humility, is the only path to us opening ourselves up to fresh insights through Him that will finally herald our reawakening to our previously buried but, we will soon begin to see, Infinite Nature.

Virtually from my formative years when I was aware of being alone and crucially silent, God's voice left echoes within me of a deeper truth resonating for me to tune into. Echoes not just of my spiritual identity or consciousness, but of a loving and unifying consciousness rather than an individually competitive one. The narrow vision and pressures of our world quickly forced me to ignore these echoes, but God never gave up.

How could He when He is intrinsic to who I am? To who we

all are?

Experiences of frailty eventually opened me up wide enough to let them flow right back in. Since then I have slowly begun to realize how my gift of awareness and sense of the miracle of life were always open to me, even though I could not initially hold onto them. As I gradually learned to live both accepting and even at times celebrating my periods of marginalization in this capitalist world, however painful it has been at times. I accepted them because it somehow felt sane to be marginalized in such a world, to feel ordinary in such a world. Knowing that those emotions – not the tragically ego-led ones demanded more and more by the system – have always been essential for God to demonstrate just who He is to me.

Until the time came when He was gradually able to bless me with His extraordinary spiritual understanding, which we all seek in the end. Indeed His genuinely peaceful and yet vibrant presence, which we have all ached for so long.

God resides beyond the illusions of this capitalist existence, waiting for all of us. It is up to us to reach out to Him there. Even or perhaps especially those who may feel content within what can become some kind of comfort zone of religious reassurance, but are perhaps still drifting within the machinations of the present system.

It is critical each one of us moves entirely beyond its endemic values of self-preservation to inspire and attract not just an eternal awareness of who we actually are, but for the restoration of the true and limitless life that God always intended for us.

That even now is available to us.

What an extraordinary transformation that will provide, not just for us, but for all our relationships with each other and, at this crucial time, for our planet and its peoples.

(There is always much debate about the use of the term 'God' in spiritual writing. For in the eyes of many the title can relate to a judgmental, unforgiving and tarnished image often prevalent within elements of religion. Yet, for billions of other religious followers, of course, their image of the Divine is anything but this. What is critical, for the purposes of this book, is that God's loving spiritual nature within each of us ultimately reflects our Higher Selves. I will continue to use the word 'God' in that context. At the same time, any use of the pronouns 'His' or 'Him' should not, in any way, be seen as an attempt to limit our infinite God to the masculine, but merely to allow for ease of expression in describing our relationship with the Supreme Force at the heart of all life.)

Meditations

Meditation is absolutely critical for inspiring us on this journey of reawakening, and while it may sometimes be seen as some kind of optional activity, it is most emphatically not.

Its committed practice is both imperative and indeed urgent for the stirring, experiencing and vitally the sustaining of who we really are, and therefore the unveiling of each person's higher and unique role in our communal and global welfare.

It is not just that it lifts us into a whole new dimension and out of the mindset of this increasingly frightened and divisive capitalist world for periods of time each day, something which is essential for breaking its psychological stranglehold on us. But it also, in its humble, silent surrender back to our Creator within, re-initiates our primary source of communication with Him and literally allows us to connect with all that flows from Him. As well as the instinctive eternal spiritual unity we share with all.

When you think about it, it is hardly surprising that the ego-centered, agitated mind cannot find God. For God reflects the self-less peace which has always been deep within each of us and which resounds outside within so much of nature beyond man's noise.

Who knows how many books have been written on meditation down the centuries, which tell us how important it is. As in its committed and radical practice, it finally allows us to confront and, in time, let go of our personal fragility and apparent sense of isolation by seeing through our illusory perception of our world and our role in it apart from God. Meditation therefore can be at times a desperate, weeping surrender that yearns to be embraced by an understanding and deeply empathetic God.

Crucially though, in its observance, it is not about trying impatiently to get God to respond, but with being content with surrendering and with being absolutely still in our direct contact with Him.

For as hard as it is to accept, if we try and force a response from God, we get no response, because it would not be coming from God. It would be coming from our own strenuous efforts yet again, like so much in our anxious, even faithless lives.

The God within, through His grace, will reveal Himself in His own time, in the silent, extended gaps that emerge in our thinking, the more we put aside whatever constitutes our limited selves. As we literally move outside of our minds and allow Him to fill us with insights that reflect His nature, which gradually go on to reveal and redefine our sense of who we really are. And through that to influence and empower our everyday actions, thereby fulfilling our ultimate potential through Him.

Indeed it may be helpful as well as true to say that meditation, far from being a technique of attaining spiritual awareness or enlightenment, is, in reality, and in time, an acceptance and experience of pure enlightenment itself. Reflecting the awakening of our spiritual being, which has always been intuitively linked to God and to all we share this life with.

Now, of course, it cannot be emphasized enough that meditation demands great perseverance. In the early stages of our journey, our minds are invaded with thousands of thoughts, reflecting the speed with which we live our lives. In which case, I must have been touching 100mph.

Most, I repeat, are based on past pains, some on future

anxieties, connected to these more superficial identities. Meditation belongs to the present and the present alone. A deep experience of which lets go the past and doesn't anticipate the future in any way.

We must not allow ourselves to become over-tense about these distractive thoughts or feel we are failing because they keep disturbing us. They are perfectly normal and we can recognize them by the sense of weariness and overall negativity they bring to our lives. To counter them simply let them float away and refocus calmly, breathing very slowly and very deeply each and every moment. There are no numbers left to calculate how many times I have done that. Eventually the thoughts and the anxieties that come with them will subside as the positive, calming silence that so deeply reflects God's nature really does embrace and then energize us.

All of which helps us to understand why there is such an emphasis on our breathing.

Another possible obstacle to our connecting to God will inevitably come when we fall asleep while meditating. But again let's not be harsh with ourselves and certainly not feel guilty. Considering the pressure most of us are all under and just how tired we can become it will hardly be a surprise. In any case, it will probably only be for short periods and then we can refocus.

There are also a few things we can do to counter this.

For example, many people ask about saying a mantra or repeating sacred verses just prior to and in the initial stages of meditating. I personally do not like the term 'mantra' as it can imply some kind of mesmeric technique with which to invoke the Divine. However, a repeated word or two – for example I, like many, simply say, "Let go... let God" – can build our concentration, our confidence and our inspiration. Saying it very slowly can also calm us, at the same time dispersing tired old thought patterns. In addition, focusing on a single item such as a candle can help us, at the same time creating a sacred atmosphere, especially when we begin to view the candle in a whole new way.

Equally, with regards to the position we adopt when we meditate. Some people lie flat and open their hands out in submission. Others sit up with a straight back because they feel it helps their alertness. There are numerous other positions. Whatever, what is important is that you select your most relaxed but at the same time attentive posture and then stay with it. After all, it is the ease and concentration of our position and approach that counts, not whether we do it standing on our heads or sitting on top of the garden shed. With the presence of God feeling less and less resistance as He begins to flow through us.

The time we spend on meditating is another question often asked. It takes a while to settle into a meditative state and to let go. So 30 minutes twice a day is generally considered a minimum especially in the initial stages. Even a few minutes here and there on top of regular times (bathrooms are good places when you have kids!) can help us to refocus throughout each day on just what is true and real amidst so much illusion. At the same time giving us the opportunity literally to restate and thereby reaffirm our relationship to the Divine. Be assured every action, every effort will have an effect, not just on us, but on all those we go on to connect with.

Walking and even slow running meditations – importantly, of course, in quiet spots and mindful of each and every step – can also be very effective in immersing us in the present moment beyond our daily busyness, allied to the peace and silence that nature can bring to our often restive souls. They also provide a welcome and inspiring contrast to indoor sessions. Some people I know do one walking and one sitting meditation each day, interspersed with other short, quiet periods.

Wherever and however we meditate, however, what we should always remember is that there should never be any competitive and therefore stressful element to it. We are free of all that now. What really matters is that we trust our instincts and propel ourselves forward both in the depth and quality of our surrender and our awareness of who we are actually surrendering to. It is to the God who is within each of us and to His all-loving nature, which ultimately is our true nature. Never take this for granted. In time, we won't just believe it, we will experience and know it.

For meditation is not just a fresh, alive and powerful antidote to all that we face each day; but with its direct links to God and our awareness of who we are in God, it is the ultimate antidote. As finally we allow His consciousness to transform our personal perceptions (as well as global) and to embrace, nourish and fulfill us fully. Not just for our benefit, but, in the end, for the benefit of all those who we feel inspired to communicate with, to share our natural peace with, spirit to spirit, further dissipating any vestiges of a self-centered, mere survivalist ego. Until over time the practice becomes a lifetime's commitment and absolutely central to our very way of being. As well as offering an example to so many others.

I appreciate all this may sound very difficult at the outset with family and work pressures. But I can assure you that the time spent meditating on and unveiling what has always been right at the heart of us is immeasurably more beneficial than so much of what we do when we pause from our daily activities.

Again, it is a question of choice.

A choice that can liberate and empower us.

By revealing nothing less than our selfless, eternal state.

Both in and beyond this world right now.

Now, as to this book and the meditations at the end of each chapter. I have discovered over many years that reflections and even inspired experiences prior to meditation have helped me focus so I can more easily open my heart up to God.

These appendages are certainly not intended to hold up your own meditations – for your own surrender, your own outpourings, your own spiritual reawakening in God are what are important – but they can help. They also come in multi-various forms, as you will discover, because variety and freshness, I firmly believe, can only aid us.

As I have said, we live in a world, very often, of preconditioned, pre-programmed, secondhand thinking that in the end can dull, drain and deny any instinctive feelings about who we really are, and has for so long now that many of us struggle to see much beyond it. So much so that we can lose not just our sense of the astonishing miracle that is our daily lives, but vitally of just what our all-creative nature can express authentically through us.

Consistently opening ourselves up to God in silence and in depth, to nothing less than an emerging awareness of His unifying presence within, which then flourishes over and over in all we do, literally lifts us into this whole new way of being. A new and fearless way of being, which, in the end, expresses our Divine identity for the betterment of all.

Modern-Day Parables

For the most part, the modern-day parables interwoven within the chapters ahead reflect the many ordinary (and yet, what is potentially true of all of us) extraordinary people we have all shared our time on this earth with over the years.

They do not appear to indicate, on one level, overly dramatic lives – most real people's aren't. Yet they do reflect what so many of us endure during the great struggle within innately eternal beings, who increasingly feel something eating away at them amidst such a limited and enslaving economic and materialistic existence. So much so they become desperate to be awakened and to see through to a sense of who they truly are.

We are not alone. That is what these very personal accounts tell us. We never have been and never will be alone in our courageous search for our ultimate identity. As we discover that every single one of us has the potential to connect not just to our higher spiritual self within, but then through that to each other.

These stories, in the end, are a testament to this. That is their essential message. They are happening right now throughout our world in so many lives. That is why it is vital to read them and to relate them, inevitably, to our very own. As God seeks to implore each and every one of us to confront our own everyday agitations and anxieties, at the same time choosing to be transformed by His infinite power. A power which reveals an all-loving quintessence that is, in fact, innate within each and every one of us, and which we must unearth and express at all costs.

Part I

Conflict: Confronting Our Enslavement Within the System

Chapter 1

Miracle of Birth

When we are born, our mums, dads and even grumpy old granddads all have their hearts melted by the sheer miracle of who we are.

No wonder.

We are a miracle.

Each and every one of us.

Anyone fortunate enough to be present at a birth knows it is one of the most incredible experiences of our lives. There is something amazing (and painful!) about experiencing creation at work. And it's live too, not on TV, or via the recorded highlights at 10:30pm with slow-motion replays.

It can even inspire questions about who we all are, about our actual identity, our eternal identity, which we may have sensed and explored when we were younger, but which in our pressurized daily living, may have, unsurprisingly, become dormant.

But it all comes back at that moment of our baby's birth. "Yes," we suddenly realize, "life is a miracle." So awestruck, are we, so somersaulted out of our often rigid routines.

"It's a boy. No, it's a girl!" shouts dad. So overwhelmed is he, everything can become confusing. Asked to put on the first diaper, he almost puts it over the baby's head.

Maternity staff that have been through it a thousand times are still moved. They hug the dads as everyone dances about like lunatics, losing themselves completely. Well, I did at any rate. Mum, already in a delusional state, perhaps through various drugs, as well as total exhaustion, now believes she is really in the land of the fairies. What the baby makes of it, Heaven knows. The moment remains with us for the rest of our lives.

The moment does.

But for the reasons I am touching on, not the constant realization that our entire life is a miracle.

But we should realize it as a God-given miracle. The light from which must not be dimmed. It must not get lost somewhere. Because what a thing it is to lose.

It is not like losing your glasses.

Especially since during those magical, if tiring, first few days when our baby is first brought home we may be put more in touch with our instincts for life than at anytime perhaps since we ourselves were children.

As, in our new family's fragility, which we can feel so acutely, many of us may sense forces far greater than us at work. Now that we are taken out of our zone of relative security into an unknown (more noticeably perhaps with a first child). And forced to trust in that unknown, and not just in the health visitor, whether we realize it fully or not.

Particularly as dad, in these early days, may continue to act hopelessly. Often upsetting the baby by picking her up the wrong way. Indeed, the more he tries not to feel awkward, the more he may look like awkwardness personified. "Here, she's not a bag of coal, give her to me," granny may tell him frequently.

Another reason it is such an extraordinary time is that many of us allow nothing to intrude into our private celebration of new life, away from the daily thought patterns of work. Indeed everything becomes refocused for this all too short a time as we surrender wholeheartedly into an extended present moment that reflects so much about our natural state. And can be such a wonderful opportunity to connect intimately with that natural state.

As we may even encourage the baby's siblings to join in as they are introduced to their new sister or brother, bringing offerings of scrawled drawings and bits of half-eaten chocolate brownies. For they too are discovering and celebrating this miracle of a new life.

Some of it perhaps sparking memories of the story of the baby Jesus in the stable in the Christian faith, with Joseph on paternity leave from his carpentry business. The sense of miracle from that story and the image it represents, both in our hearts and minds, remains one of the warmest and most poignant many of us will ever envisage.

And it is hardly because of the consumerist, sensationalist overkill that has been made of Christmas. It is, of course, in spite of it. Our hearts cry out for it to be reenacted somehow in our lives, together with the genuine hope which it generates.

Even for those of us deeply skeptical about our relationship with God or the spiritual, it can still somehow represent a whole new, yet inherently familiar, inspiration in a world crying out for a whole new inspiration.

Inevitably, however, lurking in the background is our re-immersion into our all-engulfing, work-obsessed age – closer to 5–9 today rather than 9–5 – with all that that entails for many of us and our new families.

Because just as the Christmas scene must end for another year, so perhaps does the sheer wonder of our precious allotted time with our newborn baby, as either dad returns to work or mum, or more than likely both, very often with increasing haste nowadays.

We feel our reluctance and instinctive pain deeply, because of the often overwhelming nature of what is really involved, but we will just have to get on with it.

In any case, what else can we possibly do, we are forced to accept. We have completed our maternity or paternity leave, which at least we were grateful for.

So, in the end, we cuddle our baby, perhaps even cling to her as we say goodbye for the day, almost as if we sense we are clinging to something even more precious than a newly born child (which in many ways she is).

Of course, if we are fortunate enough to be able to afford it, and if we choose to, one of us may be able to stay at home. But for the majority, the West (never mind beyond the West) is an increasingly expensive part of the world to live in nowadays. The capitalist and consumerist system, by its nature, demands that we work more and more, to pay for more and more, so that we then have to work more and more. On and on. With our humanity, with who we really are at a deeper level, under ceaseless strain.

Whatever happened to one wage being enough, which it was for many when we were somehow supposed to be less well off? But now we're better off, it seems impossible. As so many of us are tragically driven to need more of what we don't really need (and which doesn't last) at the expense of focusing primarily and caringly on everyone we are close to, especially our families, never mind ourselves.

And therein lies the true source of our torment – not our need to work, but far more the often intense and blinding pressure of the system that now drives it and affects us so deeply and in so many different ways.

To such an extent that *Who Wants to Be a Millionaire* won't be some unlikely fantasy very soon. More and more of us will have to be millionaires simply to pay our ever-increasing bills, and those of us who aren't able to will be cut adrift, as so many already have been (especially across our wider world) and many more will be soon.

Cut adrift more and more from what we require simply to subsist, after being cut adrift from a deeper exploration of the spiritual by our absorption into the system's all-pervading forces. So that, in the end, we may be left desolate and terrified by what is happening to us, especially in a climate of overall economic volatility and, in time, general global depletion. A desperately vulnerable state which may at least force us to search for the ultimate purpose behind all our lives, to explore and rediscover our deeper connection to the spiritual. If only we are courageous enough to surrender ourselves to that.

Peter's Story

For months Sally had been on about buying some new Greek temple-like conservatory. The planners must have been off their heads to accept it in the middle of a housing estate but a few had already been approved.

"Pete, for once in your life, splash out," she said right in front of the salesman, who had been there an hour before I even got there, but wasn't put off by me reminding Sally about our lack of money. Whatever, maybe I did need to let go for a change, especially considering what Sally seems to go through every day. So, what the heck, in the end, I did.

Stop worrying, it'll work out, I kept being told over and over.

"A Greek conservatory will be different," Sally said later. She wasn't wrong there. Though, looking at it, I doubt Aphrodite ever sunned herself in it, despite what the brochure claimed.

Soon after we signed the contract came news which meant we'd also be having to find enough to design a baby's nursery as well. Something I didn't begrudge, don't get me wrong.

In spite of everything, I was ecstatic about becoming a dad, particularly as Sally had been uncertain about having kids and we'd had to wait quite a while. It was just the timing with the 'Greek Temple' around my neck.

But still, for our first child, for our little girl (Sally found out the baby's sex so she could make plans), there was nothing I wouldn't do for her.

So I simply tried to suggest to Sally that maybe our baby could live in her room as it was for a short while. "But what about that ancient wallpaper? And those secondhand curtains? Not to mention the wardrobe space that she'll need," she replied.

"But she'll only be a few days old when she gets here, love. I doubt she'll need to hang up her diapers," I made the mistake of suggesting. "Nor will she be into color schemes just yet, will she?"

"What are you trying to say? You know how important all this is to me." I'm not altogether sure where she was coming from with all that but still she knocked me down.

Stupidly I had one more try, especially as it was Christmas time, which was also killing us money wise. "Talking about Christmas, Sally, what about Jesus when he was a baby? I bet he didn't have designer curtains in that stable, did he? I bet he even had a few drafts in there," I suggested.

"Yes, but our daughter will not be Jesus," she replied, and walked out.

There was no real answer to that.

Back at work after the birth, my boss and everyone else were decent enough at first, trying not to put me under pressure straightaway, but the pile on top of my desk said it all. Anyway, they were all under increasing pressure. So it was fair enough. I'd just have to get on with it.

I'd enjoyed my new job up to then, I suppose. But it was just that the extra stress I was feeling was happening at a time when I couldn't take my eyes off my daughter, who we called Jessica. Seeing her with Sally, the two of them together. And with my mum, her gran, of course.

"She's so amazing, Peter. Beautiful. I can see you and your father in her," Mum said.

"Hasn't your mum been here long enough? She'll start crying in a minute," Sally responded.

My mum's my mum though. Emotional and all that. Never has a bad word. Believes in God even. Old-fashioned.

I missed Jessica and Sally, needless to say, in the office or out trying to win new clients or checking on existing ones. But at least when I was out I could phone on the mobile to chat to them for a minute or two.

I must admit I had to dig deep just to keep my head above

water. I overheard my boss, Geoff, saying, "I'm sure Peter'll get round to it soon enough." Even though he didn't mean to be like that. I don't know why I wasn't keeping up.

Pretty soon, I started coming home late from the office. And had to phone Sally to tell her. "What! Your daughter wants to see you. I've had her stuck in here working all day. How long are you going to be?" I told her I was on my way.

Eventually I got my workmates to answer the phone just like everyone else did. "Peter? Yeah, he left five minutes ago."

Part of me was sure it would all get easier but then there was talk of us failing to meet targets and rumors of offices being merged, with the consequences we all know of when that happens.

It wasn't the first time, but you didn't know what to believe. It was just with me having a wife and a baby, as well as paying off so much, of course. I managed to keep the rumors from Sally, but she heard it from someone else, needless to say.

"Well, are you getting the sack or aren't you?" she screamed, banging the doors around the house. Restricting me to the Greek monstrosity, which seemed to shake quite a bit for a temple and certainly wasn't paradise. "What do you expect? Me to go back out full-time again? And how am I going to manage that?"

I eventually reached the stage where I decided I had no option but to bring work home with me, if I was going to make it home at all, even if it wasn't what anyone wanted. Especially when a big part of me was just desperate to spend some quality time with my family, with Jessica, during the evenings. Even if it was just for a short while.

Wanting to cuddle her before bedtime.

And watch her gently fall asleep.

Minding her every movement for a little bit.

Listening to every beat of her heart.

Being with her... who is part of me... part of Sally.

All of it something somehow amazing that... that was, I don't know, in some ways, way beyond me.

"She's part of God," Mum said to Sally.

"Tell your mother to go," Sally demanded. "She's been here all afternoon."

"She's just trying to help," I said, knowing just how much Sally missed her own mum, who was stuck down south and seemed incapable of leaving her own house and coming up.

"Well, she's not helping!" Sally replied.

I know this all sounds daft and sentimental about what I felt about Jessica and all that. But I couldn't seem to help it. If I'm honest, I still couldn't fully believe that she was actually here now, living with us. And more than anything I'd never felt so... I don't know... oddly alive, I suppose. And yet kind of... insecure about things as well, in a weird kind of way. All since she was born.

"That's part of just how wonderful it all is," said Mum, when I told her, even though I didn't really understand what I was feeling.

I began to realize that something strange was happening to me because of the way I felt about Jessica. It was affecting the way I was looking at a lot of things. That's maybe why I wanted to be with her more. Not all the time, of course. Just a little more than first thing in the morning and last thing at night. To be with this overwhelming... love I felt for her. And Sally despite the increasing strain.

In truth, I'd never felt anything like it.

Not that I would have tried explaining it to some of the guys at work. But on my own I was struggling to understand it. And somehow didn't just want to let it go.

The only way I could truly explain it was to say that I'd die for Jessica. That best described what I was feeling: I'd die for her and Sally. And for some reason, I wanted to hang onto these feelings. Increasingly it irritated me when I had to ignore them.

In the end, I had to keep working till midnight or after, two or even three nights a week, so I could spend some time with my family during the early evening. So much so I even began to doubt whether I was really up to the job it was taking me so long. Maybe I wasn't.

Things with Sally also started to get more and more difficult but I knew she was trying hard most of the time, by building up orders for her clothes-repairing business from home. And I really felt things would work out in the end.

She went to bed before me every night, of course, but occasionally when she woke up, she would come down and put her arms around me for a moment. Almost like she was a different person, more relaxed being half-asleep. Even though I felt tenser and even grumpy, maybe because I had been in front of the computer for so long, someone at work said.

"Just coming, darling," I would always say. Getting cold, she would quickly go back up, no doubt knowing that I wasn't coming. I was cold too, as well as tired. But I couldn't afford to keep the heating on that late.

Then suddenly – just as I thinking things were getting a bit more stable – we were all told we would have to work all day Saturday, not just some Saturday mornings. To "maintain the quality of service our customers are increasingly demanding," my boss said awkwardly. Another smaller office nearby had been shut and we had to take on their workload. No one in our office wanted this, of course, not even our boss.

Needless to say Sally stayed angry about the Saturdays for weeks. But what was I supposed to do? We were both getting upset and frustrated with this special time of our baby growing up with us.

Very slowly I felt more and more... tension building inside me, day after day. I held it all inside at work because I had to. So you can guess where it was going to come out. So finally it exploded around those I loved the most.

But we all have limits, don't we? Or was I just becoming the "bastard" Sally suddenly said I was one night?

"Had another enjoyable day at work while I've been stuck slaving away in here?" began to aggravate me more and more when I drudged in exhausted. I knew Sally didn't really mean it, but still she said it. We were both beginning to say a lot of things we didn't mean even though I still felt we loved each other.

Like it was... not really either of us who was saying it.

It's just that I couldn't get that ridiculous Greek temple out of my head, which Sally just had to have because her friend, Jenny, went on some fancy holiday to Athens. And this was the best she could do to imitate her. Or to comfort herself in here. Because increasingly she just doesn't seem to be able to go out of the house like her mum, for whatever reason.

A... a fad, that's all it is, which I began to throw at her every time we went in there! But then, just as if everything I had said had made absolutely no impact, she suddenly showed me yet another catalogue which had a such and such deluxe bathroom in it. Almost as if she was totally deaf, and we weren't in debt already, far more than she realized. No wonder with how increasingly expensive everything now was.

Every few weeks I began to feel like I was... crossing some kind of limit of what I could cope with. Like I was desperately trying to hang on. Because of the love that I felt, even for her, who I still managed to cuddle in the few hours of sleep we had together.

It was the only time we felt truly close.

When nothing could get at us somehow.

When we were almost in another world.

Some peace, even... intimacy at last.

I even whispered, "I love you," and snuggled closer.

I'm not sure she heard me.

She was probably asleep.

But still I said it.

Then, a few hours later, we woke up.

Initially we felt warm to each other.

Even caring.

As we had once been.

Then we were forced to release.

And to go our separate ways.

A separation I just couldn't seem to do anything about it. So much of what I now did felt like it was something I really didn't want to do.

I didn't really want to... live like this.

Even to... be like this... if that makes any sense.

"But I can't stop it!" I screamed inside myself. "I just can't seem to change things." I didn't know what was up with me. Never getting on top of things!

And this also came back... somehow... to Jessica and even Mum and what I felt when I first saw her born. To this... I don't know... feeling of being so insecure about things more and more. But also the... love.

Wanting to feel... really alive through this love somehow. Some hope of something... different through it... even, I don't know, of some... kind of meaning through it... whatever that means. But I didn't really have time to think about it or even to talk to Mum about it. So, in the end, I was just left feeling that my family and I were being shoved and dragged here, there and everywhere, except where I really wanted us to go.

"We need you to work out of our city office twice a week, Peter. The company is trying to widen its catchment area," our boss suddenly announced to me at work, again totally out of the blue, as I passed him in the corridor.

I simply stared back at him, quickly trying to work out the time I'd have to leave in the mornings... and what time I'd return at nights.

"Look, I know..." he smiled, kind of uneasily.

"Well if you know what this is going to do to me and my family, why the hell don't you stop it?"

No, of course, I didn't say that to him. In any case, it wasn't his fault. Nor would it have done any good. It was just the way it was and I would just have to get on with it like everyone else. What else was I going to do?

Miracle of Birth 2

It's vital we make time, however difficult that can be, to look into this question of our underlying sense of unease and vulnerability, which so many of us feel deep down, but may never fully confront. Whatever may finally spark our awareness of it, in order to move forward positively from it (and, in time, inspirationally), we must explore just what is at the root of it and why we very often struggle to face up to it.

It is ultimately, of course, generated by our deluded sense of separation from God, which blocks us off from nothing less than His eternal and therefore reassuring presence.

No wonder there is such an undercurrent of anxiety about us.

Cut off from our instinctive realization of who we really are.

From the Source of all we require to live to our maximum potential.

And no wonder we try to compensate for this in so many tragic ways.

By primarily responding to the demands of the governing system to attain and then expand on an economic and materialistic identity which cocoons us (and, for some of us, our families) from our apparent sense of spiritual isolation, mortality and, in the end, oblivion.

A cocooning, however, that only exacerbates our feelings of disconnection from God as it focuses us continuously on our own attempts to secure some kind of impossible earthly salvation, rather than on surrendering ourselves to His all-sustaining spirit in our lives. On trying to build up our own sense of all-knowingness and even indestructibility. Even though our deeper sensibilities suggest there just may be one or two limits to them.

Never mind our deeper sensibilities about globalization's continuously egomaniacal, very often toxic approach towards the fate of our planet and its peoples during these highly unstable days. Which is even leading more and more of us to ask whether anything really seems indestructible anymore (apart from God).

Indeed, did it ever?

Those suffering the ongoing effects of mass corporate greed and economic volatility; those whose lives have been devastated by environmental catastrophes increasingly brought on by man-fueled global warming (even in the West, of course); together with the peoples across our world who live in terror of violent reprisal perhaps following peaceful protests over multinational operations – would all tell you otherwise. And so would the many individual folk everywhere increasingly struck down by stress-related illnesses, a whole variety of addictions, family disintegration, social breakdown and an overall sense of bewilderment.

Therefore, many of you closer to home may well know this too.

However, if remarkably some of us still think we can entirely determine our own fates (or our governments that of our world), we may be far more in need of therapy than anyone has ever imagined.

As we fail to summon the humility and courage that is vital to inducing any essential admissions of vulnerability and then, in time, a gradual stirring of our primary spiritual identity. Until, tragically, old age is on the horizon or we face some overwhelming personal crisis somewhere along the line. As we continue to content ourselves with a superficial relationship with God for most of our lives or none at all, enduring so much random fear and anguish along the way, cut off from His guiding presence.

All of this reflected over and over in our often wayward, frantic modern-day struggles for life, which continue to ignore so many warning signs on a daily basis:

"Look, I'm late for the meeting, that's why I'm driving fast! The car's only doing 80mph. Stop worrying, for goodness sake!"

"OK, maybe they were chest pains! But I'll be fine. I'll get them checked out when I've got time."

"Who cares about rising global temperatures right now? The sea's not going to engulf us overnight."

Gambling recklessly with our lives (and those of future generations) far more than many of us realize, while, at the same time, ignoring completely the extraordinary awareness and empowerment that is potentially alive within us right now and has been all along.

In our heart of hearts we also know that our failure to confront more fully our personal and indeed worldly vulnerabilities (seemingly separate from God) is perhaps because we see them as indicating a lack of individual strength to succeed ourselves. Something that we know will not be tolerated within this largely competitive economic order which we adhere to, and therefore within our increasingly pressurized and even manipulated minds.

Therefore they must be buried. Or we may appear less than super-efficient and suffer some desperate humiliation, disgrace or even dismissal. As we are coerced into believing that it is solely our illusory ego which we ultimately must have faith in. And that we really do not have the time to nurture our own inherent spirituality in any depth, even if some persistent part of us is still appealing for us to do so.

So that our real god, I repeat, then becomes the god we surrender to within the capitalist system or our role in it. A god whom more and more of us now realize will accept nothing less than increasing demands of us, as well as profiteering and exploitation by us, whether directly through various forms of work or indirectly through our ignorance with regards to so much of our consuming and investment. All part, very often, of the gross subversion of our humane instincts and even of our care for our fellow human beings in this world.

Reflecting the system's manipulative nature and the inherent fear that drives it, to the point where more and more of us, and society in general, end up trying to submerge this schism within us.

Whether it be with regard to the credit company that we may work for which forces us to exploit those who we know cannot afford the loans we try to tempt them with. ("Yeah, why not borrow £20,000 for that brand new car you desperately need?")

Or our bank investments in the giant corporation that chops down the rainforests across our globe. ("If we don't some other foreign company will.")

Or our purchase of fruits from our nearby supermarket which have been sprayed with insecticides by unprotected workers. ("We are constantly vigilant about the practices of our local supplier.")

All of these conflicts nagging away at our essentially caring souls so much that they may even start to torment us. As we struggle to wake up fully to the inescapable truth that it really is not possible any longer to have faith in such an increasingly destructive order for our survival and an all-caring, all-unifying God.

Eventually the recurrent discord in our hearts and minds will begin to lend more and more of us becoming dysfunctional or ill long-term.

Indeed, of course, it is already doing so.

If some of us still somehow doubt the severity of the division within us, and continue to justify the so-called 'moralistic' capitalist existence many of us live, we have only to ask ourselves whether we – that is our true and Divine natures within – would really countenance the exploitation, enslavement and preventable deaths of millions of our fellow human beings every year in the name of profit? The reality of what has been happening and continues to happen globally through the tragic actions of an economic elite.

Actions which are responsible not just for the impoverishment and starvation of these lives, but for the suffocation of the spiritual breath of so many more of us, who would respond far more decisively in confronting their misery if we knew the full truth. But instead have become compromised, tormented and, to varying degrees, lost within the system.

Very few of us are immune to its debilitating effects, whatever we may appeal: "This has nothing to do with me. I don't enslave the poor. I give to charity. I do!" And this will, very likely, be the case, as very many of us are indeed genuinely caring as that is one of our inherent qualities deep down.

But until more and more of us consciously choose (for God has always given us free choice) in favor of surrendering entirely to our greater spiritual identity, we will continue to get caught up in, however unintentionally, some aspect of a system whose primary aim will inevitably be larger and larger excesses for itself, all in order to help preserve and even intensify what is, lest we forget, an illusory sense of who we really are.

For whatever capitalism/globalization may claim about itself, whatever changes it may claim it is making for the better (and, I repeat, it does work for the greater good in some areas), the problem is still and will always be the system's primarily survivalist and ever-expansive nature, with its actions, in the end, determined by us, its operators and our sense of spiritual disconnection and resultant fear.

Actions not only at the cost of upcoming generations across the world, but also, more and more of us are beginning to see, at the cost of our own children's disconnected, turbulent and increasingly fragile futures.

The irony and tragedy though is that there is no disconnection from God and never has been. There is only our authentic selves united within His love and care, and through Him, all of humankind. Something we will only start to recognize the more we are able to surrender to who we truly are and then, in time, react intuitively to what we truly feel, to what is crying out deep within us, rather than merely continuing to do as we are told.

So that in time we may finally be able to join with so many others in facing up to our underlying vulnerability within the system, and then, through God's revitalizing presence, start to gain some enduring insight into what has really been happening to us all for so long.

Until eventually, in our growing spiritual reawakening, we all begin to express the voice of the Sacred within and to challenge en masse the stranglehold that is being intensified every year. To such an extent that we might even go some way to following the peaceful but challenging path that the Christ of the Gospels pursued all those years ago and which He now wants us to take. He the ultimate representative of ultimate truth, who confronted those in power in His time.

As we start to die to our egotistical selves and, both liberated and liberating at the same time, become more and more conscious of the greater journey ahead for all of us.

One thing is for certain, each one of us must never feel there is no option to what is increasingly bearing down on us, which is so often rooted in this faithless system. We do not simply have to step into line anymore or to turn consistently to the whole variety of 'must haves' or other addictions on offer, or simply to apathy.

As tragically we bury this critical vulnerability of ours, which God is desperate to embrace. And which, if we are brave enough to face up to it, brings us genuinely alive not just to a conscious and eternal sense of who we really are in Him, but to a sense of what He can truly accomplish through us during our free and extraordinary life on this earth.

The alternative is to accept our lives being taken more and more out of our hands, until it feels like we are mere hand puppets in a game of Punch and Judy.

There is not a lot of slapstick fun, however, in getting beaten regularly about the head, even if it is just psychologically. Until, eventually and inevitably, our inherently peaceful natures become more aggressive and, in time, we scream back.

Dehumanized ourselves, we may eventually, of course, begin to dehumanize those around us. Not just at work but even more at home where very often we feel compelled to control and mold those we love, especially our children, so we can manage them within the limited time we have with them. In other words, their behavior must come within the parameters of what we can cope with under the level of harassment we endure.

"Put that thing down, put the other thing away, don't get that out!" In other words, sit down and shut up, or, inevitably, "Oh, go on then, stick on your smartphone!" We've had enough.

As we reluctantly decide that their freedom to explore, play and to express themselves instinctively, creatively, wondrously, even naively within God's extraordinary earthly realm (which we, of course, begin to lose sight of under this level of pressure) must be curtailed. Because there is only so much unpredictable and disordered activity we can deal with when we need to be so ordered ourselves.

So we rein them in pronto and they had better obey or perhaps suffer the consequences of unrelenting nagging and worse in some cases. When our tension finally snaps and any true vision of who we all really are gets lost altogether.

"What's wrong with the belt now and again? It never did me any harm!" may even be the desperate, desolate, not entirely stable defense of some, at least some of the time. As others of us try to contain our frustration by merely strangling a toy hippopotamus under our children's terrified gaze.

It is, of course, a persistent pestering and even abuse that we are suffering ourselves and are now transferring on, such are the stressful demands of our work, not to mention so many other areas of our life that the system invades.

Until, in time – hopefully far sooner rather than later – we emerge from this wholesale conditioning and are opened up to the most horrific realization of all: oh my God, we have merely been preparing our children for what we ourselves have been going through all along, against our better instincts!

Generations programming generations for the same increasingly automated and tragically misdirected way of life. At the same time, limiting our infinite Divine potential to reach out way beyond the desperate parameters that the system has set for us.

Peter's Story 2

"Quickly, Jessica. It's time for bed. It's half-past six, no nearly ten to seven." I exaggerated the time, of course, so hopefully I could put her and her brother, Robert, to bed early. What else was I supposed to do?

Asleep, the two of them couldn't distract me so much so I could quickly finish the work I had left while Sally was unloading our online Saturday shopping, which increasingly seemed to take half a day, we ordered so much.

I suppose I sometimes found it a strain looking after them, I have to admit. I wished to God I didn't, but I did. Even though I still loved them to death, of course.

I tried to play football with them earlier and managed it for about 20 minutes. I was actually enjoying it so much that I forgot the time. Then the sun went in for a moment, I remembered my work and said, "It's going to rain. Get in, the pair of you."

It was just a passing cloud. I felt terrible, of course. And they moaned, "Ah, Dad..." Their surprise and even... sparkle, I suppose, at having me out playing with them disappeared. They became naughty, especially Robert, who's only three and a half.

But then they don't realize just how much I have to get through in order to keep Sundays clear.

Even though that was just an excuse. Because the bottom line was I wasn't prepared to play with my children for more than a few precious moments. And what's worse, I knew it. Every time I knew it.

My mum said I should try not to get so tensed up and take it easier. "But you don't know just how far behind I've let myself get," I told her. I could see from her face she was sympathetic.

"Things'll work out, love. Least you've got a job," she said, which I suppose was true.

Whatever, I kept trying to convince myself that if I could earn enough to ensure that Jessica and Robert got a decent education and a better job than me, it 'ud all be worth it. Then they could earn loads of money and could afford all that they wanted and everything would be OK for them. Thinking like that kept me going.

I also listened to Bob at work telling me exactly what steps he was already taking to get his kids "ahead of the game," which seemed to make sense.

Whatever, with my two in bed at last, I got back to my work. Quickly, before Sally came through with our special dinner she was preparing. She was trying to "put the spark back into our relationship," she said, with chicken biryani and a new DVD called *Mayhem in Chicago* or something. So the time I'd got now was important.

The last thing I needed to hear was what I heard. The dreaded footsteps and whispering. Robert was creeping downstairs, frightened. "What is it this time? A pigeon on the roof?"

"No, I... I saw something in the dark, Daddy. It looked like an alien. I want a cuddle," he said.

I realized he was more frightened of disturbing me than he was of the alien. My own son was frightened of me. But still he reached out to me so, of course, I cuddled him.

I cuddled him, and then, after a short while, felt so... comforted myself, I suppose, that I... almost found myself clinging to him. Relieved, strangely, at what it brought me. From what I... constantly seemed to feel...

I sighed deeply into my son's neck and sensed this... permanent kind of... worry of mine, or whatever it was, but also, at the same time, feelings of deep, deep love for my children... my family. The only way I can describe it all.

I kissed Robert back in his bed. He asked for yet another cuddle and to have the light left on. To hell with the electricity. I left it on. I went back downstairs with my emotions bouncing off the walls. I felt like some... gaping wound, or whatever, that kept opening wider and wider.

But I still had to face what was in front of me and the reality was that more time had been lost. So I had somehow just got to shut off these emotions and quickly start again. The phone went almost immediately. Instinctively, I picked it up as if I was in the office, which was where I really was, of course.

Immediately, I regretted it. It was my mum.

She was lonely and needed to talk. Dad had died two years ago the day before. I had meant to phone.

I tried as hard as I could to listen and to respond, but it became increasingly difficult. Especially when she began to ramble on about anything and everything, not just about Dad. Just wanting to be close to someone. To me, her only son, naturally enough.

"Yes, Mum... yes, you told me your old friend Barbara has cancer... of course... of course I remember her... yes, we're all fine... yes, Jessica's fine... Robert too... hey?... no, Sally and I haven't had tea yet... yes, of course, I heard what you said... you had scrambled egg on toast for tea... no, nothing's wrong... I'm just a bit tired tonight, that's all."

Not just tonight but most nights in truth. I was even tempted to hang the telephone over the computer screen so I could carry on working. Especially as I could hear Sally reaching boiling point in the kitchen.

Finally, Mum said, "Well, take care, love, you and Sally take care." I could tell she was worried about me, though I tried to reassure her. She knew all about stress. Dad was 67 when he died. She'd warned him to take it easier, but he found it difficult.

I put down the phone riddled with guilt, needless to say. This time I left the phone off the hook but sensed it was all going to be too late and true enough a couple of minutes later Sally announced, "Dinner's ready!" I leaned back in my chair in frustration, screaming inside.

She cheerily popped her head out of the kitchen, "Come and help me bring everything through then!" she said, trying so hard. I wanted to pull down the house with my bare hands.

"Would you uncork the wine as well, darling?"

The coup de grace, however, was still to come.

"By the way, I've been looking through a Laura Ashley catalogue and I've just seen a really lovely couch, which would be perfect for us."

I now felt like Robert's alien in his space rocket on take off. A rocket that had already counted down. There was no stopping it. Sally came in and put her arms round the back of my neck. Trying to put the spark back into our relationship. "Come on, this is our night tonight. I've been looking forward to it all day."

Something that I knew was true. And which I knew was important for someone in her situation, who for the life of her just couldn't seem to stop herself getting so anxious so much of the time. Like more and more people nowadays, she told me. According to something she saw on some TV program.

But still, for all that, what Sally didn't realize was that she really shouldn't put her arms around the neck of someone who is sprung as tight as a coiled spring.

I struggled desperately to fight it but my wife's touch began to make my flesh crawl.

So much so I just couldn't stop the tension inside me from

exploding any longer and I jumped up yelling, knocking her clean over.

Jessica's timing could not have been worse. She's seen and heard so much in her short life that she should not have seen and heard. She came downstairs in tears after a bad dream about a monster, just as her daddy was finally turning into one.

Perhaps I **was** the monster in her dreams.

An increasingly out of control monster, who more and more had less and less to give. Any goodness or kindness in me, whatever you want to call it, felt like it was being sucked right out of me. As hard as I kept trying to stay calm and to stop it happening.

Sally's bewilderment quickly turned to screaming and even wailing. Jessica was mostly just terrified. However much I loved them, I felt that who I was turning into was largely out of my hands.

Or was it? Maybe it was just me. It was all my doing. I just couldn't cope with anything. As simple as that.

Needless to say, as much as I apologized, the meal Sally had cooked and the Laura Ashley brochure were thrown into my face. And it'd be a Saturday night and Sunday of sheer hell with her before I returned to work on Monday. I had that to look forward to.

As I was forced to sit in tortured silence in front of *Mayhem in Chicago* as if there wasn't enough mayhem all around us. As our love for each other continued to disintegrate under the pressure I was putting everyone under.

Indeed, far more than pressure. For I was also left to reflect on how I had just managed to scar my daughter with the sheer ferocity of the verbal abuse I hurled back at her mummy, for what she screamed at me.

Miracle of Birth 3

The economic powers can not only end up controlling, but also consuming and agitating so much of our lives that any glimpse, not just of the spiritual and eternal, but also of the compassionate and peaceful that are innate within us can fragment from time to time.

As the competitive and sensational are promoted and paraded.

While the loving and sacred are demoted and debased.

As we, and even our children, become faithlessly and fearfully absorbed into a predominantly inflexible mentality of work and materialism certainly for ourselves, but especially for our impatient masters.

"Root out the under-performers and the unproductive and those not responding to the demands of the market," the industrialists and politicians tell us indirectly and even directly, their language so often confirming the rigid and unforgiving nature of the governing order.

So that very often over-driven and alienated, as well as disconnected and depressed (no wonder, apart from who we truly are), many of us may search around for some sort of temporary cure to the schism that pulls us apart. Some form of addictive relief (however normalized, I repeat, in today's society) that, in our deeper bewilderment, will at least keep us functioning within this capitalist system. And keep us responsive on a daily basis to the demands of our bosses, who, so often, are so utterly indignant that anyone could possibly want anything different.

"The rewards are there for anyone who works hard. So what's the problem?"

It's as simple as that apparently. As simple as the myth that any one of us can make it to the top, whatever our background. So we can achieve the lofty status of the rich and superrich. Even if we somehow see that as the ultimate purpose of our lives, as reflecting the sheer miracle of who we really are no less.

Examples of ordinary folk becoming successful and powerful (and now even celebrated as almost godlike, of course) are constantly wheeled out onto the media stage. "Let's give a big Tuesday morning welcome to billionaire entrepreneur and business guru, Sir Elliot Elbowgrease!" who then proceeds to tell us how his master plan is open to each and every one of us.

Against this barrage, we can even begin to lose any sense of fulfillment and indeed gratitude for an inherently calmer, more contented, more balanced vision for ourselves and our families. Never mind a vision of God at the heart of who we are, guiding us all, providing for all.

With instead the ultra competitive, expansionist perspective slanted and glamorized as if it is the pinnacle of what we ourselves should be aspiring to. Where we may judge others (or feel judged ourselves) according to our individual wealth and material standing, or lack of it.

Judgments that:

Merely classify and categorize us.
Undervalue and undermine us.
As well as disunite and disconnect us.
Both those who believe in the superficiality of their poverty.

And those who believe in the superficiality of their riches.
As the extraordinary potential within each of us is blocked out.
As Divinely-inspired and therefore genuinely free individuals.

And these are not judgments which just delude people of relative prosperity in the West, of course, but these are judgments that are tragically dividing, degrading and even destroying the lives of millions of innately spiritual people across our world.

With increasing numbers manipulated by their apparently less 'developed' status and even more vitally what globalization entices them with that they very often feel compelled to sell off rural, communal and supportive ways of life, linked to their spiritual heritage and culture, that may have been passed on from generation to generation. (That is providing they have not already been bulldozed from their land by some multinational project or impoverished in numerous other ways.) Before trudging off with so many others to swell the numbers of the unemployed or exploited in some large urban expanse somewhere.

Either that or their younger folk are duped into choosing to emigrate to potentially luxurious lifestyles in economically wealthy Western countries. Without fully appreciating the conflict and sense of estrangement that may engulf them as a result of surrendering who they ultimately are and what they already have to alien, often far more demeaning, meaningless ways of existing in various sprawling international cities.

The system meanwhile is largely unconcerned with the large-scale fallout, on so many different levels, of its one-track ideals. As it focuses instead on continuing to export itself and thereby undermining the ideals of the innately self-sufficient, frugal and content wherever they may be.

"Capitalism works for anyone. It gives us all the chance to grow within it. In any case, it's the best system we can come up with. Man needs the sense of drive it brings. He is a competitive, aggressive animal. What else would he do?" is the desperate plea of some that completely disregards the truth about how the more fear-driven, ego-led effects of the economic order are undermining more and more humankind's instinctively caring and peaceful nature.

By crucially ignoring who we are first and foremost. With little time available for us to stay connected with or to reconnect to our spiritual awareness and all that it expresses through us. In public or even personal denial too of the natural fragility that we dare not show and which just might open us up to God's genuinely transforming presence.

As either we exploit millions of our fellow souls on this earth in order to rake in totally unnecessary excesses or we ourselves are spun in a continuous cycle of demand, stress and reward, which aims to 'get the absolute most out of us.'

All of this, of course, reflecting a way of existence that, I repeat, so many of our children are increasingly being prepared for, wherever capitalism's ideals are paramount, including within many of our secondary schools through the burdens being exerted on them. Where more and more pupils are primarily being molded for various profit-obsessed sectors despite the best efforts of many aware teachers. And very often against the calling of their higher spiritual natures, which are given little opportunity for nurturing at such early ages.

So much so that education can even begin to take on the air of a punishment rather than a pleasure.

Is there really so little value in encouraging the kind of silence and contemplation in their daily lives which would allow a connection to a deeper consciousness and creativity essential for a wider perception and empowerment of life? Where unfettered by habitual fears, pressures and perpetual noise their hearts and minds could reach out way beyond the competitive and consumerist horizons that are laid out for them. In order to discover whole new insights that, taken together, might begin to help address humankind's crisis of meaning today.

Each of our children is capable of instinctively absorbing so much more about who they really are and through that the miracle of their earthly lives and the extraordinary possibilities they present.

But instead and tragically, they are being designed to fall into line with the same limited concept that economic success encapsulates the ultimate meaning of life or largely determines people's worth both individually and on national scales. As measured by the apparently sacrosanct Gross National Product of countries (unless you happen to come from happiness-centered Bhutan). Reflecting a blinkered ideology which isn't interested at all in other features of what makes us who we are, on a far more profound and, indeed, definitive level.

In many countries of our world, of course, children are forced to compete in the workplace from primary school age on in acts that can only possibly be described as child slavery. With poverty the root cause of parents' tragic decisions to let their children grind away in factories for a pittance, with multinational companies and other businesses callously exploiting them in the name of increased profit.

Many children are even forced to work as domestic servants or sex slaves from very early ages around the globe, with forced labor in the private economy now generating an estimated $150 billion a year, according to the International Labour Organization in 2016. With God, no doubt, in tears that humankind could ever conceive of, let alone tolerate, such brutal treatment of her young.

Whatever happened to our children's hearts being allowed to roam free, their intuitive links to the spiritual and nature being given the space to be unveiled, as well as their individual personalities the chance to unfold gently. All of this underpinned critically by allowing their deeper instincts the opportunity to take root by, in effect, trusting fearlessly in God. As instinctively they are guided by Him to fulfill their unique potential.

Inevitably, there can be a tragic consequence to all of this. Our Western world is a testimony to the increasingly dysfunctional effects of whole generations of youngsters (and in time, of course, adults) being faithlessly separated from their innately spiritual sense of who they are.

So much so, whether still in education, or out trying to survive in this competitive world – whatever brash or even aggressive front they may put on – more and more now feel frightened, insecure, lost and mutinous like never before. Rebelling angrily against continuously being torn away from something they may feel so passionately, even if they do not fully recognize it for what it is.

Indeed they sense the anger of other teenagers at this.

The anger of their parents.

Never mind the anger of other adults.

And, unlike their elders, they have not yet gone through the years of assimilation and addiction within the system that programs them into controlling that anger.

Well, some of us control it some of the time!

At their still-vibrant age, they are fervent enough to be in touch with an instinctive call to be free. So much so that continuously pressurizing them into becoming 'responsible' young employees and accumulators in such an increasingly desperate way only alienates them further long-term, storing up potentially destructive and self-destructive problems.

Until, fractious and increasingly in turmoil, they finally unleash this rage. Not just at home, school or in college, but on our streets and in our bars. And the established order responds again by saying, well, if institutionalizing them isn't enough, we will have to incarcerate them.

What a desperate, terrified policy, which always fails to get even close to answering the question as to 'Why is this happening?' in the depth required and is therefore doomed to failure. Just so long as we continue to come up with yet tougher solutions of 'how' to deal with what are, in the end, the divisive consequences of the system.

All of which is playing a very dangerous game. As denying what is instinctive in us all may well explode into a wholesale disaffection or even a desire to drop out altogether (from living) if you keep suffocating the essential consciousness of people more and more.

Either that or they sink into the abyss of wholesale technological addictions, which involve them in subsisting in virtual reality existences.

Throughout the Western world, in particular, we have been seeing signs of all this for a long time now. In the United States, capitalism's chief headquarters, the whole world looks on and senses the seething resentment. Indeed, it hardly came as a shock that a UNICEF report released in the spring of 2013 put that country fourth from bottom of a league table of the world's most advanced economic countries examining child well-being. However, it was right at the top when it came to putting people in prison and having the highest rate of both illicit and prescription drug use.

But still so many of our leaders and even some of us continue to go along with this desperately limited vision, however reluctantly or not. A vision perhaps conditioned by our own rigid upbringing, which very often insists that only a strict re-imposition of moral and religious education, which critically, of course, does not root the spiritually experiential and truly transforming into daily lives, will somehow restore some sense of order.

Policies, which, of course, suit the established order as it hardly wants our children and young adults questioning its core values from such a potentially radical and genuinely liberating perspective. Such is the depth of fear of its advocates and their need to maintain their control and security, however illusory it may be.

A depth of fear and a failure to confront it that, in the long run, is the most critical obstacle to us discovering our ultimate being in God and living our lives far more in harmony with who we are for the good of all.

For where else will a genuine reawakening of humankind spring from and crucially be sustained? Other than from our absolute surrender of this fear to the spiritual, ultimately to the supreme and universal force that created each and every one of us.

However enormous the task – and the enslavement of so much of our lives within the collective thinking of such a seemingly omnipotent economic superstructure is extraordinarily intimidating – we shall, in the end, discover that there is no alternative to submitting to this revolution deep within ourselves. Something which we gradually come to recognize by the initial turbulence it creates in our lives. With our whole sense of identity very often ripped apart and our underlying vulnerability exposed like never before.

A state which, over time, if we find the courage to embrace it and to go forward with it, will almost miraculously and paradoxically allow us to feel both broken and deeply loved, and both insecure and increasingly secure. As we begin to reconnect, however gradually, with our original natures.

Something we may begin to glimpse and then realize the longer we are able to sit peacefully looking out in wonder from a panoramic hilltop. Or we make the time to immerse ourselves in the vital silence of a vast cathedral, temple or mosque. Or perhaps even more significantly, while right in the midst of modern family life, we insist on staring longingly and lovingly into our baby's crib... all the while fragile and yet becoming incredibly alive... recalling moments of pure instinct from our own early childhood.

At these points, and during a multitude of similarly enlightening moments, each of us has the potential to grow more and more intimate with God's everlasting presence, as gradually we become assured about what is really required of us for our daily lives on this earth.

Through acting according to His selfless nature.

Rather than our egotistical selves.

Acting according to His Divine will.

Rather than what we are programmed to do.

Or are often compelled to do.

Now that we feel inspired to make daily positive stands wherever God leads us.

For example on behalf of our own children, by switching off the advertising on TV, which tries to make demanding consumers of such susceptible minds. Or we may even decide to join campaigns against those who are content to poison young bodies (never mind ours) with the additives they throw into our food. Or finally (and most crucially), we may at long last challenge head-on the dogmatic mindsets of large corporations and governments that, by their very actions, are threatening the very future of our planet.

All the while as our reawakened sense of who we really are emerges and finally we act not just upon what we feel but indeed upon what we now know is right for ourselves, our families and people everywhere. So that our lives are no longer filled with unfulfilled regrets, especially in the case of the nurturing of our own flesh and blood.

But the realization, at the very least, that we have tried our absolute best to give them the opportunity to unearth their spiritual inheritance no less. So that it can begin to guide and sustain them in all that they say and do.

Peter's Story 3

Jessica still dropped in to see Sally and I now and again when she left home. I always loved seeing her and, if I am honest, dreaded her leaving... especially, I suppose, the older I got. Even... the lonelier I felt if I'm honest. She was still, in so many ways, the little girl I couldn't take my eyes off all those years ago.

OK, I had to accept, she had developed a different kind of smile, a slightly... strained kind of smile maybe. But then that's fair enough, it was just her age. Many of them were like that. I was forever asking her, "How are things, love?" And all she ever said was,

"Fine."

Sometimes though, I had to admit that I felt like I couldn't quite reach her, like I used to. You know, inside her. Like... I don't know... there was some kind of... barrier between us.

She'd done well at the two schools she went to. She was very bright. Don't know where she got that from. Certainly not me. Though she only had a few friends, a couple of her teachers said. Then she went onto university, which I couldn't really afford, but I'd been left a bit of money by my uncle and I had secretly saved a bit myself, so we somehow survived, making sacrifices as you do.

She did well at university too, but it was then that she really grew more distant from me. In fact, she seemed sort of... distant and disinterested in a lot of things except her work. I put it all down to her age again.

"I'm just busy, Dad. What can you expect?" she said.

After she left, she was so well qualified she became a chartered accountant for a top company that dealt mainly with the larger businesses in the area. I couldn't believe it – my daughter! My hopes fulfilled. I couldn't believe her salary either. She didn't actually tell me what it was, but I accidentally saw it on a bank statement when she visited once. I was very proud.

Looking back on it, though, I couldn't really remember when I began to have doubts about her state of mind.

I recall meeting her friend, Rebecca, who she brought home one night. The two of us sat waiting for Jessica to come downstairs. There was an awkward kind of silence, like she was trying to say something, before she asked a strange question.

"Do you know how Jessica is?"

I didn't know what to say. "She's... fine. She seems fine."

"Yeah...?"

"Yes..."

Then Jessica came into the room. The following day I spoke to her myself. I asked her how she was. And, of course, she said she was, "Fine."

I suppose that should have been some kind of clue to me that everything wasn't right. Maybe it was a sign of my generally... weary state that I didn't really look into it enough.

The phone call from her boss was the beginning of the ordeal.

Jessica had not been to work for over a week and no one knew where she was. She had left a message on her desk saying simply that she was going away. She didn't answer her mobile or reply to e-mails, and there was no sign of her at her flat either. We weren't in her contacts' book, which she had left at work, so they had had difficulty contacting us.

"Just what kind of communication do you keep with your daughter?" her boss asked, almost angrily. It didn't make any sense. Needless to say, I became really worried, almost frantic.

All I could say was that I didn't know where she had gone but I'd ask about immediately. Jessica hadn't in fact been in touch for nearly two weeks. Or… even a bit longer, I suppose. I didn't understand how I had allowed that to happen. Or why she had not said anything to me. Why hadn't she?

The only person I could think of who really might know was her old friend Rebecca and fortunately her name was in the contacts' book. For a couple of days I left increasingly anxious messages on her answering machine. But she didn't phone back.

I was even on the point of making enquiries with the police when suddenly, right out of the blue, I got a postcard from somewhere in the middle of Australia. All it said on the card was:

"Hi, Dad, I'm fine, love, Jessica."

Nothing more. No explanation. Nothing. Was she on holiday? Without getting permission from work? It didn't sound like her. Had she met some guy and gone off with him? Why was she almost giving everything up to go to Australia? It didn't make any sense to me as hard as I racked my brain.

I eventually got round to telling her mother one day. Not surprisingly, she couldn't throw any light on it either. "That girl's always been a mystery to me," she said.

I should say here, by the way, that her mother and I were living apart for a time by then. A time that was getting longer and longer. With me living in my mum's old house, after she had died. I just called around now and again, more than likely when she was having another panic attack. I'm afraid I hadn't a lot left to give her by then except some financial support. I felt like I had tried, for so many years, but somehow I had just become so tired of so, so much.

In truth, I felt like I'd nothing much left to give anybody, except somehow to my daughter…

Then suddenly, one night, very late, her friend Rebecca finally phoned back, sounding a bit drunk. Despite the state she was in I tried asking for more and more information. I even pleaded for it because I felt she must know more. But there was none, she insisted.

"She sent you a postcard and told you she was fine, didn't she. What more do you want?" was all she would say. As if that should just be that.

I didn't understand. Didn't understand any of it.

Over the following weeks and months, carrying Jessica's postcard wherever I went, I began to be really affected by the thought of just why she had gone away. I kept going to work, of course, but if I wasn't really there before, I certainly wasn't now. And, needless to say, they noticed quick enough.

Deep down, I… slowly became aware that what was going on inside me may even have been more than about what Jessica was up to. As alone, back at my mum's, I finally had some time to myself. And slowly began to wonder about something that I had perhaps sensed a long time ago, but had failed to think much about. So much so I had almost forgotten about it.

When somehow I hadn't… allowed myself, or more likely, knowing me, been… brave enough to look into… I don't know… the possibility of something more… something more about my life… however difficult that might have been, of course, with Sally and the kids and the house.

And the bottom line is, I suppose, that I had somehow regretted that failure… wherever it might have led. Feeling that either I had just taken the... easy option or more likely was just not up to... exploring something different or... even looking at things in... another kind of way somehow.

Whatever, one night, I suddenly wondered just what would my mum make of me now? If she was looking down on me? She'd still love me, of course, because that was the way she was.

But I felt somehow that she might be in tears at what 'ud become of me – living on my own, no future, sitting here, with, in truth, not enough money put away despite all my years of work. Perhaps all along, I don't know, she had been trying to tell me something as best she could, which just may have offered something...

But why had I never made the time to listen to her? Or to reflect on what she said?

Why was I always so... anxious so much of the time, I felt?

Could I be in any worse state than I am now if I had listened?

All these feelings, in time, began to overwhelm me. So much so that I didn't just begin to wonder about growing old, I really felt that I was and fast. Nor did I seem to be able to do anything about it. Except stare at some postcard from somewhere in Australia that nobody had ever heard of like it meant something...

Maybe it was all too late for me. I was probably stupid to think it wasn't. But eventually things all came to a head one weekend when I got so low that it suddenly dawned on me that I had got absolutely nothing to lose by making drastic changes to my life.

I sensed somehow that I was heading for an incredibly... lonely existence here in this small house. And it scared the hell out of me.

So I swore from that moment on, as ridiculous as it sounded, that no one would tell me what to do anymore, whatever might happen to me. OK, it took another week to really build up the courage, but I finally decided to resign from the job I had been doing for so long. Despite all the fears that were hurled at me both from outside and within.

"What'll you do? You can't do that at your age. You're getting old. You'll end up living in a garbage can," I heard a hundred times. And I woke up terrified every morning while I was working my notice. But the one thing I somehow felt certain about was that nothing had any chance of changing without big alterations in the way I was living.

Of course, I was also desperate to see Jessica. But something again told me that this wasn't really about her.

Especially as I began to put a few of the pieces of her life together. And I sensed that, just maybe, I don't know, she really was a bright girl, who was... somehow working out what was really right for her, whatever that meant, whatever I may have previously thought... as slowly I began to see her... life in a different light. Something I told her in a letter addressed to the post office of that small place on the other side of the world, which she may or may not get.

I also believed that she still cared for me, and who knows even loved me deep down, sending me the postcard, which gave me hope and made me feel a little less alone. And just as she was making major changes in her life, maybe I would try to do the same, wherever it led me, however late in the day. Even if it meant it was the end of me.

So what?

I was already dying in my mum's old house.

I had died in my marriage.

And I had long ago died in my work.

As I finally realized just how depressed I had been for so, so long.

Realizing all that was what... freed me, I suppose.

Realizing that was what really opened me up...

At least to the hope, who knows, of some new possibilities?

That demanded that I try something different. Even if I had to work in the local diner or the nearby zoo, or wherever, to make ends meet. I was under no illusions.

All I knew was that change was the only way.

Of getting me out of this desperate rut.

That was much more than about work.

Sally, my ex-wife, not surprisingly, did not respond very agreeably to my new ideas about things. "What are you talking about?" She had always been terrified of change despite the state both our lives were now in. I had no idea just how vicious people can become when they feel their security being ripped away from them. But then Robert, Jessica's brother, had moved out six months ago and I suppose I was now exposing her completely by leaving her and who knows even the area.

But I knew there was little else I could do to help her anymore. Me hanging around only seemed to make her even angrier. All I could do was what I did, which was, yet again, to suggest some counseling through her doctor, but she just got irate with me as usual. She just seemed to have been a victim of something, which over time has increasingly overwhelmed... and even paralyzed her for some reason.

No one has any idea what it is like to live with someone who is so scared so much of the time!

The thing was I had loved Sally once upon a time. When we used to get out. And even in our early years at home before the house... everything in the house... everything about the... nature of the house... seemed to... close in all around her.

I still thought back to those days and nights with her and Jessica. But sadly there was nothing left between us now whatever may happen to her. I had not been able to see a way out of the... way we were living and still couldn't for her. In the end, I felt I'd failed as a husband.

At least though, there was still time, however late in the day, for me to try something else, however... vague and even... ridiculous it all seemed. By stepping out into something completely... different. Which may or may not end up with me reconnecting with my daughter Jessica at some stage in the distant future.

And maybe even... I don't know... apologizing to her or not. For perhaps not always... listening to her as I had wanted to... or talking about things as we used to... even though, at the time, most of what I did seemed... OK.

But nothing seemed right, or wrong, or certain any longer.

Everything seemed incredibly... uncertain.

Not just for me but for all of us.

And, more than anything, it was terrifying.

But somehow... strangely... that did not seem all bad.

Somehow... strangely... there was some hope in it all.

Meditation

Looking back, those of us who are older may view our childhoods as, to a degree, idyllic and even dreamlike, largely devoid of responsibilities and worries. All at a time when we were allowed to develop freely and securely in a largely unthreatening world.

Few of us would claim that is possible now, however, for many of our own children. Nor does it take studies and reports to tell us what we are already know. That many family homes, in so many ways, are increasingly out of control and even dysfunctional, with parents or adults, unsurprisingly many would say, projecting their own anxieties and fears in such a pressurized daily existence onto those who they cherish and love the most.

We do not mean to, sometimes we are desperate not to, even as we are doing it, but when it comes down to it all that we have left, very often after years of conditioning and manipulation, is raw emotion, with little sense of tranquility, even in our reserve tanks.

Nearly 200,000 children phoned Childline in the United Kingdom in 2008 desperate for help, according to the Children's Society in that country. With one in five children and young people having mental health problems at some point, and one in ten having a clinically recognizable mental health disorder, the report stated. And they are the ones who were courageous enough to phone up.

UK children, the report concludes, are stressed by schoolwork, worried about their futures from an early age, and at the same time having to deal with issues such as peer pressure, bullying, emotional or even sexual abuse, poverty and difficulties with family relationships.

All of these familiar issues in our fragmenting culture, but issues nonetheless which we are not allowed enough time, space and, above all, an atmosphere of calm to face up to in the depth required. How can we, with parents and even children absorbed as we are within such a frantic desire to accumulate, merely to survive or simply to fit in?

So what do we do? And what do those in power do?

Merely very often, of course, declare that this or that report is yet another "wake-up call" or "reality check" for our society. While little or nothing is done radically to respond to the vulnerability so many of our children and indeed so many of us clearly feel. With our dormant sense not just of what could effectively sustain a far more harmonious daily life – our inherent spiritual reality – subdued and, very often, overwhelmed by the multi-various pressures and technological addictions of our age.

Just as soon as we possibly can, we must begin to counter the effects of this existence on ourselves individually and then, in time, as a family, through frequent (not just intermittent) submissions to the Divine, and therefore, in due course, a re-empowering of our true natures in Him. As we focus primarily on our very being rather than our always doing.

Initially, in order to aid us, we should experience something we may not have experienced for a long time that won't cost anything. As we try to reacquaint ourselves with the extraordinary miracle of just who we are and what is already before us on this earth by spending time, as often as we can, surrounded by nature. Whether it is right out in the wild or in the quieter part of a park if we live in the middle of a city. Urban life often makes it tougher but it does not have to disconnect us from that which is vital to us.

For, in the end, the aim is not to walk as far or as fast as possible, but as slowly and patiently as we can (step by step) for as long as we can, which in itself will not be easy. And to absorb as much as possible of all that is around us each and every moment, while trying to keep our minds clear of all our preconditioned and often anxious thinking. By repeating over and over a few words that reflect our yearning for our actual Creator, who is present everywhere, including within our very selves.

We should try to take in not just what we see along the way, but everything we listen to, everything we smell and everything we feel. Becoming increasingly silent and then aware, each precious instant, of our extraordinary connection with the aspect of life we are focusing on even beyond the form we are witnessing. But we must give it time to affect us, while vitally not allowing our minds to pass judgment on it. Indeed, I repeat, let's keep our minds as still as possible.

So often so much of our lives pass in a blur. We don't realize how fast we are actually moving. Anyone who has stood on the hard shoulder of a motorway will know what I mean.

We need to slow down and indeed stop. Right now.

And very gradually begin to recognize in nature, and then similarly in ourselves, life simply as it is in all its multifaceted glory. Observing something, perhaps for the first time, in the silence beyond the bustle, in the feel beyond the brush-past and in a light beyond its physical and material body. Sensing an eternal energetic presence within creation, which is nothing less than the essence of God, which, I repeat, is within us too, calling to us from within.

But, I cannot emphasize it enough, don't rush this experience.

And don't evaluate it too much. The smallest, apparently most insignificant detail can begin to enchant and to affect us. And we have an absolute right to pause and spend time over it simply for what it is, as we did as a child. And we still may do with our own children.

Again, at times, we may have to wait for our minds to be liberated from all the fears and pressures of our agitated existence that will inevitably try to drown our emerging sense of who we really are. But we should simply let them flow through and refocus over and over in this present moment, which is all that counts. Breathing in some of the slowest, deepest breaths of air we have ever taken.

Then sometime during our walk, when we feel ourselves to be altogether calmer and more alive, let's find a quiet place to sit and to stop altogether, and to meditate quietly on the sheer wonder and inspiration that is perhaps beginning to transform us. Even, in time, the humility and gratitude we may feel for all that surrounds us.

Do not worry about what other people may think if we are in a park and they are passing by. They will probably think we are sleeping or simply relaxing and wish they could take the time to do the same. Some of our growing harmony may even pass over to them. Perhaps they may even realize that we are meditating and it may enthuse them.

Never underestimate what may be going on in the hearts and minds of people. Remember, we are all instinctively at one within God's universal spirit, whether or not we are yet aware of it, and deep down wanting so desperately to reconnect and be renewed by that. By a sense of who we really are. And, in truth, always have been, if we only realized it.

After returning home, we may very quickly find ourselves confronted with the demands of our children or other loved ones. Now is an opportunity not to view their presence as perhaps an infringement on our newly-discovered peace and emerging awareness, but as an opportunity, quite naturally, to express that peace and awareness, to transmit it to them.

For example, by taking time to ask them about their day and focusing selflessly on their response. Not necessarily demanding things from them (especially if they are teenagers!), but recognizing that simply in the listening and encouragement we offer that we care. Over time perhaps very subtly touching on the journey of renewal that we are going through and that is open to each one of us.

All of this may be a lot harder than it sounds, depending on how stressed we have been. Whatever, none of it will ever be wasting time. Being at peace with ourselves and then with all those we love or simply meet is integral to all our lives and the first step on the road to learning to trust in God's all-loving presence, which can and must be awakened within us all.

At the end of this day we should again create an opportunity to be on our own, and to be still, as we discover just how we feel after these experiences. Crucially we should also reflect on just who has inspired them within us. (Experiences we should repeat as often as we can.)

Chapter 2

Separation

Very many of us live a tragically schizophrenic type of existence, to varying degrees.

Something that may sound rather extreme, I know.

But then is it when we take time to consider just how much we live blocked off from our instinctive connection to our spiritually assured and peacefully eternal natures? While feeling forced, very often, to scramble about as agitated, competitive individuals within the multi-various illusions of the capitalist system?

Scramble about determined to prove, rather bizarrely, that we can survive apart from the Source and therefore the constant resources of our actual Creator. And therefore alienated from and totally at odds with who we actually are and can potentially be in this world.

Why on earth would we be driven to do that, you may ask?

Unless we were so deluded by those ultimately frightened and belligerent souls directing the system, who try to scare us into believing that their relentless, ego-centered existence is the only one open to us too. Their fear, of course, being induced by their rampantly dysfunctional spiritual faithlessness.

So much so that many of us end up acting so frequently in such frantic, and even, at times, in such highly desensitized ways on behalf of our so-called economic and political masters. But against our own inherently caring instincts.

As if the consumerist, materialistic way of living that is supposed to compensate us for our inner turmoil is somehow our only authentic route to long-term contentment and joy, which many of us, of course, have long since felt it isn't. Especially with its draining, demanding, often destructive effect not just on our overall lives, but primarily, as I say, on our sense of who we actually are.

No wonder we feel it isn't when we bother to ask:

Is working from dawn till dusk till we're 65 (or beyond) selling some apparently essential product really as good and free as it gets? Or shoving fellow shoppers out of the way to grab some half-price shoes at the latest 'sales'? Or earning enough to convert the loft into a private gymnasium to stave off the coronary that is brought closer by this way of existing? Or voting for decrepit political parties with virtually the same, blinkered policies?

Is that really about the pinnacle of it? Is this really what life on earth is fundamentally all about for most of us? For our loved ones? Never mind any considerations of what is beyond this life.

Most of us, despite all the propaganda, suspect – indeed we may know – at whatever level, that there is something more fulfilling, something we yearn for increasingly, year after year, if not day after day.

Especially those of us who may have asked questions or even glimpsed a deeper identity of ourselves at some point, which we are given little time to explore. Even though, sooner or later, we increasingly feel that they could inspire a wholly different and liberating sense of who we really are and what we could experience in this world. Where we discover that, in order to live, we don't need, out of mortal fear, to be focused primarily on expanding more and more in order somehow to survive, in order to feel secure. Because, at long last, we can summon the courage to face up to the transient nature of our present lives, knowing that our spirituality, the essence of who we are, within our all-embracing, all-sustaining God, stretches out way beyond our deaths into the timeless and eternal.

No wonder there is so much strain within ourselves and

therefore within our societies. As we constantly do what the economic order that controls us dictates, to preserve or advance our identity within it, while at the same time many of us are crying out for that something which we sense is far more profound, yet, in so many ways, simpler.

A schism that is highlighted for so many of us when, for however short or long a time, we are finally allowed or are forced to decelerate within the system.

It may just be when we manage to take some kind of break or holiday and are less driven and frenzied to produce results. Or it may hit home even more intensely when the life of a close family member or friend, or even ourselves, is threatened with an illness (very often stress-related) or worse. And perhaps we are left lying in bed with no alternative but to plead for a recovery, rather than stumbling about trying to achieve it ourselves.

It is at this point that our consciousness, jolted back into a more awakened state, may finally realize the extraordinary opportunities that our lives are and how close we have come to not fulfilling them as we could. So we appeal for a second chance to explore and to express them more fully. And, more surrendered in our convalescence and in our time of reflection, we hopefully receive one. As our bodies are gradually restored to health and our souls to a deeper sense of what is vital to us.

At the instinctive level I have referred to, so many of us may have experienced and understood situations like these. Where, suddenly, we are freed of our worries, enslavement and addictions within the capitalist system and can glimpse a way of being that is finally in accord with who we really are. And hopefully cling on to it as we pursue it mindfully, and then unceasingly and even fearlessly.

But, for others of us, it may be sadly for all too short a time. As perhaps we don't fully appreciate what we have experienced and, in any case, we are all too quickly sucked back into the system's mass indoctrination and, yes, mass aggravation. An assimilation, which tells us that, for all its drawbacks, it would be utterly reckless to reject who we have become within its narrow but at least 'safe' categorizations. Even though our status within it, however lofty or debasing, may again force us to begin acting in ways which are in conflict with what we truly feel. Very often to the detriment of all those we are close to or work with, never mind ourselves.

As once more many of us become wearily resigned to the fact that 'there really isn't anything better.' Especially if we are soon no longer able to summon the inspiration to see beyond it in the depth required.

"I've no time to pause for breath, let alone to think about anything. What do you expect of me?" is, of course, the perfectly rational excuse we may offer. As we return to roaring around the kitchen, running out of the front door and revving off in our cars most mornings.

Absorbed into 'working all hours' and 'shopping till we drop,' however much it torments us. Even though we may sense at some instinctive level that God or our Higher Spiritual Consciousness is far more critical to unearthing our deeper selves, whereas ten hours of stress followed by 24-hour shopping probably isn't.

So that in the end, whatever our circumstances, we may well be tossed back into capitalism's enormous blender again, waiting to see what turns up or what it turns us into. But, at least, we may content ourselves that it is the blender we know.

But it is not all we know by far. There is nothing less than a whole other dimension to who we are waiting to be awoken within us. A whole other spiritual dimension that demands daily exploration, daily living and daily expression.

But what we all need, above all now, and desperately, is the freedom and space to allow for this exploration. The freedom and space to surrender to and experience a loving, eternal and omniscient force amidst such a limited, ego-dominated existence. So that our vision may be transformed gradually but, in the end, radically, with our perceptions now coming from a whole new direction, inherently connected to who we really are.

If only we can find this space facing the level of stress we are under! Work. Houses. Cars. The bills. Overtime. Children (perhaps). Rushing here, there and everywhere. No time to listen attentively. No time to talk with any sense of real meaning. Surely that is a sign that there is something wrong, very wrong.

For goodness sake, this is our God-given life!

It shouldn't be so much of a struggle either, as a consequence of this stress. Life just shouldn't be so difficult. "So bloody hard!" Like trying to eat cement. Reaching breaking point so often. For so many of us increasingly. For so many individuals and families everywhere. Communities. Whole segments of our society. Fragmenting.

Yet still, not only do those within the system that governs us largely ignore the underlying and widespread causes of all these conflicts and even personal tragedies, but crucially they will not even consider linking any of them to the nature of the system itself.

Not for one second do they conceive that *it* could be the root cause of so much that is breaking apart all around and within us. As, rather bizarrely and even insanely, they blindly ignore all the evidence and merely insist we continue on and on, as well as faster and faster, needless to say.

Meanwhile, we, the vast majority, are left sensing so much that we want to be calmer, more sentient, even more loving far more of the time. After all, this all seems to come so naturally during those increasingly rare moments when we manage to be in touch with who we really are. But very often we are just not allowed to be like this, especially with those dearest to us, perhaps just when we most need to be, facing the strain that they and we are under.

The strain to be somebody successful within the system or even just to stay afloat within it.

The system even encourages us to feel proud of our egotistical qualities the more we battle within it, even though the battle is, of course, relatively superficial and only succeeds in taking us further and further along this illusory and exhausting path to nowhere.

And away from the essential time we all need for the unearthing of our ultimate selves within God. As we desperately try to relax not just at the end of our five- or six-day week, but our hours of fixing things around the house, never mind all the damned ironing.

However, almost inevitably, all we may feel capable of doing after all this is to plonk ourselves in front of our brand new widescreen TV or to sit out with a beer under our brand new gazebo, which leaks after a few weeks and sends us into an uncontrollable rage. "Why do they make things that only last five seconds nowadays?!" (As if we don't know.) As inevitably perhaps, we become too tense and taut to open ourselves up to any spiritual surrender of depth.

Especially when the gazebo boys then phone up to remind us that we got their "extraordinary offer" credit free for two months with a free ice bucket. "So why don't you buy our latest King Neptune water fountain too?"

And we're supposed to think, "Hell, why not, what more could we want? Let's order some more of this junk."

Sometimes it can take years and years of this, of being drugged and deluded within the capitalism system, before finally, after a succession of particularly bad nights on the razzle (or whatever), we are finally brave enough to look more deeply into the mirror the following morning. And to realize what is becoming of us really is not a pretty sight. Little of what is happening to us is. As it suddenly dawns on us, to varying degrees, that we're living with a conflict that throbs right through us.

We desperately need help we realize, and not just toward some superficial lifestyle change, but so that we can be transformed to our very core. Consistently saying to ourselves as we begin our search: "There has to be some other way! There is some other way!"

Especially as our despair may by now be affecting us to such a degree that we feel as if we are existing with this sense of schizophrenia, or sense of separation from who we really are in God, on an almost daily basis. With the increasing and multi-various intellectual and behavioral disorders that can come with surviving in that state.

As many of us rush and race, and bawl and scream, and then overspend and over-consume as part of a fairly regular routine. Until the day finally comes when we recognize and accept that our behavior does, in fact, reflect others who we previously thought were losing it.

Schizophrenics aren't just people in various forms of psychotherapy. Some of us, to varying degrees, of course, are actually walking the streets, surviving with our numerous dysfunctions, many of which, I repeat, society has long since accepted as normal. As what is deemed normal is solely in the hands of the established powers of the day.

Something which explains why it is now deemed normal for so many worn-out parents to run round like lunatics all day at work before returning home to act in similar ways with their families. Drinking glasses of red wine as they exchange volleys of abuse with their children as they plead with them to get off Facebook, to turn off their mobile phones and to do their homework.

It also explains, on an even more pernicious level, why it is also deemed perfectly sane for some people to work every single day for companies that design, produce, market and sell foods and substances that are damaging to the human body and therefore to countless numbers of people.

Or even to be involved in the manufacture of instruments of oppression, destruction or so-called 'security.' Some, even more bizarrely, are even allowed to enjoy a high level of esteem within society because of their work, while at the same trying to justify their various actions, even if what they are saying is palpably Orwellian.

All of this, we must always remember, against their own and our inherent sense of who they really are.

The list, needless to say, of the conflicts capitalism stirs up within us, and how we try to deal with them (or not), is endless.

However, some may argue, very few of them relate to instruments of torture or killing.

The truth though is that millions, particularly in the US and the UK, never mind the rest of Europe and the world, are working directly or indirectly in industries involved in human rights violations or other far from caring enterprises that damage our fellow souls in this world.

People who we know may even be. However inadvertently through the provision of seemingly innocent parts, for example, or, I repeat, by investing in companies involved in such ventures. And what underpins many of these activities, I repeat, is the system's faithless and insatiable thirst for ever-increasing profits, and the need to protect the workings of that system at all costs.

In the end, we are all victims of an economic order that demands we all must pay any kind of price to preserve and indeed expand on a 'luxurious way' of life, which most people across our world have no hope of attaining. Nor perhaps, deep down, do we really want it. Certainly not at the widespread cost it takes to acquire it.

Above all, what we must all do is to wake up from this mass deception of our lives, and finally realize that our time on this earth is potentially about so much more than this.

As we face up, sooner rather than later, to the unavoidable truth that we have been abducted from our eternal spiritual identity, cut off from our moment-by-moment relationship with our actual Creator and been brainwashed into surviving in such a limiting and even destructive existence. With the inevitable large-scale fallout related to this disconnection.

In these circumstances, many of us may well have become largely what Western society makes of us when our time on this earth is as controlled as this, against our deeper instincts.

However, it is these spiritual instincts which are now beginning to awaken many of us to the full horror of what has been happening and what is now being committed, on an ever-intensive scale. As they keep penetrating our trance-like state in order to help us confront our deepest fears and apparent sense of isolation. Until finally, in time, we begin to glimpse a real sense of who we are.

Liz's Story

Each morning I wake up at 6:05 when my "machine-gun" alarm clock, as Joanne calls it, goes off.

"Why do you have to use a firing squad to bring you into the world?" she screams at me, which is ridiculous, as it does its job.

All this uproar before I've even had the chance to do my usual exercises.

I always try to get out of bed with plenty of time so I can have a calm morning, while Joanne, needless to say, turns over, wraps her pillow around her head, and wishes the day would go away. She's a fool. It won't. I tell her this every single morning.

"Why don't you go away?" is her response.

Ludicrously, Joanne does not stir herself for a further hour, not actually rushing out to her beautician's job until well after eight. I've suggested till I'm blue in the face that she should re-timetable her mornings, but she never listens.

Another reason I get up a little earlier is to do with our faulty ironing board. Every morning I try to iron my blouse for work and every second morning, or thereabouts, it collapses on me. Quite often, it seems, just when it is not going to. Then it does.

"You bastard!" I yell at it, though my real anger, of course, is directed at Joanne, who broke it in the first place and for some reason has dug her heels in about us not buying a new one because it never goes wrong for her. Or so she claims.

This fury about the ironing board, together with the inevitable headache I have woken up with, wreck how good I feel after my exercises and the power shower which we paid goodness knows how much for last month.

So I try to relax instead with my regular fruit, yoghurt and decaf coffee. Compare that to Joanne's crunchy nut corn flakes and croissants for breakfast. And figs rolls at work. I tell her nutrition should be higher on her list of priorities.

"And I keep telling you, Liz, that fig rolls are nutritious," she replies ridiculously.

Her weight is a cloud which descends over her entire life. I am the opposite. I am comfortably underweight, and therefore, for most of the time, feel good about myself.

Despite all this, I would still say that Joanne and I are... well, yes, we are still close as sisters. We always have been.

Whatever, at least we have each other.

The early rise I have made, I have to admit, is then partially wasted, as while sipping my coffee, I annoyingly start gazing out through the kitchen window into the park opposite and start daydreaming. Something I have only recently started to do and which I cannot begin to explain.

It usually involves my mind drifting back to an earlier period of my life for some reason. Or no reason more like. Until I finally wake up and suddenly have to leave the flat in a rush, which is, of course, absurd. Pulling out the plugs that Joanne will inevitably fail to pull out en route, of course.

Before I embark on the part of the day I both dread – but have also oddly started looking forward to – the 30-minute train journey to work.

The reasons for the dread are obvious... having to mix with so many strange people in such a confined space and the possibility of breaking down and being late for the office. The reasons I now look forward to it are a little more... awkward to explain – even, I have to admit perhaps, a bit embarrassing – as they involve the... vague hope, if I am honest, that we will break down.

Why would I want that? Or even think that? OK, my work is pressurized, like everyone's. And one or two of my colleagues are... well yes... highly peculiar and anxious, and therefore difficult to deal with. But it is still work, which I am grateful for, and it pays the bills. I work in insurance, by the way, which is not as dull as most people think.

Of course, bearing in mind the erratic nature of the trains, I should really go back to taking the car to the office as I used to. But bumper to bumper for 40 minutes sent my stress levels rising to boiling point and my dental hygienist, Denise, suggested the train.

Whatever, the switch to the train now means I have to leave the house at ten past seven. And, rather irritatingly, as when drinking my coffee at home, I've also recently found myself daydreaming out through the carriage window into the usual blur of green and grey.

Fantasizing that the next points' failure will not be in some grim, damp tunnel but opposite what looks like a newly harvested field on some light early autumn morning. And the railway companies (whoever is responsible, I've no idea) will surpass their usual performance with an even longer breakdown. And ask the passengers to get out and go and sit under a few gently swaying trees while repair efforts are made in vain.

And somehow under those trees, I will again return to those memories... yes, I suppose, those... strange memories for some reason... from when I was younger that have long since slipped from my mind.

All the disembarking passengers remove their jackets and coats, the men even their ties. The early morning sun is warm already and there is this refreshing breeze blowing up over the open field, which then begins to instill a gradual sense of… calm, I suppose. So much so that fleeting words that I recently heard somewhere, which I now realize I may have been sad to ignore, begin to reemerge over time, seemingly from nowhere. Words that I believe may have… suggested something to me, but I was preoccupied with other issues at the time.

Some of them may even somehow have… connected me to these memories from when Joanne and I were not just younger – we're both in our early 40s now – but when we somehow… lost ourselves… unconsciously in things. Especially while exploring the multitude of rocks down from our gran's bungalow. But where are these memories coming from? And why now, for goodness sake? My gran's been dead for nearly 20 years…

Until the ticket inspector suddenly breaks up the scene before me and I wake up to the fact that I had merely slid into yet another fantasy again! Why do I keep doing this? It is so infuriating. Losing myself completely and wasting so much precious time. I'd be better off reading a newspaper or a book like most other people. But newspapers are full of nonsense and books take far too long.

The train, needless to say, is still rattling on. And my anticipation of work quickly reasserts itself. I check my watch. We are just over seven minutes late. Like most people, I always allow for this by getting the earlier train. I open my laptop, which I didn't use to take on the train, but now I do.

Part of me is angry that I have to use it but with all the daydreaming I have recently started getting behind… at this crucial time with two important reports to complete.

"Stupid fantasies!" I chastise myself.

So I start typing quickly. Typing something that I should really have completed last night. But I have been so tired lately… so very tired… yet unable to sleep for some reason…

… I even remember building a raft on the beach down from Gran's bungalow. With Rosemary… John Knight… Catherine and Robert Thompson who were on holiday nearby... as well as Joanne. We seemed to spend a whole lifetime building that raft. An incredible adventure. Even though Gran yelled at us all the time. Lunch... tea... bed!

While Joanne and I... well... yes, deep down we just wanted to sail right away somehow. We even planned to sail away. Not from Gran and the beach and our friends, of course... but away... from... so much that seemed to... weigh us down...

Not again! Dreaming again! Now we're even coming into the station! And I'm still sitting down. My laptop isn't even packed away yet. Normally I get up opposite the plastics factory and walk down the carriage to be at the head of the line.

But I have now missed that opportunity, of course, and am instead in the middle of the carriage forced to look at a bald man sitting directly in front of me who is staring deeply into space. He glances up at me glancing at him. I quickly look away. The doors open. We shuffle forward as quickly as possible. There is no time for anymore of this daydreaming thankfully. From now on, there is no option but to focus on work.

As usual, the pressures of the day build quickly as the demands on me build. Regrettably, I have a new assistant who is not performing. Somehow I had completely forgotten she was starting today which is ridiculous. She seems nice enough. A nice older lady. But she is not performing.

"Nice is not relevant!" I quickly remind a colleague. "Yes, whether or not she is happy to make all the cups of coffee! And, yes, whether or not she has baked nice cakes for us as a sign of welcome!"

I can also hear her talking incessantly about her son, who is doing something or other in Nigeria. "I wish she would go to Nigeria," I say to another colleague, not quite so loud that the older lady will hear. Something inside nags at me for saying it, but she really is starting to irritate me.

Particularly as everything she does is agonizingly slow. And she keeps rechecking things. She is creating more unnecessary tension. She spills the coffee. I mean, I do. But she's responsible. She's over-fussy and over-apologetic tidying it, offering more of her cakes. Almost like she is wanting me to be fat, which is bordering on... on spiteful!

I come under pressure from the production manager, Melissa. I can't tell her about the older lady, of course. After all, I OK'd her.

"Next time, I'll be more ruthless," I say to myself. "No picking nice old ladies. Out of kindness." Part of me would like to. But I can't afford to. On reflection, I realize no one picks older ladies now. Why did I? The woman must be nearly 50. I need someone quick and efficient for this job.

"Not someone who bakes and chats and apologizes all the time!" I suddenly say aloud.

Monica was super efficient. "But she had to have a baby... which is fair enough... don't get me wrong," I again say to myself. My sister may be lonely and desperate for a partner and children. I am not... at least not at the moment.

The older lady has now started sniveling for some reason. I accidentally crumble one of her crumbly cakes.

Why is she so sensitive? Another assistant is comforting her and glaring at me. What does she expect? She has been doing the older lady's work as well as her own. Now nothing is getting done.

I start to breathe a little more deeply, which sometimes has a beneficial effect. However, I hear that Melissa, who is wearing a horrendous blood orange top apparently, has threatened to come down things are getting so far behind. I was supposed to be at a consultation meeting five minutes ago. A report on the marketing of a new life insurance policy was supposed to have been submitted to another department half an hour ago.

"Where is it?" everyone's complaining. I don't understand why everything's getting behind. Normally I am on top of everything. All because the older lady is crying. What is the matter with her? Finally, I decide that enough is enough.

"Right, take her out of here!" I demand of the other assistant.

"What...?" she whispers.

"Take her out to calm her down," I insist. "She is disrupting all the work. She can't possibly work in that state. She may need a doctor."

She whispers something back about the older lady only being upset, not ill. And then says something about me, which I can't fully make out.

"Why are you whispering?" I shout. "What is going on in this department today?"

Nothing, in truth, seems completely real today. Like, I don't know... everyone's acting very peculiarly or... or it's all some kind of dream. That I'll wake up from in a minute and everything will be back to normal.

"What is going on?" I again demand to know.

The older lady is now almost wailing. The other assistant says it's because of all my shouting. And quite ridiculously suggests I should calm down. When it is they who are all gossiping as usual and not getting on with things.

My deputy now says I should sit down. "Why should I sit down?" I shout. "What about Maggie Smith?" I scream, pointing at the older lady.

I sense everyone is puzzled at this reference. Perhaps because her name is neither Maggie nor Smith.

Then I realize that I am initially puzzled too. I don't fully understand why I called her Maggie Smith... until I begin to recall that I OK'd the older lady because she looks like the actress Maggie Smith. And Maggie Smith played the teacher Jean Brodie in some ancient film I watched on the telly a few weeks ago. And Jean Brodie was like my gran who brought Joanne and I up after our mum died suddenly. I was just nine, Joanne seven. Our dad fell apart.

But why in God's name am I thinking about all of this right now!

A part of me is suddenly aware that everyone has been staring at me while I have been reflecting on this. So I quickly snap out of it and realize that someone in my position cannot allow this to happen. With this amount of work to do. This amount of work that, in truth, I realize, has been building up and worrying me for weeks.

Whatever, I must pull myself together and act responsibly right now. I have worked hard to get myself into a solid position with this company. The last thing I want to do is lose it. So I really must get on top of things like I usually do. So, I quickly begin issuing instructions to everyone, which sounds authoritative and normally works.

However, today I somehow sense it is all sounding rather random. So I quickly go off to the toilet to regain my composure. Because I also sense that I haven't entirely got a grip of myself yet. I need to take some time… just a moment or two… to refocus. My headache from this morning has gotten worse and is now throbbing. I take stronger painkillers than I took earlier.

I try to breathe deeply in front of one of the mirrors. Slowly, over and over. Until irritatingly I hear someone following me into the toilet. It is the other assistant. She looks strangely at me.

"Yes? Can I help?" I demand of her because of the condescending way she is looking at me.

"I think you should know that that poor lady's recently heard that her son's got some strain of malaria out in Nigeria and unsurprisingly she's very worried about him," she replies.

She walks out. I shout after her that I can't possibly be expected to know all about the current affairs in Nigeria. But still I feel a sense of guilt beginning to build inside me. Guilt and… and pressure. Part of me senses that somehow I may have acted… unsympathetically, even uncaringly, towards this person, to whatever degree.

"How though? Why?" I ask. "I am not uncaring. I am a thoughtful person deep down. I am!"

I keep breathing deeply. Now desperately hoping that this will somehow help me recover so I can at least start to function again.

But the production manager now walks in.

I stop breathing.

Her blouse is more sunset than blood orange but just as garish as others are suggesting.

I shrink back as she comes closer.

I realize I am now trembling. And feeling utterly desperate. As well as terrified.

Indeed, I suddenly realize I haven't felt so terrified since... since way back... way back... I can't remember when.

The next thing I recall is waking up in hospital...

Separation 2

Times of crisis, ignited on the surface by the strain of the unceasing masquerade many of us feel forced to put on within the capitalist system, can in the end bring us to the brink of some kind of personal disintegration. When surviving from one day to the next can become fraught not just with a whole variety of relentless pressures, but by some long-standing torment, which eventually comes to the fore in often unforeseen circumstances.

Many of us have been there, and there are few more frightening places. Where we feel confronted with a sense of unraveling and then nothingness not only devoid of the reassuring, eternal presence we may have felt once-upon-a-time, but now of the superficial identity we may have clung onto for so long, which is beginning to fragment way beyond our control.

Certainly it can quickly become a place reflected in under or overweight bodies, or overflowing with empty wine bottles, or new tech or numerous other addictions, as well as various other (perhaps less familiar) dysfunctions. But above all it can be a place screaming aloud for the opportunity to give expression to some unremitting pain that has previously been buried by our frantic desire to survive within the jurisdiction of such an all-pervasive system.

So much so that when this traumatic experience finally emerges and begins to run amok, it very often creates a sense of helpless terror in our present, which not even our vague hopes for a secure future can do anything to becalm. Such is our sense of abandonment and isolation in that present, which is threatening to collapse all around us.

We are not, however, abandoned in this present, if only we knew it.

For God has never been separate from us at any stage.

Indeed the present is not to be feared but ultimately provides the opportunity to experience nothing less than our ultimate spiritual and eternal reality. And is therefore to be bravely faced up to – whatever we may have endured.

So much so we may discover a whole new healing, meaning and vibɩancy to our lives, as we literally come to realize our oneness with (not disconnection from) the true Source of our very being and also with each other.

At the desolate stage, however, it can seem like we are a million miles away from realizing our true identity. When we may sense that we are gazing across some battlefield strewn with so many bewildered and lost victims of our consumerist, capitalist modern-day life. Until something prompts us to move closer and we stare directly into this apparently overwhelming abyss and gradually we become aware that one of the latest bodies to be curled up down there could, in fact, be ours.

And the more we stare at it we reflect back and try to understand, with God's help, just what led us to fall into such a state.

Recalling pertinent times throughout:

Our yearning for security in our childhood.

Our striving for success at school.

Our perhaps turbulent relationships with our peers.

Our longing for love within our families.

Our searching for love outside our families.

Our chasing after some kind of employment.

Our search for recognition within society.

Our struggle to be an understanding parent.

Much of what we call life, which has always been, at least for some of the time, so indiscriminate and fragile (and therefore limiting and even potentially destructive) when lived with a sense of separation from who we essentially are. While offering obedience and servitude to another master, which deludes us into imagining that we could be safe and sound with our status in the system. With the system as the chief custodian for our lives.

But the more honestly we examine it now, the more we can see that we never could be totally secure in that status. As, in reality, all that the system ever offered and still offers us is, at best, transitory and very often distractive. Even inciting us to resort to the many illusions offered by the grandest illusion of all as temporary fixes.

Instead of encouraging us to withdraw ourselves completely from these excesses and face up to the piercing cold of our apparent brokenness apart from God, in order to find the absolute truth about our relationship with God.

Or rather, in order to allow God to find us.

As finally we allow ourselves to stumble about in this seemingly abandoned world, in defiance of everything this system has ever instilled into us about securing ourselves for the future. For, ultimately, God is to be found in this stumbling about, in what we ourselves can't fully comprehend or even grasp. Where, gradually and at long last, He takes over the vacant space previously occupied by our insistence on who we thought we once were.

Indeed, very slowly we begin to reconnect with our intrinsic nature in this space, which, we discover in time, is filled with His presence alone. Until, in due course, we become dynamically alive in Him, in direct contrast to our previous way of existing – our previous prearranged, prepackaged way of existing, careering along the production lines to some 'insured' way of being alive that is a mere imitation of life as it should be.

Reflected in judgments often summed up by, "Her path is well and truly laid out for her," or, "He's set himself up for life."

Is that really all we are? The best we can hope for? Exalted or denounced, I repeat, merely according to our work, financial or social status? Our lives done and dusted? Without the wonderful potential for God to heal us of so much of what has gone before and then guide and empower us in whole new and more vital directions.

More and more of us no longer accept this.

As finally we begin to deal head-on with deeply honest questions about the meaning and purpose of our lives. Such as:

Just what is at the root of why I continue to feel relatively happy one day but dissatisfied, depressed and even insecure and alone the next?

Is living like this really helping me to confront this right now?

Is it allowing me the space to explore what I really want out of life?

And what about my unrelenting fears about life... and death for that matter?

Indeed, how can I alter the structure of my life so it relates... I don't know... to whom I may have sensed at different times that I really am deep down?

But why do I keep feeling such a profound fear connected to any real desire for change?

Again, is it somehow connected to my everyday life? Or even the trauma of something at the back of my mind that I sense I may have been trying to work through for so long?

All of these questions ultimately related to that same old question: Who on earth am I in all of this?

That same old question that, in the end, can only discover an answer in the vast silence where God is to be found. As we sit still before Him, surrendering everything to His presence, to where He can awaken us, to where He can guide us, His voice, His insights, the place of true fulfillment.

Where we no longer seek to limit Him by searching for answers from manipulative prayers initiated by our own egos, as we cling to being in charge. But increasingly at ease, we become content to remain still in the quiet of our apparent nothingness that is a gentle slowing-down, a humble letting-go and a sincere expression of faith.

"But it is impossible to surrender that much, to be that quiet," we may say. "To... to accept I am absolutely nothing! People will say I'm mad. I'm vulnerable enough at the moment. I'll cease to exist."

All of which may seem a perfectly reasonable response to what is being asked of us. But then again, have we not searched long and hard enough already in this life for something more profound and transforming, for something far more caring and compassionate, for something that at last answers vital questions about who we really are? Isn't that really the truth?

So why don't we at least take the chance? And set out on a journey that could lead to us discovering an alternative way of being and living than the one many of us have scavenged about in for so long. Like lions wondering where their next warthog is coming from.

Well, that's what it may have seemed like for so long to so many of us.

But yet again we may hear a voice inside striking fear into us about just what it would mean to accept and then own up to any vulnerabilities. Because for so long we have survived under an economic order that has insisted we must cover up or drink away any feelings of weakness.

In order to get on.

So, wouldn't it really be easier just to be content with a superficial recovery to what we may have been going through and to get back to some kind (or any kind) of work or 'normal' living as quickly as possible? Never mind the superficial rewards of the system, especially if we are weighed down under a pile of mounting financial obligations, which so many of us are?

Surely 'keeping ourselves busy' *is* the only answer.

After all, not that many people in general (perhaps not even our family or friends) seem to be talking much about another plane of living, a spiritual sense of being, to guide us beyond this one.

Nor do many churches seem to be admitting much about *their* vulnerability and brokenness, which would at least be a sign that it would be safe for the rest of us to do that. But perhaps that's just the image you get of them through the media.

If we're really honest we may even have felt intimidated about God up to now because of the image of these 'respectable, powerful, even authoritarian' churches.

Some people talk about just how loving He can be. But just how genuine is that love, we may have wondered, especially when other impressions you get are about just how judgmental and even unforgiving He is. Especially when some of His followers merely seem to reflect what those in overall authority say? Or worse. Without being radically different. As many say Jesus of the Gospels was.

So what could God possibly want with us? With me? "When I'm clearly not good enough. Especially now, when, if I am honest, my life feels so... fragile so much of the time. I mean, I don't want to be the only one shown up or humiliated. And, in any event, He would only condemn me even more if I did approach Him, wouldn't he? And I certainly can't take anymore of that! What I need above all else is to feel... loved for who I am, I suppose. To feel... accepted. To feel... safe... and at peace."

Don't we all?

The instinctive plea of our world today perhaps – which is hardly surprising, considering that is exactly where our God of love is to be found, in the silence, in the peace, that is out there all around and even, of course, potentially within us.

Within us individually, but also very often within the shared stillness reflective of small, supportive groups in communities in many places. Something that is indicative of altogether gentler, humbler gatherings, for example, with fewer rules and regulations and less airs and graces even. Where folk are drawn together and welcomed simply for who they are. Not only un-judged, but allowed simply to sit quietly, to sigh deeply and to slow right down.

Somewhere where we are all given time – as long as it takes – to reveal and release personal torments. And, crucially, where we sense we are joining a kinship of shared frailties. With each of us helping the other to awaken God's presence in our lives. So that He can then begin to embrace and to heal us, now that we are no longer overwhelmed by feelings of shame, bewilderment, loneliness and separation, which we may have felt for so, so long.

Indeed, over time, we may find that these gatherings inspire periods of hope, creativity and empowerment, as well as ones of refuge and tears. Places perhaps far more like many recovery meetings, where, in time, God's spirit reaches so deeply into our hearts that we all begin to inch forward and then, in time, flourish through His very Being. By expressing His universal truth and love, which reaches out to people and cares for people. In silence, words and action.

Tragically, however, without the awareness and encourage-ment to join one of these of these havens, even if they should be available to us, many of us very often put a plaster over our various crises and slide back into what the economic order expects of us.

Assimilating ourselves back into something where we can at least appear to be efficient and, above all, in some kind of control. At the same time perhaps, trying to convince ourselves that nobody has noticed that we may have been going through some kind of traumatic experience or even breakdown.

Jean Vanier, founder of the worldwide L'Arche communities, used his years working with the disabled to express just what those who go to work alongside them must face up to with regards to their own brokenness. His words speak to us all about what we experience on our journey through vulnerability toward realization. And how we should try to respond:

It is not easy for them to let go of their security
and to enter a world which is different
and which is so full of pain.
There is a temptation then to avoid facing it
by doing many things,
to cover up feelings of loneliness and insecurity.
There is always the danger of throwing oneself into work
in order to feel useful, appreciated, and wanted.
It is important to take time
and not rush into things.
There are many forms of culture shock,
so people need to be patient and gentle with themselves.
People need to be reminded
that they have not come so much to do things
as to learn to be,
and that they must not come
like a mechanic with tools of knowledge and theory
to repair what is broken.
They must come to discover a secret,
like a treasure hidden in a field,
the pearl of great price.[1]

The faithless, frightened and therefore constantly agitated capitalist system cannot, of course, begin to understand why it is actually instinctive, never mind vital, to our nature not "so much to do things as to learn to be." In order to have any hope of being in touch with deeper aspects of ourselves. So much so that tragically many of us have even forgotten what simply being can feel like as we are forced to respond to the system's perpetual demands on us.

As capitalism's bustle so often drowns out God's peace.

As capitalism's tension so often tears away at God's gentleness.

And as capitalism's competitiveness so often stamps out God's harmony.

As time and again we hear its voices of propaganda telling us just how irresponsible it would be even to think of slowing down and therefore, as a consequence, allowing ourselves to discover something that is ultimately so precious about ourselves.

In any case what gives us the right to think we can take a new direction outside the edicts of the system? This is the way we live. Unless we want to end up penniless. So we work. Not just full-time. But overtime. Individual responsibility. It's up to us. To earn and survive. To pay for this and that. There is no other way. The absurdity of denying that! Just get on with it. The clichés. In so many of our heads. Doing their job. They're good. Very good. The first thoughts, very often, that penetrate our consciousness each waking day and separate us from the time we need to nurture our deeper selves.

However, somehow still managing to cling onto our intuitive sense of who we are, some of us may still waver from time to time about the oppressive way we live. Is there really no other way?

That is until we hear a phone-in on the radio. The theme is the 'Idle in the Workplace' which hammers home the message conclusively. A retired man is more than adamant, he is vitriolic.

"I worked for every penny. I didn't get handouts off anybody.

I didn't look for anything for free. Like some people who lounge about. You shouldn't get anything for free in this world. Not like some layabouts! They don't know what work is."

This tormented message, that deep down we may sense cannot even begin to admit some buried anguish, still drives fear into our hearts.

It sounds so powerful, so right, so black and white.

Sweeping aside any questions relating to the ultimate purpose of our lives. To any long-term healing. Or to the discovery of the space and peace we need for this through, for example, the possibility of job shares, part-time work or other lifestyle changes, where we may decide we can survive on less.

"He's right! He's right! What will people say? What happens when the money dries up? I must get back to work full-time. I can't miss a day. There's so much to pay for nowadays. The price of things. I'll be on the streets. The humiliation. My children."

Liz's Story 2

The woman in the bed next to me, who is clearly deranged, tells me the nurses stopped me walking out of the ward a few times when I was first brought in.

She even claimed I kept shouting, "What am I doing in here? I need to get back to work!" which is nonsense. In any case, tell me one sane person who actually enjoys being in hospital. Especially when your work is piling up even as you think.

One of the younger nurses keeps telling me to try to be a little calmer. But that's easy for her to say – she's got a ward full of patients to keep her busy. How am I supposed to keep calm when all day long all I have to do is lie down with nothing to occupy my mind, here in this suffocating building!

At least Joanne visits, but as usual doesn't help by asking me over and over whether she should restart an old failed relationship with Simon or Steve or somebody. Asking me why it fell apart in the first place.

"Why do they all keep falling apart?" she goes on.

For goodness sake, I tell her, how would I know! "I'm supposed to be the patient in here!"

I'm so tired of it all. Tired of so much for some reason. The only consolation is that at least my headaches aren't as severe just now. The painkillers are even stronger, the nurse said, though they don't appear to have much idea what is causing the problem in the first place – none that they are telling me anyway.

But still Joanne keeps on, "Aren't you lonely? How aren't you lonely?"

"I told you, I'm too busy to be lonely. Except when I'm stuck in here like this. Why don't they let me out?"

But all that they do all day is take my blood pressure when what I really need to know is when is the damned doctor going to turn up and sign me out of here.

Instead though I am forced to listen to the television of *Attack on Uranium 5* that some children have put on in the ward rather than speak to their mothers and grandmothers. I tell the staff nurse that I really need to go back to work for my sanity. This time she takes my pulse.

A coughing, skeletal old lady comes up to me, head bowed. She mumbles something about wanting me to help her work out how to use her phone card. I can't be bothered but at least it is a distraction from what is happening on Uranium 5.

She seems to be hopelessly deaf which I suspect may complicate the call. Whatever, after finally getting through I leave her to it. Unfortunately, almost in tears, she says we haven't got through. I take the phone and her husband is indeed on the other end of the line. I explain this succinctly to her but she goes into another coughing fit.

I end up having a conversation with her husband.

Two complete strangers having a conversation about nothing.

"I don't need this, I don't need this…" I keep saying to myself. But as I am repeating this for about the 50th time, what he is saying gradually begins to register with me. And, very slowly, I somehow feel compelled to listen to him.

His wife isn't deaf at all. She just can't talk to him. Even though she calls him now and again. She apparently left him and their two children just over 20 years ago. They had all adored her. Most mums are the heart of their families.

Even I can remember...

Whatever, she was lured away by some man who part-owned some business or other and made an absolute fortune at it, before buying a second house in Florida or somewhere. She wasn't able to speak to her husband or children for years. Now she is close to the end of her life she is desperately trying to. But still she can't.

Her rich boyfriend, if that's what you call him, left her after a few years. Partly because her own guilt apparently. She is 66 now, her husband tells me.

I look at her – what is left of her that is – curled up on her bed.

She looks more like 86.

She has lung cancer.

For some reason, I am suddenly dumbstruck, I realize, listening to all of this. And particularly dumbstruck by the wretched, pitiful state of this woman.

And, above all, I think... by just how utterly alone she seems.

"Part of me can't help loving her despite everything," her husband admits to me.

His apparent... torment, I suppose, coming together with his... extraordinary sense of compassion, considering what his wife did, seems to melt away my initial indifference. And, as he hangs up almost in tears, the sheer depth of my own... yes, I guess, my own... self-absorption suddenly hits me.

There is absolutely no... escaping it.

"What has happened to me?" I begin to ask myself over and over. The question almost ringing in my ears in the face of this couple.

"I am not like this," I swear to myself loudly. "I have never been like this."

I cannot seem to put the phone down as I stare at his wife turned away from me, utterly desolate in her corner bed. Away from everybody. Away from... I don't know... life itself, it suddenly seems.

At this point, again right out of the blue, something within me just seems to pour out to her. As I simply gaze fixated at her for whatever reason. I have never felt anything like it.

After a while, I approach her gently trying to whisper to her. But the words barely come out and in any case she is totally unmoved and mute. As well as wholly and utterly... empty of... everything, or so it seems. It is impossible to know what is eating her alive more, the guilt or the cancer. The two working hand-in-hand, killing her.

The image of this woman, after talking to her husband, together with everything I am going through myself, now terrifies me so much I actually find myself starting to tremble. In time, to tremble almost uncontrollably. As I stagger backwards towards the edge of my own bed.

I don't understand what is happening to me. All I can say is that it feels like I am being shaken to the... very roots of my being. Losing any semblance of the control which I normally have. Which I have learned to pride myself in.

All of it somehow connected to the... fate and inevitable death of this woman before me now.

As well as... I slowly begin to realize... to the inevitability of my own... yes, my own death... whenever that comes.

Even to the inevitability of death itself – maybe sooner than any of us realize – seeing the impact of this woman's... life choices... all our life choices.

All of this as I then suddenly begin to recall the terrified feelings surrounding some young girl's response to the shock of death, another death... a long, long time ago now... the longer I am left here simply to sit and reflect, which I just can't bear anymore!

But how can I stop these thoughts invading my mind? When I haven't got anything to occupy it?

As I slide back into my bed, pulling up the sheets and covers as far as I can, turning on my side, utterly desperate for any kind of comfort, relief, to come to me.

All of this at the beginning of an ordeal that, in the course of time, would seem to go on not just this day, but for days and weeks, tormenting me over and over. As I was moved from one ward to another and then to some other place I didn't really want to move to and made to speak to endless, prying people I didn't really want to talk to.

Feeling exposed more and more while all the while I was desperate to go back to my old life... my old daily routine... my old secure job... where at least I knew what was going on!

Until... eventually... at the end of what seemed like months... I at last began to question... whether this was all something that I, in truth, really wanted to keep fighting anymore... to keep exhausting myself with anymore... as just maybe, somebody suggested, and then it gradually dawned on me too, finally accepting I would have to go through it all was probably far easier than continuing to... wrestle with it over and over.

In fact, it was far, far easier.

So much so, after a time, I began to find myself at least able to face up to some of what had happened to me... both when I was older and gradually when I was younger... without feeling it was all just too much for me. I managed to hang on, initially for short periods of time each day... but then for a little longer.

Around the same time, just as strange, it became OK for me simply to go for a walk with absolutely nowhere to go or to sit still with absolutely nothing... to do.

In fact I was encouraged to do this and allowed myself to do it... without feeling guilty or that I was wasting time... or wasting my life.

Overall... I suppose... I began to become far less... harsh on myself.

Just to be... waking up and not... worrying about everything at the beginning of each day, I finally started to realize, was a... relief... after all I had been through, I suppose.

For a long while, of course, I couldn't express any of this clearly and certainly not openly. But, in time, to some degree, I could. To so many... I must admit decent people, who I was surprised to find were trying to help me and not always take advantage of me.

As the... anxieties that have affected my life for so long, which somehow I had managed to be largely unaware of, very gradually gave way to a slight but emerging sense of... I don't know... assurance... from somewhere. Even, at times, of... hope... however vaguely.

In fact, I eventually began to recognize the... field of my recent fantasies as reflecting much more than some immature desire simply to run away. But instead as being some kind of attempt to reconnect, I was told, to that little girl within me. And all that she was maybe trying to work through, desperately, on her gran's beach all those years ago. Offering at long last some... glimpses of... understanding of all that went on... even of compassion for it?

So much so I could finally learn to be more... accepting... and loving of myself. Even... perhaps... having faith in myself, I suddenly realized. And therefore, I suppose, in other people. Other people, who I may even have gotten much closer to. And become friends with, I suppose.

In the end, I suddenly realized, very few people have ever truly known or experienced just who I am. Let alone me.

"I have never lived as I was meant to live!" it again dawned on me one day.

Nor chosen so many of the things that have happened to me, I thought. Maybe they just happened... out of my control.

Gradually over the coming weeks, the more I found myself responding to what happened to me in hospital and after that, the more I was able to take time somehow to... think about certain deeper questions... perhaps for the first time.

And as for what my life still held for me, I finally woke up and realized, "I'm only 43!" Incredibly, part of me had been feeling that my life had not long to go. Even, at times, that I wanted to grow old quickly and get it all over and done with!

And yet I haven't done anything with my life as a reflection of... of who I truly am, I now thought. Not gone anywhere nor really experienced anything of myself as a consequence of my actually... being there, if you know what I mean. Even reacting to different... emotions within myself and others in different situations outside the usual, outside the workplace.

All I have basically done is college, debts, work, debts, more work, paying off more debts, with my life. "I have sacrificed my life to paying debts!" I finally shouted aloud one day.

That day in hospital when I was struck dumb by that woman curled up in her bed still, even now, comes back to haunt me every so often about what can happen to... any of us, I suppose, if we are not... more aware of who we are in our lives.

She made a tragic, tragic decision at a very difficult time for her. When perhaps she... did not appreciate what she already had. And she slowly died of regret and guilt from that very moment. Never forgiving herself. Never... freeing herself.

Just why couldn't she forgive herself?

Just why couldn't she be freed?

Why couldn't she make amends?

Either in her old life?

Or by discovering an entirely new one?

As for me, however long it took, I now realized I had been given an incredible opportunity by everything I had gone through. By the whole... at times... agonizing experience... which stopped my old life in its tracks, and finally... finally gave me some... space to breathe.

So that... I don't know... I could start to live... not just differently... but from an entirely different perspective from the one that had overwhelmed me up to now.

Separation 3

More and more of us are beginning to link this growth-obsessed capitalist existence to the increasingly restless, divisive and even at times destructive life it demands of us, the more we question it at its roots. And in time, once we have embarked on a journey that begins to dismantle its power over us, we can just maybe seek its evolvement into something that far more reflects our instinctively peaceful, assured and caring natures. Perhaps, who knows, as part of a popular mass movement.

In the 1980s I faced a crisis of direction, relating to conflicting forces stirring inside me that had seemed incompatible for a long time and finally had to be confronted. God had, of course, always remained quietly alive within me ever since an early sense of disconnection at school. But, at that time, I obviously did not possess the depth of awareness to surrender what I was enduring to my Divine identity, so the spiritual remained a largely suppressed influence in the ensuing years.

Even on into a career in journalism, God seemed to assume a peripheral role, but eventually, over time, these deeper questions about my ultimate being not only resurfaced but just wouldn't go away. Some of the work had also begun to seem more superficial, though in reality it wasn't really about that. It was just that I was under increasing pressure to explore something that had, of course, never left me. To explore it by walking out into the relatively unknown and defying fears within me.

In essence God, or the spirit within me, just wouldn't take no for an answer.

To be honest, at that time, many aspects of my existence were literally stagnant and dying. Things just had to change. Though for me and others who embark on these initially solitary and seemingly lonely journeys, it was merely the very first stage which, at its heart, would tear apart our still relatively cocooned existences and leave us desperate to be embraced by the liberating, unifying and loving force that we all seek in the end.

A force that at the outset, in fact, led me deeper into the mental anguish of my apparent isolation, not out of it. A path essential to us all confronting the truth about our absolute poverty without God.

There were months, indeed years, when I was so broken at times (reflecting on the conditioning of my past), bewildered (in a haphazard present) and frightened (about a totally unknown future) that it perhaps seemed miraculous that I managed to hang on at all. As I struggled to allow my marginalized, 'freelance' status (which embraced much more than work) to become subservient to the greater potential of my true spiritual identity.

However, in time, I felt compelled to surrender so frequently and to such depth that God's presence gradually began to be reawakened within me more and more. Once I had learned to calm my impatience for insight by accepting that my transformation was always likely to take a long time. I had to fall absolutely because of the degree of fear embedded within me. Something some of you may be able to relate to in different ways. At the same time, I had to demonstrate as much faith as I could, even amidst so much apparent pressure, confusion and estrangement.

But also, at times, the extraordinary periods of illumination I was given.

After all, like so many other people, I too was trying to overcome the addiction of my image within the system, the addiction of my desperation for some individual status in order to 'survive' in our seemingly 'detached' world.

So I could allow God unrestrained access to help me realize what, in fact, already embraced me – His eternal, all-sustaining presence – which is open to each and every one of us at any stage.

The alternative, I repeat, was to keep re-submerging myself in illusion, with an even greater intensity of regret once I had already embarked on the journey of discovery. In reality, none of us can do that without increasingly going mad. The daily sense of suffering from a 'hangover' becomes unbearable, the cynical approach poisonous and the negativity overpowering living such a lie. Never mind the overall sense of fragmentation.

Once we have seen through the whole masquerade there is no turning back. We must courageously see it through to the end whatever our suffering. Until finally:

The fears endemic within us are becalmed by our loving reality.

The capitalist becomes submissive to who we really are...

Not the other way round.

As we emerge into a whole new awareness and vision for our lives.

So adrift is our age now, however, that this new vision can seem to be way beyond most of us. With our conditioning within the system, if we are honest, even leading some to deem not only that the actuality of God is unproven, but that it is, in fact, inconceivable. Such is the demand for instant experience of everything, and our insistence that our way is the only way. Such is the prevailing bewilderment and antagonism towards an unseen Divine, which is very often reflected in headlines such as, "What's God got to do with anything?"

But what we must ask ourselves is why are so many so adamant that it is impossible to believe in, let alone experience:

A Supreme Creator, intimately within our hearts, who just could be an omniscient spiritual force guiding our lives?

Ensuring they are not lived in such haphazard and even chaotic ways?

Indeed an eternal and therefore liberating consciousness, which just may offer some greater insight into some of the schismatic decisions that we continue to make, whether on a personal, national or even global scale every day?

And just how much of our blindness is to do with the capitalist, materialist suffocation of God's higher consciousness within us? As, desperately, fearfully, we insist on our plans for our salvation. Our pride, our competitiveness, our aggression, whatever the consequences, entirely separate from Him.

Reflecting an egotistical approach that makes it so hard for us to accept, of course, that all that God offers is given for precisely nothing. The concept of something for nothing being incomprehensible to the economic order (beyond the superficial, of course). Therefore the startling, free offer of eternal salvation – central to the Christian faith through the sacrificial Cross – seems totally irrational.

"How can it be free? When we've not worked for it. When we've not striven for it. Or at least invested in it!" is the system's deeply skeptical attitude. And is therefore the attitude of so many of us, if we are really honest. We, who are tragically locked into its prevailing mindset from childhood (to varying degrees) and therefore inclined to judge so much through its core ideals.

So much so we are very often not alive to (and therefore ungrateful for) all that we have already been given and all that is before us. As we turn predominantly instead to what the system offers as our only 'real' hope for our long-term futures.

All of this making it so hard for us to break through to an alternative, Higher vision just at the moment when it is so critical for our world and for each one of us to join together, and, through God's awareness, begin to find a way out of this mass indoctrination and fragmentation of who we really are which we have become so entrapped in.

The consequences of which have led to so many divisive, ruthless and even destructive global policies, which prove beyond doubt that the coexistence of the system's uncompromising values with those of a unifying spiritual life rooted in the love and empathy of God are impossible any longer for any genuinely awakened person to countenance.

All of which we will eventually realize at the culmination of a journey that demands our all and we could not possibly, of course, complete by merely continuing to pray to God to lead us down our chosen paths. Rather than silently imploring Him to take over our entire beings, never mind lives, entirely according to His will.

A will therefore which demands our all and especially, I cannot emphasize enough, our poverty.

And yet it is a demand and a way of being that so many of us have so much difficulty coming to terms with. With the edicts of the system ensuring that poverty of the soul – our essential poverty – is a bridge too far for many to cross. Because of the system's underlying doctrine of frightened self-preservation, which has ended up diluting the Gospels' self-denying radicalism in the Christian tradition (and others) beyond recognition.

Something we must not let it do.

We cannot let it get away with this.

For it is our essential route to exploring and experiencing what is our spirituality and our inherent union with God.

As over and over we seek our liberation from what is an ultimately illusory and addictive existence, until the moment comes when God finally reveals Himself fully to us, indeed potentially to all of us.

Meditation

Very slowly, as we build up the regularity of the time we spend absorbed within God's calming, illuminating presence, we begin to let go not just of the acute stresses that infect so many of us so much, but also our discordant conditioning generated by a daily existence apart from our awareness of the spiritual.

As we are encouraged to accept that periods of not struggling, not accumulating, not-doing and, yes, even not-thinking are all vital to experiencing our unique and unifying state within the Divine.

On extraordinary days of acknowledged poverty and silence, we may even feel God responding so intimately within us that we can almost feel propelled forward by the encouragement, guidance and inspiration that He offers.

However, there will still be many apparently empty, difficult days when, overwhelmed and lost amidst our feverish activities, we sense our old frightened and egotistical selves getting on top again. And, perhaps frustrated and alienated, we may call out seemingly in vain at the desperation that we feel.

It is precisely then that we must surrender utterly within our hearts, at the same time determined not to succumb to the multitude of habitual distractions out there to fall in line with the collective mindset. Instead we must take a leap of faith over and over and respond courageously and resolutely to what we will begin to feel is stirring within us.

I recall one of my first knowingly bold decisions as a teenager at some party that was supposed to be the high point of the week. I had been to a hundred such parties, the purpose of which had always been to try to get off with a girl or to get drunk depending on which came first.

I was not confident at this pressurized game, having absurdly long and unappealing hair and acne too. A bulbous spot on the end of my nose was the icing, or more like the cherry, on the cake. I couldn't even get drunk properly.

Finally, at this party, from deep within me, a voice inside told me at last to be brave enough to act upon what I really felt. It told me what I knew to be the truth, which was that I really couldn't stand the falseness of all this nonsense anymore, so for goodness sake stop it.

In reality, of course, it reflected a wider schism at the heart of who I was.

Whatever, after finally summoning the nerve to follow my instincts (and therefore accept the authenticity of this voice), I walked straight out of that party into the twilight of a beautiful late May evening. I then climbed over a wooden gate into some field and scrambled to the top of a small hill. I could barely sense what was fully happening to me at that age. All I could remember feeling was increasingly liberated about the decision I had taken, as I was enveloped not only in nature, but also by the stars that were above me, with my senses becoming alive like never before.

From the depths of my impending Saturday night humiliation (and Sunday morning depression), I suddenly felt entirely at peace, not just with the sheer brilliance of my surroundings, but crucially with my spiritual self, which, in the vast silence, was resonating within me.

By now all my fears about what people back at the party might think had evaporated. And after nearly an hour alone, I learned a very important lesson, when a group of them came looking for me and joined me at the top of the hill.

Indeed, we all stayed up there till one or two in the morning. For the most part still and very definitely in awe at all we were experiencing. Even though I don't believe many or indeed any of us were fully aware of the profound, meditative connection to the Divine that many of us were experiencing at that time.

Or why therefore it was one of those magical moments in life that you never forget. One of those magical moments when, perhaps for the first conscious time, we have the opportunity to sense not only our oneness with the spiritual – but also with each other. Rather than to accept that our lives will only ever be pulled this way and that.

To do that is finally to live in truth.

To experience the extraordinary nature of our eternal being.

By finally waking up not only to God's presence within.

But also to our empowerment through His grace.

To ignore it, on the other hand, is to live a lie.

To be separated and enslaved by who we are not.

Absorbed into some disconnected mass collective.

Seemingly in control, but ultimately lost.

So let us celebrate our true inheritance right now or just as soon as we can. Don't put it off. God wants us to respond to His calling straightaway by instinctively choosing to show faith in and give expression to His spirit within. Even if we are taken out of comfort zones and there is some cost to our apparent sense of security or especially our own personal egos.

As, following our regular meditations, we feel guided to break out of our routine way of thinking or doing things by choosing to act on something from His far greater perspective. By, in effect, taking a chance and stepping out into an unknown, however small or dramatic our action may seem to be.

For example, instead of simply sitting in front of the TV one evening, we venture out to some meeting we may never have attended before. Perhaps a guest speaker has returned from some strife-torn part of our world and suggested campaigning actions we can take with others as a united response. We may even be tempted to attend a peaceful protest march or to move beyond our generous but perhaps conservative approach to giving.

As another example, instead of putting off confronting matters that have been on our minds for a long time, we may opt to spend an evening at home writing personal letters/sending e-mails or making phone calls to friends or family who we may have not contacted for ages. Deeds, which perhaps involve us in reconciliations which may be difficult or even painful, but which will be liberating for all concerned at the end of the day. We may even go and visit someone out of the blue who we have not seen for a long time or have become estranged from.

Finally we may choose to include in our weekly routine an evening at a local class, perhaps yoga or tai chi or something similar, a positive activity that we share with others and determine to keep up. Especially when we increasingly start to revel in the long-term sense of calm and inspiration it brings us, particularly in the immediate hours after the sessions. Not forgetting the new connections and friendships that we may make.

All of these, and so many more actions, which are ultimately a reflection and expression of God's nature becoming more alive within us and our acting upon it. A relationship which we continue to nurture after each activity with a further period of silence and a releasing of our old selves. As, more and more, we feel compelled to follow wherever He leads us.

Chapter 3

The Collective

In the early part of the last century theologian, Albert Schweitzer, pointed to the decay of human life and the world through the practice of an industrialized existence that is underpinned by collective thinking. He warned about the developing weakness and dependency of people:

> Because society with its developed organization exercises a hitherto unknown power over man, man's dependency on it has grown to a degree that he has almost ceased to live a mental existence of his own.[2]

Schweitzer highlighted even then the oppressive, even destructive effects of existing under such an organization or system and it is clear that for two or three centuries now many of us have lived chiefly "as working beings and not as human beings." In denial of ourselves primarily as spiritually-inspired and therefore instinctively selfless beings.

Indeed by surrendering ourselves at an even more accelerated rate to the prevailing ideology of this collective mindset, we are now not only exacerbating our loss of faith in the truth about who we really are – but limiting our eternal and potentially miraculous individual lives to existences that can spiral dysfunctionally out of control. Something which is hardly surprising if we refuse to be guided by the all-sustaining, all-loving nature of the Supreme Force within us.

As, out of our sense of disconnection and therefore fear (seemingly apart from God), we predominantly compete to secure our egotistical role, however esteemed or demeaning, within the system. Even as we face up to its classification and judgment, perhaps even its condemnation, of us. All of which, of course, very often serves to block out the unique potential of who we can become under God's free guidance.

Yet, both staggeringly and ironically, it is this same freedom which those in power claim is on offer within the daily operations of the economic order, however superficial and even fraudulent their claims may be.

"You can achieve anything yourself! You are free to do what you want. To build up your own private nest egg for life," they tell us.

As they confuse individual self-fulfillment (and apparently long-term security) within it – which is rarely fulfilling in a genuine sense (never mind any questions of eternal assurance) – with just what God can express through each one of us. When, at long last, we become unshackled from a whole variety of artificial 'must dos' and 'must haves' that are imposed by the collective demands of the system.

Indeed our true individuality, revealing God's distinctive and visionary plan for each of us, can only blossom when we finally offer ourselves back to that life-force from which all creation originates. Finally embraced and at peace within the grace of His vast presence, way beyond our past conditioning and future fears.

As our senses are finally reawakened to act according to our already Divine and unifying nature, which begins to emerge so instinctively the more we are released from our enslavement.

Rid of our own personal delusions and even denouncements within the system, we soon discover God expressing Himself lovingly through us for the good of all, including ourselves. As our lives become refocused and reenergized by being reconnected to the Source of our very being.

To have this denied to us not only cuts us off from our bond to spiritual living but can ensure that our time on this earth remains not only programmed and all-consuming but, even worse, continues to be random, and even destructive, lost in a sense of apparent abandonment both for ourselves and all those around us.

What follows is inevitable. As Schweitzer again tells us:

> Later on, himself subjected to over-occupation, the adult person succumbs more and more to the need for superficial distraction... Absolute passivity, diverting attention from and forgetting of oneself are a physical need for him.[3]

Reflecting, of course, so much of what is going on in modern-day society. In our increasingly frenzied, bewildered and chaotic society, at its most extreme and desperate stage, however collectively secure some of us may claim to be in the 'security' it offers. Though in reality deeply insecure at what we may really sense is going on to whatever degree.

As yet again, in company with so many, we seek to take the edge off the anxiety we may feel after yet another day of fierce and perhaps desperate struggle to accumulate. Demanding our right to our daily distractions, which, unsurprisingly, many of us feel we are fully entitled to after all we have had to endure.

But even more critically, so that the acuteness of pain many of us may feel at continuing to turn our backs on our submerged, yet instinctive sense of who we really are can be deadened.

Maybe even our submerged sense of something we once glimpsed but weren't fully aware of, something we may once have aspired to. All of it now increasingly suppressed amidst our often persistent struggle for personal survival.

Even though it should be becoming increasingly clear to more and more of us by now that the more that any of us amass, the more fixated on it and therefore potentially addicted to it we will inevitably become. And the more we will continue to demand at the expense of others everywhere.

As the scale of our personal hoarding – our unquenchable,

unsustainable hoarding – merely reflects and indeed intensifies the mounting spiritual hunger, anxiety and sense of separation we feel. Seemingly cut off from that which alone can satisfy us – our realization of our true selves in our eternal God.

Something that we cannot possibly experience if we spend most of our time insulating our roofs, insulating our lives, insulating our futures, insulating our very hearts. As we not only keep all the draughts out, but the energizing wilderness out, the essential raw courage out, the winds of inspiration out, the liberating truths out.

Still though, those who are enamored with the system will inevitably go on denying all of this and continue to tell us that there is nothing wrong with working long hours and then splashing out on loads and loads of fun.

An after-hours' celebration to which God (or a deeper sense of who we really are) is, of course, the last person you want invited. They'll also state that anyone who attacks capitalism and its materialistic rewards is merely a killjoy or some kind of renegade from reality, or their tragically limited concept of reality.

But that is to ignore blindly just how the system, by its continuously agitated nature, will always end up dragging us, and society in general, in one relentless, though, at the same time, illusory and manic direction – and away from facing up to these, in the end, urgent questions about our mortality and spirituality, which just have to be faced up to.

As collectively we remain obsessed with the fate of our egotistical selves, whether economically or materially, at the expense of a far more contented, holistic and genuinely harmonious approach not just to our lives and those of our families, but to the fate of our planet.

In line therefore with the thinking of the faithless and wealthy, who will tragically do anything to preserve their established order. Even devoting so much time and energy to controlling, manipulating and denying the full scale of the truth about what is really happening in our world to ordinary people everywhere. To protect and uphold the core ideals of the system. Even if it means deliberately enticing millions of already struggling folk into debt, excess consumption and overall enslavement.

Yet just how can so many of us, indeed whole societies and cultures, have allowed ourselves to become so conditioned and lost, we may ask? How can so many of us have become so compliant and so complicit within this mass indoctrination? So much so that our instinctive and empowering sense of spirituality continues to remain largely dormant?

We have only to look throughout history, however, to see numerous examples of just how that can be achieved on national and even international scales by those in power through their control of most means of communication. How even the instinctively humane can be led astray by those who have become so indifferently or even insanely inhumane. How people's inherent care and compassion (which we all possess at whatever level) can be submerged under the power of the ruthless if assurances are given that the majority or the herd will be saved or even advanced, and critically their desperate fears alleviated.

Throw in, perhaps, the inevitable base nationalistic or even xenophobic appeals, and more and more then becomes permissible under the power of the state. Anyone or any number of people can then be thrown onto the altar of mass marginalization and impoverishment – even 'collateral damage.'

Maybe, in the end, who knows, even ourselves and our families, depending on what fate throws at us in so many ways.

Today, of course, despite the large-scale protests of so many enlightened souls, a great part of our world is still allowing itself to become increasingly absorbed within a worldwide web of short-term economic expediency for a relative minority, at the expense of weeping, suffering voices everywhere. Never mind the devastating effects on our planet. All of this, as I say, exacerbating the everyday conflict so many of us have to endure between the lifestyles we are supposed to aspire to and the true cost of achieving them.

Until in time, and at long last, enough of us begin see through this wholesale masquerade. And we begin to ask ourselves what it is we truly want from our lives. As finally we become courageous enough to confront our deeper insecurities by surrendering to God's spiritual presence within. A surrender that is essential to emboldening us to activate the lasting changes we so urgently need to make.

So much so it then becomes impossible any longer for increasing numbers of us:

To ignore the plight of the bewildered and broken at home.

And the plight of the despairing and dying throughout our world.

As at last we start to recognize that their plight is ours too.

Through our realization of the unity we all share in God.

As we all begin to react to the instability and torment prevailing in so many places, and the individual, family and social disintegration breaking out in so many more. All of it rooted ultimately in this delusional sense of separation from God and His empowering nature.

A sense of separation, I repeat, that we will only intensify the more we focus on merely trying to secure ourselves. Through the all-pervading influence of a system that, in reality, maintains a virtual dictatorial control over our lives, however subtle and duplicitous in its actions and despite its claims and stated pride at its democratic ideals.

A system within which manipulated servants called politicians are, of course, paraded as mere 'personality' choices, who, in the main, can only be differentiated by the ruthlessness with which they will carry out the policies that perpetuate its power. On behalf, of course, of their principal bosses in big business, who now rule like a multinational elite over and above individual countries. Forcing our so-called elected representatives to act with all the deviousness associated with any desperate-to-impress subordinate. As, very often, they try to prove that:

> We're tougher on you at dealing with this. We'll do anything to get the job done. To ensure growth and 'prosperity.' Whatever it takes.

So largely in awe are they of the collective thinking of the all-glorious system that governs them. Committing themselves obediently and relentlessly, often against their higher instincts, to so much of what it demands and commits.

Indeed, as soon as they attain office so many of them lose any sense of a genuinely alternative vision and fall tragically into line with its more hardcore, yet normalized expectations. Frightened of what will befall them if they tamper with deep-rooted principles of what is perceived as the primary purpose of our lives – profiteering, largely irrespective of our wider humanity and urgent need for sustainability, at all costs.

The Dow Jones Index and the other stock exchange indicators of the globalized system give the game away, of course. Going through the roof in ecstatic anticipation of the more ruthless candidates being elected, especially if there is the prospect of safeguards against 'free,' or rather unregulated trade, being torn away so that the 'big players' can operate even more unchecked across the globe. Just so long as they can secure their own pockets, rather than genuinely showing concern for the bodies, minds and souls of people everywhere.

An approach which demonstrates not just the extraordinary degree of ruthlessness and recklessness that pervades in these corridors of 'power,' but more critically the extraordinary depth to which the system can, if unchecked, sink, because of its very nature.

It is a callousness, however, which more and more of us are now seeing through.

As the veneer of moral respectability is finally exposed for what it is.

By the wails of the downtrodden and dispossessed.

Indeed, very often by our own suffocation.

Until at last we refuse to be ruled principally by a craving to accumulate.

By addiction and the addicted.

By mental instability and the mentally unstable.

Or more simply by a wholesale lack of meaning.

As deep down increasing numbers of us yearn for dramatic changes or even awakenings in our alienated lives. The more we are courageous enough to confront the sense of isolation and indeed spiritual unease we may have felt for so long.

Now that finally, we are beginning to ask ourselves, why on earth are we collectively pursuing lifestyles which bring such global misery to so many and, at the same time, can be so ultimately unsatisfying, limiting and even harmful to us?

As we perhaps start to be healed of years and years of, in truth, feeling that we have merely been molded as tools to be slotted into some economic machinery. As submissive tools to be withdrawn and then reprogrammed for some new consumerist inventions.

"You must respond to demand. To increasing and decreasing production levels," we remember being told over and over. All part of our conditioning and reconditioning. With our deeper hopes and dreams, as well perhaps as our compassionate hearts, so often hammered and nailed to the floor. The hardly subtle vocabulary of the media and corporate public relations people really has given the game away, we can now see ever more clearly.

As, at long last, in discovering the fortitude to face right up to these mere images of ourselves, we begin to catch fleeting glimpses of something not just far more vital, but even inspiring from deep within which we were perhaps seeking all along.

Something, of course, that only an absolute and silent surrender to the Divine can possibly unveil, something that only direct contact and experience with the Divine can possibly reveal.

"Can we trust what we now feel though?" many of us may well have asked and still do.

How do we know that it is really related to our ultimate sense of being and is not merely a product of our imagination?

Who are we to feel that that something stirring within us is actually emanating from what many call some kind of Supreme Creator or God? Indeed, believe it or not, an all-caring, all-sustaining God?

Just how can we trust these feelings to break free of the prevailing mindset?

Precisely because we are feeling them. Right now.

We are.

An essential part of us. As we start to accept that, just perhaps, He really is within, guiding us in a whole new, radical direction that is genuinely reflective of our true natures.

Natures which now react with increasing frustration and distress to the proclamations of our leaders, who in response to all the warning signs of our times merely say that any fundamental changes aren't really necessary – "We can deal with whatever comes up. We can find a way around any problems."

There always has to be a way around any problems, of course. But what is absolutely crucial is that the system is sacrosanct and cannot be called into question. It cannot be modified or especially slowed down. Because it cannot possibly be at the root of our present difficulties, can it? And as for politicians trying to force multinational bosses into contemplating, never mind carrying out far-reaching change…

The superficial gloss of 'business as usual,' however, can no longer disguise the sense of instability and escalating fear prevailing globally. As more and more people everywhere begin to see through and rebel not merely against the preservation of such unjust institutions that underpin the system, but against the ever-widening gap between those living in rampant opulence and those who, who, in certain parts of the world, are starving to death. Never mind the environmental consequences of such insane short-term decision-making.

This book is not one for recording statistics, when there are literally millions out there, but these few put paid to the shameful lie that the 'trickle-down effect' of the system could ever eliminate poverty through the sharing of economic growth:

> The gap between rich and poor in Western economies is at its widest in 30 years, according to the Organization for Economic Co-operation and Development (OECD) in 2011. The gap is also increasing in China, India and other parts of the global south.
>
> Even at the height of the recent economic crisis, in 2009, when the living standards were plummeting for the vast majority of people, average Wall Street bonuses were back to being nearly the highest in history, and the following year there were a record 1,200 billionaires in the world, up 28% on 2007.[4]
>
> Finally, at the beginning of 2016, Oxfam reported that the richest 62 people had as much wealth as the poorest half of the global population. This figure has fallen from 388 in 2010 and 80 last year.

Statistics, I repeat. But statistics that yet again prove that capitalism and globalization work in direct opposition to our inherent inhumanity by serving primarily those in power, while the lives of the vast majority are increasingly enslaved and impoverished.

And plainly it doesn't have to be this way.

A United Nations Children's Fund report at the turn of the Millennium ("Poverty Reduction Begins with Children") stated that the "worst manifestations of poverty can be eradicated in less than a generation...Through the investment of a very modest share of the world's annual income, all children could achieve a minimum standard of living... The investment needed is estimated at $80 billion per year – less than one third of 1% of global income."

Indeed Oxfam stated in 2012 that the income of the 100 richest people in that year was enough to end extreme poverty suffered by the poorest on the planet not just once, but four times over.

Meanwhile, insanely, for the rich, this ever-increasing disparity in riches only serves to draw them further into a tragic state of self-delusion with regards to their true sense of identity. As on and on they seek evermore excessive ways to placate their sense of spiritual disconnection and mortal fears.

Often grinding any hopes of a genuine spiritual awakening for the poor and marginalized into the dirt of a sweatshop 50- or 60-hour week or no work at all. While, so often, losing any sense of the instinctive empathy they should feel from their blind and divisive perspectives that very often go on to manipulate and limit us all.

Robbie's Story

Most of the time I've done whatever it took to get what I wanted from life. Fair enough. After all, that's the way the world works, my dad used to tell me, so get yourself ahead of the game. Everyone knows that.

"You're the boss, son. Never forget that. You can sit on your backside and get nothing. Or you can work your socks off and grab it all," he said.

Wherever you listen, you still hear everyone saying the same things he did. Especially the politicians. And they're running the country.

There was nothing wrong with the way I was brought up, despite what some weird person says. I heard someone say my dad was quarried, not born. Sure, some of the blokes who worked for him at his haulage business may have been frightened of him. But I wasn't. No need to be. He was my dad. They all looked up to him.

A few days after my 19th birthday he was killed.

His car was involved in a head-on collision with a drunk driver. It was the other guy who was way over the limit. But he never even got charged. I'd have gone after him if I knew where he lived…

I missed my dad, of course. Maybe I missed him a lot if I'm honest. But there was no use moping about. I just had to get on.

"You're clever," he'd always say. "Nearly as clever as me. You'll do alright." So much for not really loving me.

My grades at school and college had been great. I got on with it. I could have gone on to do anything. My music teacher even nagged me about carrying on playing the piano because I'd won some competition. But where would that have led? Especially when I was desperate to get out there and earn as much as I could. Like everyone else.

I eventually heard there was a lot of money working offshore on the rigs. So I trained up and got a job as an electrical engineer. Those oil companies – they don't know what to do with it they've got so much. Well, they can give it to me, I decided.

Two weeks on, two weeks off suited me at the time too. But it quickly didn't suit my wife Jane, of course. We married four months after Dad died but she wanted me there 24 hours a day.

"Fix this, fix that, Robbie, do this, do that," as soon as I got through the door. She was the one that needed fixing.

"Joey's a right handful," she moaned, blaming it on our kid. That was no excuse. She only worked four hours a day over lunchtimes. Then just stuck on the TV or chatted on Facebook. She was bone idle. That and the drink, of course.

"I'm so depressed, Robbie," she whined.

"Depressed about what?" I replied.

"Every… thing…! Working… you telling me to work more. How can I do that?" she sniveled.

"You don't need to be bloody Einstein. Stick your alarm on and get up," I told her. We both should have been working full-time with what we were paying out on mortgage payments and the car and furniture loans and the rest of it. But she wouldn't work. So in the end, I'd had enough and walked out.

Walked out, OK, a bit suddenly – and a small part of me maybe felt wrong about it – but who wouldn't have? None of my friends, I can tell you. I also quickly discovered it was great being free again with the money I had. If I'm honest, I'd married too young. Everyone said that.

Anyway, I had lots to spend after I got rid of Jane. I couldn't have much fun on the rigs so I made up for it when I got back and went berserk. OK, maybe a bit too berserk at times, but everyone was at it. Drink and the rest. I did up the house a bit when Jane moved back to her mum and dad's and I had a few women back. Women like a guy with his own house. It was a great time.

What more could you want? And why not, I thought?

I'd earned this life.

Why should I feel guilty? No one else was. There was money everywhere at that time. There was no stopping us.

Jane kept nagging me that she wanted some of it, of course. But why the hell should I bankroll her drink, I thought? Someone said she was even smoking joints. So how could I be sure the money would go to the kid?

Her dad even came to plead with me. "We've not got enough to support her and Joey. You should see the state she's in. She can't look after him," he said. I was sure he was going way over the top but I gave him a few hundred quid, though God knows why. Fortunately, he hadn't heard of that child support agency or whatever you call it.

Her mum virtually brought the kid up, which... I suppose I may have felt a bit guilty about... but what was I supposed to do?

Anyway, after all that I bought a beautiful blue Porsche despite a couple of mates laughing at me. It was secondhand, of course, but, I must admit, the power when I first pressed that accelerator was incredible. Even my dad never had a car like that.

My God, he would have been impressed. Who wouldn't have?

There was one special girl I was after at that time. From outside the usual ones and our crowd. Maybe she wasn't the most incredible looking one I'd ever seen. But there was something about her that got to me.

I spotted her at the club we started going to. She was there with a few friends. I danced with her even though she turned me down the first couple of times. My mates said she was too young and laughed at me for even trying. They also said I was only after her because she was sort of posh, which was nothing to do with it. They were just jealous.

"No one's better than me," I told them straight, something else my dad always told me.

Suzannah was from somewhere or other down south, and was studying at college up here. I reckon she was impressed I worked offshore and was my own man. She giggled at the Porsche, which I didn't understand and irritated me a bit.

Whatever, we started going out. Well, we did and we didn't because she just couldn't seem to take me that seriously some of the time, which I didn't understand. Because I was serious, very serious. But then when she realized I was, things changed. And she became sort of... I don't know, worried, in a funny kind of way.

She seemed a bit confused by everything even though she also seemed dead keen on me and I was sure I had made absolutely all the right moves.

"I mean, what the hell is there not to like about me! I've got it all!" I joked with my mates.

I became really determined not to mess this one up, like I sensed it was a real chance to make up for the total mess with Jane. And she was even the type of girl that, I felt, I wanted to end up with. Why not?

Not that I was in a rush, of course. But just because I had married the wrong girl the first time, it didn't mean there was anything wrong with marriage, and Suzannah really did have something all the other girls didn't have.

So I carried on doing things the right way and taking her wherever I felt she wanted to go. You know, not cheap places. Though she still didn't seem that bothered about that for some reason, which left me kind of frustrated. Though at least my friends began to accept her into our group without laughing anymore.

Whatever, I then went offshore for a couple of weeks, and when I came back to my amazement everything suddenly changed. She had been home for a couple of weeks herself and, totally out of the blue, she seemed really happy... relieved almost to see me, giving me a huge hug and kiss when she first met me. And things just seemed to take off from there. Though God knows what the difference was.

Don't get me wrong, I was really keen on her and... I liked the change. But deep down... I was the one who suddenly wasn't sure for some reason. Like, I don't know, I didn't really... trust what was happening.

The way she suddenly started being... affectionate towards me, I suppose, after being so uncertain at first. Without wanting anything in return like all the others girls. It didn't make any sense.

I mean, I had never been... given anything for free just like that. I had always had to fight really hard to get anything that was really important to me and then struggle to keep it. That's just the way it was, my dad always said. But this didn't happen like that. Especially with what she was giving me, for nothing, which was special. Something... that made me feel kind of different... I don't know... about myself.

I even asked her why she was like this one day.

"You're kind to me, that's why. Caring. Something that's... important to me right now. I'm very fond of you. Maybe... who knows, maybe I even... love you."

Where the hell did that come from!?

It blew me away.

No wonder.

She was the first fucking person who had ever said that to me.

And no doubt would be the last.

I was stunned. And, not surprisingly, still stunned a week later when she suggested we go and visit my mum. What was going on here? Obviously I had told her about my dad. But I don't tell anyone about my mum.

I mean, what the hell is there to tell?

She's lived on her own ever since he died, off the money from his business, no doubt, and through selling his house, in some tiny cottage in some dead village somewhere that I don't visit much.

I mean, OK, she's still my mum and maybe there's some small truth in her claim it wasn't always easy with him – but it wasn't as tough as she makes out. Whatever, she barely exists now, spending most of her time just floating about smiling vacantly as far as I can see. She works in the local flower shop and is always digging away in her garden in the evenings. Hell knows what Dad would make of her now. He'd have certainly shaken her up. She's not altogether there if you ask me.

"Why on earth do you want to visit my mum?" I asked Suzannah.

"Why not...? Isn't she a nice person?" she said, surprised.

"She's nobody special," I replied.

"So..." she said.

Whatever, even though Mum was OK and polite enough to Suzannah, she managed to make her feel... uneasy just by the... awkward way she always was with people, especially me. Staring at me all the time, not really paying attention to what Suzannah was saying.

Then, of course, out of the blue, she just had to ask Suzannah whether she played the piano and whether she kept it up. I knew where she was coming from with that, of course. But, in the end, Suzannah didn't seem to bother too much and simply said she liked Mum and her tiny cottage, and that seemed to be that.

"She seems very happy. You're very lucky to have her for a mum," she said on her way back to the car, not making any real sense. Even becoming a bit upset for some reason.

Something about nothing was my verdict on the whole afternoon.

Gradually, I have to admit, I began to find myself missing Suzannah more and more when I went offshore, missing what she was giving me... especially... I suppose the... affection she continued to show me.

However, work was work, I never forgot that from my dad, and I still felt that I would only continue to be my own boss if I kept earning as much as I could. What with the new bathroom I'd just had installed in the house.

Not forgetting the money I kept giving to Jane's dad now and again. Why did I keep doing that?

Never mind all the usual bloody bills, which only ever seemed to go up. Bunch of sharks running the country.

At the same time, I also wanted to keep taking Suzannah out to the top places and to buy her decent things, however strange her reaction still was, which I still didn't understand.

After all, how else was I really going to show her how I felt about her? After all she was giving to me?

There was also the fact, maybe, that I was a bit worried about meeting her parents, which I felt would be the next step, after she had wanted to meet my mum. If I'm honest I wanted her to be able to tell them where I took her and all of that. OK, I know that wasn't everything, but it was still important to me.

At least they would be impressed with my job and what I had already done with my life, I knew. But they probably wouldn't think I earned as much as I did if I never spent anything on her. Which I would if she would only let me!

So I asked her why she wouldn't. I even mentioned my feelings about meeting her parents. Something that seemed to... surprise her and then began to make her angry.

"I never want you to meet them," she said, out of nowhere, totally unlike her to be so... outspoken.

At first, I was taken aback and didn't say anything. But my mind quickly started filling up with the reasons why she said it. Increasingly I grew irritated about what the answers might be, and even though I sensed I might not like them, I just had to ask her.

"So why don't you want me to meet your parents?" I said.

"Because... because you won't like them," she replied.

Her answer was nonsense. I was bound to like her parents, I told her.

"No, you won't!" she insisted.

I didn't say anything for a few moments because of how upset I could see she was becoming and because of what I... felt for her.

But then I felt myself getting more and more angry because I simply didn't believe her. It just seemed an excuse for something that was dawning on me. Of course, I would like them. And I really wanted to meet them.

One day, however soon, I might even have to.

In any case, I was confident I would get on with her father.

Someone in his position was bound to be impressed with the start I had made in life and the hard work it's taken to get there. I knew he would respect me. I could talk to him about it. I could talk to anyone. I was confident that way, just like my dad. I could even chat to her mum.

"How can you say I won't like your parents? They sound like good people to me," I finally insisted.

"How would you know? I've not told you anything about them. In any case, they're not. He could be but he's not. And she… she just thinks what he thinks."

"How do you mean, 'He could be but he's not'?" I asked, totally baffled.

"Look, why are you so bothered about this?" she suddenly asked, again taking me aback.

"Because… I think it's… important."

"Why? What do you need to meet them for? There's no reason at all."

"Why not? You met my mum…"

"Look, he gets tense. OK? Very tense. And I really don't want you to meet him."

Something was telling me to let this go, and a part of me was really trying to, because she felt so… strongly about it… but I began to feel a kind of… red mist or whatever they call it coming over me. As it was becoming clearer to me exactly what this was about. And she was totally underestimating me, everything I had achieved, and everything I was going to achieve.

"So he gets a bit tense. Everyone gets tense from time to time. There's nothing wrong with getting tense," I tried again.

"He gets… he gets out of control. Do you understand? So… please… just leave it…"

And so I did, for the moment, because she was getting even more tearful. And obviously I didn't want that in spite of the turmoil inside me.

But still I was adamant she had absolutely nothing to worry

about with me meeting her parents. And she would soon realize why it was important to me. Even to both of us.

The Collective 2

Right from the early stages of our lives the all-pervasive world according to capitalism and globalization is so often and so tragically self-deluding for so many of us as it immerses us in a daily quest to be better than anybody else, and especially to possess more.

As with one voice its adherents try to impress upon us just how overwhelmingly in control, limitlessly rewarding and therefore potentially fulfilling it can be. Yet the often routine existence it offers can not only be divisive and conflictive but even at times manic for us, as it continually undermines our inherently assured and harmonious natures. Through the pressures it places on us at work, on our personal relationships and especially on our families. Even, on a far broader scale, on whole communities in our world, not to mention on our earth's resources. A correlation that our bosses and even many of us go on ignoring en masse as we simply try to react to the next problem or crisis that inevitably comes our way.

None of which prevents us continuing to mimic each others' demands for more and more unsustainable growth, wealth and materialistic comfort as a primary expression of life as we know it. Reflecting a deeply addictive trait that will, of course, always prevent us facing up to our fundamentally critical dilemma: our seemingly vulnerable and even mortal state apart from God.

Many of us may recall George W. Bush, that great ambassador of globalization, soon after entering office and feverishly excited over the Star Wars Defense System, saying:

It is not in the United States' interests to perpetuate vulnerability.[5]

Heaven help our world if we are not able to challenge our leaders about the consequences of constantly pursuing primarily self-serving, competitive and belligerent policies, whether military or economic, utterly in denial of our fragility, whether or not they are labeled as purely 'defensive' or 'essential.' Policies and overall attitudes that very often set the prevailing tone throughout society.

As so many of us, generations upon generations, then become focused on this collective call to secure ourselves for life at all costs. Rather than on confronting the blatant truth – which we all know deep down – that we simply cannot react to every eventuality or threat that comes our way (never mind any anxieties about what happens when we die).

Every moment we realize, at whatever level of consciousness, that we face potentially damaging or even mortal dangers, whether they arise with our personal lives, or through national or global breakdowns (whether economic, environmental or whatever).

So what we must do, above all else, is confront this inescapable reality head-on. And in particular our buried sense of feeling abandoned apart from the Source of who we really are. Until very gradually, through the growing time we spend in surrender to Him, we feel ourselves more and more liberated from our fears by His reassuring and eternal presence. With our attitudes and behavior then transformed by an instinctive and growing perception about what our time on this earth is really all about. And about the unique role that God has always had for us in this life.

As we learn to practice putting our entire trust in His all-giving spirit and nature, which does not just involve us in an awakening within ourselves, but then, in time, we shall discover, into our far more harmonious relationships with each other.

Indeed, our lives, lived from His vision, offer up an entirely fresh, selfless and vital outlook.

Within which we perceive ourselves and indeed everyone we encounter as we are in Him, whatever our backgrounds or individual situations. Rather than merely the next folk we should try to manipulate to our own ends.

As our struggles end up embracing their struggles.

Our hopes end up being energized by their hopes.

Our potential ends up being fulfilled alongside theirs.

Now that we have all finally owned up to our limitations and instability apart from God, and our terrifying dread of the unknown, and surrendered utterly to Him. Having felt, at long last and with much relief, that we have nothing left to lose with regards to our old selves – our old, random, agitated, fractured and, perhaps, forlorn selves.

An awareness of which has finally opened our eyes to a whole new vision. At the same time helping us to glimpse the miracle of life that is within us. And of just how precious it can be. All of this coming from God's extraordinary perspective.

Our ultimate redemption.

A perspective which we can now take into all the more difficult encounters we face. Recognizing that up to now we have all been undermined by the anxieties and pressures that have become so endemic within us. We have all been the victims of our spiritual consciousness being denied to us for so long by our shared delusion.

But this is no longer the case – as soon as we choose not to allow it. As soon as we choose to:

Empty our minds of today's collective thinking.

Break habits induced by self-absorption.

Open ourselves up to fresh and fearless insights.

Reach out with our care towards all.

Tragically, however, this is not the approach some are even close to taking, particularly if they follow the example of our leaders.

Something that was amply demonstrated, as just one example, by the collective reaction of many people, not directly involved in the events of September 11, 2001, when they were very quick to follow President Bush's general lead. As firearm sales went up by 50% in some states. There were also rushes on the purchase of rifles, gas masks, pepper sprays, baseball bats, canned food, water tanks and army-issue ready meals.

However, none of that, or anything that has happened militarily or internationally since, has altered their or our reality one little bit. I repeat, as hard as it is to accept, we will always feel vulnerable in this earthly life cut off from a genuine awareness of God's presence. An experience of which will only ever be intensified, ironically enough, the more aggressive and violent we become.

From whichever side the violence comes. Whether perpetrators or avengers. We just move further away from God's and our inherent peace.

Of course, worse still President Bush characterized his overwhelming use of power with two principles uppermost in his mind, prayer and power: the deluded and dangerous doctrine of the primal fundamentalist coming to save us.

A fundamentalist who was apparently blind to God's vision of universal love as he chose above all to spend billions on defense budgets, very often at the expense of more humanitarian programs across the world for the poor and the dying, many of whom ended up condemned, even within his own wealthy country. With his vision of 'god' in denial not only of what Jesus Christ stood for, but of what the Cross is all about.

The concept of self-sacrifice having been entirely lost somewhere along the way.

For these are the real effects of the policies of many of these 'religious' capitalists, effects they ignore as they assign glory to their 'god' and the strange kind of exclusive power they seem to believe He has bestowed upon them.

Personal vulnerability is, of course, not something, in public at least, that President Bush or most political leaders would ever dare show. The omnipotent economic order demands that all that they can ever display is absolute authority and apparent certainty. At the same time burying whatever fragility they may feel deep down.

As instead they remain focused on the continued preservation and expansion of the system and their own exclusive status within it. To such an extent that it should be increasingly evident to the rest of us just how impossible it is for them ever to respond positively to a truly alternative strategy for life, particularly one that is acceptable to us as primarily spiritual beings.

Nor will they ever be able to acknowledge the truth behind German philosopher and psychoanalyst Erich Fromm's 18th century assessment that the development of the collective organization is:

... no longer determined by the question: what is good for man? But by the question: what is good for the growth of the system?[6]

which, many of us can see, still holds true today.

An insanity which continues to engulf so much of humankind in an agonizing schism where continually:

We may seek the courage to be our true selves,
but instead succumb to illusions that enslave us.
We may sense the spiritual peace that is within us,
but remain agitated by the clamors of the system.
We try to respond to the calls of the fragile,
but so often yield to the demands of the elite.
We yearn to radiate God's love,
but feel coerced into expressing policies of fear.

Deceiving ourselves, and yet not really deceiving ourselves, for part of us (at whatever conscious level) knows what we are really doing and just how much we are denying God's full expression in our lives.

Torn increasingly by a conflict that, in the end, simply must come to a head. When once and for all we will decide whether we really are going to carry on with this betrayal of our spiritual birthright, of who we feel we are so passionately deep down, or finally we decide that enough really is enough.

The decision we should make, of course, should be an obvious one. Especially when we finally accept that the road the capitalist system is embarked on will only, inevitably, get more and more desperate, I repeat, because of its insatiable, yet unsustainable nature.

With those who gain exorbitantly from it continuing to take more and more, while the rest, the vast majority of us, will be left with less and less. Something that is as inescapable as night following day, as when, however long ago, due to our and the system's faithlessness and fear:

Desperate greed superseded basic need.
Care for money superseded care for people and planet.
Care for the individual superseded care for the community.
And when hyper-investing superseded mere investing.

Indeed, of course, money has long since taken on an entire life of its own, with financial wealth being produced merely for itself in various sectors of the global markets. With the inevitable disconnection from so much of what is integral to life. An accepted practice within the economic order and an extension of the mindset which has always allowed, indeed encouraged, the system of exploitation to be built upon the ruins of a simpler, frugal life. With multinational companies denying indigenous people their lands, forests and water that are all vital to providing the necessities of life within a subsistence economy. With all that that entails with regards not just to their inherent links to their environment, but even to their spiritual and cultural heritage.

The reality of the effects of the globalized market system for so many. As it brings down and impoverishes communities where profit is not a precondition for life, and makes it a precondition.

So that everyone must become absorbed collectively into the system or die.

And perhaps part of us also dies with them. For just maybe we sense their way of being as somehow being linked to God, offering glimpses of the way we might choose to live, of the way God would have us live. Not primitively, of course, but nor in such a fearfully relentless, unbalanced, egomaniacal manner either.

Do we need any more convincing of the economic order being an anathema to the spiritual and humane than this?

If we have any doubts left just look at the heinous actions in recent years of private companies, mainly based in tax havens, which have been involved in buying up the debts, at discounted prices, of the world's poorest and most ravaged countries before suing through the legal system in order to make massive profits. These so-called "vulture funds" then ensure that money released by debt relief programs and earmarked for health and education initiatives have gone instead into the pockets of already wealthy 'investors.'

There is only one alternative to all of this. There is only one alternative to all this capitalist anxiety and dread inciting such hideous acts of self-preservation. And it is the ultimate alternative of more of us first individually and then in unity finally breaking free from the mental stranglehold that this delusory system has increasingly taken on us.

By at last recognizing and accepting our vulnerability and turning back to the spiritual, back to our actual Creator and our utter reliance on Him, who alone can transform us into fearlessly and uniquely expressing who we truly are through Him. Not just for ourselves and our families, but primarily for the good of all. Indeed the survival of all.

Robbie's Story 2

"Time waits for no man," my dad always used to say to me. And a big part of me felt the time was right.

I was totally secure in my job, I was earning more and more every year and Jane was almost off my hands. On top of that, I had just moved into a bigger house.

So that all that was left for me to do was to find someone special to live in it with me and I knew I had found that person. She was even in her final year at university so the timing really could not have been better on that front either.

OK, there may have been one or two things that she insisted we needed to "talk about," which she kept going on about without actually saying anything, but they weren't much, I was sure.

We were still great together and she gave me something that I had never experienced in my life. More than just... love... and that... but, at the same time, she somehow helped me to feel... good about myself, I suppose. In fact, I had never felt so good.

There was only one person who put a dampener on the whole situation and that, of course, was my mum.

Stupidly I felt I should go over and tell her my plans – not that I needed to because I was certain myself. Surprise, surprise, she was digging in her garden. She was just as... awkward and tense with me as usual. I didn't say much for a while but then I came straight out with it.

"I've decided to get married... Well? What have you got to say?"

"Oh..." was all she said, half-asleep as usual.

"To Suzannah... Hey?"

"Yes... I heard."

She didn't seem to be shocked at all.

"Is that all you've got to say? What's wrong with me marrying

Suzannah?"

"Nothing..."

"Well...?"

There was another pause and then typically, without even looking at me, she said, "So... so soon after Jane?"

"Jane was wrong. Suzannah isn't! She's totally different," I replied. "Well..."

"Suzannah seems a lovely girl," she said.

"Hey? Yes, she is... so... haven't you got anything else to say?"

"Why... why get married so soon though?"

"Why do you think? Because she loves me and we're perfect together. All my friends think we are," I responded. "Look, anyone can make a mistake once. OK...?"

"Of course..."

"Well..."

"But... why... why married?"

"I just told you!"

"Did you?" she asked stupidly.

"Yes, I did!"

Irritatingly, after yet another ridiculous pause, she just turned away and went on with her gardening, trembling slightly.

"Yes, I did tell you why I wanted to get married, I said!" I insisted.

"Oh..."

"Oh!"

I couldn't hold myself back any longer.

"Look, what is it with you? Why can't you say something decent to me? You just can't give me any... encouragement or praise at all, can you? Whatever I do, however successful I am – and I am very successful, by the way – you just can't bring yourself to be happy for me. Why? Just because I didn't become fucking Beethoven?

"Jesus, I could be some drunk or drug addict on the streets

but I'm not. I have made something of myself just like Dad knew I would. I am in charge of my life just like he was. What more do you expect of me? Hey? And now I have even met the perfect girl.

"Do you even know who she is? The type of family she's from? What more do I have to do? Well?

"You have no idea just what she has given me. Do you? Well? Something... something that you've never been able to give me! Feeling totally... good about myself. Maybe... maybe for the first time in my life. Why couldn't you do that? Hey? You're my mother, for God's sake!"

Part of me even felt like lashing out at her sitting there like some deaf mute in her bloody vegetables. Though, very quickly, guilt came over me, of course, for the ferocious way that it all just suddenly spilled out and the way she backed off frightened. I know she's my mum, but I could understand why Dad got so wild with her because I could feel the same rage building up inside me. Not that I even thought about laying a hand on her. I somehow resisted... like my dad.

I could see she was desperately trying to stay calm even though she was shaking and breathing deeply, which I also felt bad about. Why didn't she just let it all out? She never did with Dad either. OK, what I said was horrible. But I felt so frustrated. What was I supposed to do?

We both said nothing for I don't know how long.

I sighed deeply and was just about to go when finally she started to whisper something without even looking at me, instead gazing vacantly across the fields.

"What are you mumbling about now?" I asked.

"Suzannah phoned last night, I said..."

"What? Suzannah? No, she didn't. Why would she phone you? She doesn't even know your number? Well...?"

"She was... worried about you. She didn't know who else to speak to."

"What? What are you talking about? She's not worried about me. There's nothing to worry about."

"She says you've been… irritable lately, and even… angry…"

"Rubbish. You're making all this up…"

"She's been trying to talk to you, she said, but you just keep shutting her out."

"I don't shut her out," I said. "We're really close. She loves me. Why are you saying all this?"

"She says that when you've been coming home from the rigs you've always been too busy to talk, always saying you had a lot of work to do with your new house."

"I still do. So has she. We're working on it together. Just like everyone else does with a new house if you hadn't noticed. She's really keen on the house. And moving in with me. So what are you talking about?"

"Are you sure she feels the same way about it that you do?"

"Of course, she does. It's our house."

"She said that she used to feel that you had a lot in common when you first went out…"

"Hey? We do…"

"She even… even said she sensed the same… the same… insecurity in you that she feels."

"Insecurity? What's that supposed to mean?"

"Robbie… I think… I think you know what that means… she said she told you…"

"Told me what?"

"That… there've been a lot of problems at home for her too…"

"What! No, there haven't!"

"Apparently she told you that there's always been a lot of shouting…"

"Rubbish! That's not true. She's exaggerating…"

"Her father…"

"She's blown it way out of proportion. He's not like that!" I insisted.

"She's tried to share it with you, she said. Even hoped you would open up to her…"

"Open up to her about what? What have you been telling her? You haven't been going on about Dad to her, have you? You've always gone way over the top on that."

"Have I?"

"You know you have!"

My mum suddenly turned to me.

"You don't really think that I have, do you?"

"Yes, I do!"

"And now you think Suzannah is doing the same?"

"Yes!"

"Why would you possibly think Suzannah is doing that?"

"Look I know her…!"

"But why would she exaggerate over her father shouting and… and even being threatening and violent?"

"Violent! That's ridiculous."

"Is it?"

"Yes!"

"Well… unfortunately, Robbie… unfortunately…"

"What?"

"It seems you're wrong."

"No, I'm not!"

"Suzannah… Suzannah has also asked me to tell you something…"

"Tell me what? Now what?"

"To tell you something that I'm pretty sure you already know…"

"Know what?"

"That, unfortunately…"

"Well?"

"She… she doesn't want to…"

"To what?"

"To… marry you."

"Hey? She didn't say that."

"I'm sorry. I think you know she doesn't..."

"I never even asked her to. So now I know you're making it all up. We've been starting to do the house up together. That's all. We're really close. OK, I'm offshore a couple of weeks and things have been a bit difficult. It just takes me a while to get used to being home again, back onshore, and learning to relax, everyone says that. Especially if you've been on nights. Does your head in. I never asked her to marry me."

"I'm sorry..."

"Stop saying that! Why are you making all this up? I keep telling you I never even asked her to marry me!"

"Suzannah... felt you have been thinking about it recently."

"No, I haven't!"

"Why... why do you want to get married again so soon, Robbie?"

"I don't!"

Mum again turned toward me, almost as if she was reaching out to me in a ridiculous way. I turned away. I felt... irate. And... humiliated. She was the last person I wanted to be telling me this. If I even believed it, which I didn't.

"Robbie... Robbie, can't you see that it doesn't make much sense you wanting to get married again so soon..."

"What? Who says it doesn't?"

"Why do you keep making these decisions?"

"What decisions?"

"In spite of everything that happened to you, what happened to both of us, you don't need to keep making these... decisions just to make you feel more..."

"Feel more what? What are you on about?"

"I am not just talking about marrying Jane and now Suzannah, but everything you do seems designed to..."

"Look, you don't know what you're talking about. Just like you don't know what you're talking about with regards to

Suzannah. So just leave it, will you! Leave it!"

I moved away. She was nagging me to death again. Putting me down again like she always did. I needed time to think so I could work out what was really going on with Suzannah, which was what was really important to me. Finally Mum turned back to her plants, breathing deeply for some reason, while still keeping half an eye on me. At least she wasn't suffocating me anymore.

What she was saying about Suzannah was totally ridiculous. Suzannah loved me. Even when things have been difficult, and OK they may have been a little more lately, she's still great with me.

So what if I had been thinking about marrying her. There's nothing wrong with that. OK, I have been married before. But you move on.

My dad always told me that. "Get straight back in the saddle, son, don't mess about doing nothing."

So none of this made sense. I didn't understand it. I was doing everything I was supposed to do. I had achieved everything I was supposed to achieve. And more! I needed to know the real reason Suzannah was running scared.

"What else did Suzannah say? Hey?"

"About what? Robbie, please don't shout," she moaned.

"Why she won't marry me, of course? Well, according to you at any rate. Well…"

"Robbie… I'm sorry… but I have got something else to tell you."

"What!"

"Something else Suzannah is frightened to tell you herself."

"No, she isn't! What are you making up now?"

"Something that I'm also pretty sure you know…"

"No, I don't!"

"That she doesn't even want to…"

"To what?"

"To see you anymore."

"Hey?"

"Robbie, Suzannah's lovely but she's very, very young. You do know that she's only 22, don't you? I'm... sorry... sorry..."

She again seemed to lean toward me. I again moved away, fury building inside me. This definitely wasn't true. A total lie. I tried to think. And suddenly, and finally, I woke up, and I knew there was only one possible explanation.

"Her parents...! What did she say about her parents?"

"I told you... just that her father..." she replied, puzzled again.

"She wouldn't let me meet them. She must have told her parents we were thinking of getting married. So what if he's some director of some big company. She never even let me meet him and..."

"Robbie, what are you talking about?" she interrupted, clueless as usual.

"Look, you don't know what's really going on here!" I yelled. "I do! I am actually reasonably intelligent believe it or not, no thanks to you."

At this point, I felt real hatred towards my mum about... about just how really ignorant she was... about the way things really worked in the real world. And I was doing everything I possibly could to restrain myself. She kneeled up, appealing to me.

"Robbie, I know you keep blaming me for so much... which is fine... I am responsible for a lot of what has..."

"What?"

"... but it is long past the time that you and I faced up to..."

"Look, I don't need this right now..."

"... to what... what is really going on here."

"Hey?"

"You know what I'm talking about..."

"No, I don't!"

"For so long I let myself believe that you'd somehow shut out all that happened... that you were asleep. But the walls were paper thin... what was left of them..."

"Oh, not this again!"

"I know I should have protected you when your dad came back home late..."

"Once and for all shut up about it, will you!"

"... but I'm afraid that I completely failed to function even as a... a basic mother during that time..."

"Look, just stop it, will you!"

"And, in the end, Robbie, what both of us must always remember is that we mustn't hide from what he did..."

"Nothing happened!"

"Just because your dad died it doesn't mean we should pretend he wasn't the way he was. His way of life, satisfying his urges wherever he went..."

"He wasn't like that!"

"... battering his way through life. At least Suzannah is trying to face up to what's been happening to her. So she can try to move on. As I have tried to do with the help of my friends. So I can really make a fresh start. Even though it has taken me so, so long..."

"Long time for what!" I replied, though just perhaps, for some strange reason, there seemed to be, perhaps for the very first time, a... slightly hollow ring to it, or whatever they call it. Though I certainly wasn't about to admit anything to her. Especially as I still felt she was exaggerating by far.

Well... the larger part of me did.

The larger part that was still focused on what was happening with Suzannah. And my absolute determination, still, to make things work out with her.

Something... something that it would take me a... long... long time to let go of.

A long... and extremely painful period of time, I can see now. That led to me facing up to some... incredibly desperate...

moments in my life.

That the loss of her... love for me... finally made me confront.

A love that... yes it really did break me apart...

Feeling... loved... when I had never really felt loved.

I don't know how long it took, in truth, before things finally started to get a little clearer... a little easier.

When, at long last, I... began to accept things for the way they had actually been back when I was younger... I guess, is what I am saying. However hard that was to do.

To see so many things... differently for the first time in my life...

My relationship with my mum stayed angry for a long time, needless to say, but very gradually it began to ease too.

So much so I finally manage to see a bit more of her now. Not every week, of course, but at least more than before.

And we're able to speak now without me getting... so irritated all of the time, which, I suppose, is... good.

After all... after all... yes... she is my mum.

And, as much as I still don't understand or have a clue about what she's doing with her life, I can see that she has been... and is still trying her best for me.

Especially considering everything she has been through.

At least, she seems to be doing that.

And maybe I appreciate that for the first time.

Yes, I appreciate that.

Meditation

Opportunities arise. In order to open our instinctively loving hearts and thereby liberate our often controlled minds.

So that the stranglehold that the all-invasive capitalist system has on so many of us, in so many areas of our lives, can finally be released. And we can uncover a whole other world of extraordinary potential within ourselves coming from an altogether Higher spiritual source.

Most of us have annual holidays or at least some weekends off, within which there are days and even weeks we can break out of the collective thinking of our limited lives. These represent the chance not just to unwind but to take a leap into the unknown by experiencing something completely different and, who knows, even inspiring, by moving outside of our comfort or routine zones.

For many years many of us may well have been determined to 'really get away from it all this time,' rather than just bowing to the lure of the all-inclusive hotel or all-inclusive resort or whatever.

Because deep down we want real change.

Change from what though?

For the majority, it is from the long-term work/consumerist conditioning and strains, as well as the monotony and lack of meaning, which can intensify year after year. And the lack of time and space to respond to that persistent, loving voice, which we may feel calling us from within toward the genuine transformation we may well have been yearning for in our lives.

Of course, many of us will still have enjoyed plenty of high points over the years, perhaps connected to our various pursuits or more simply by being together with family or friends, which we celebrate, and which raise our spirits for a certain length of time.

But, questions regarding a wider perception of ourselves, of our true natures and the way we should really be living our lives right now may have largely remained unexplored and therefore unanswered.

So, these holidays, or long weekends, or more pertinently these extended gaps in our schedules (any genuinely different experience) are rare opportunities to step into fresh situations and to stir fresh imaginings beyond our everyday thinking. As well perhaps as to glimpse some genuinely alternative vision for the long-term.

And yet how do many of us very often spend them?

By, to varying degrees, re-creating the world we all know so well at home, very often because of the exhaustion we feel and our understandable desire to 'chill out' completely. Either that or some of us even suffer a sense of fear about doing something radically different, as feeling safe and surrounded by the familiar has become an ingrained priority within the system and therefore within ourselves.

Once upon a time, a suitcase of clothes was all that accompanied us on our trips. Now, this cocoon of safety is augmented by mobile phones, satellite TV linking us to our home news, Internet access, home country newspapers and home country representatives.

So much so we may never truly get away from our 'home' thinking.

Indeed, from our collective thinking.

In truth, we never truly let go at all.

Nor open ourselves up to something genuinely transforming.

To the possibility of a whole new dimension to our lives.

Which isn't necessarily achieved by drowning ourselves in exotic cocktails.

Or even by white-water rafting down the Zambezi River.

As the prevailing mindset continues to maintain its hold on us.

As gratification continues to come before meaning.

And sensationalism before an authentic celebration of life.

Before an authentic surrender to life.

Indeed a life that is rooted in the eternal and therefore potentially unlimited.

Rather than simply in what money and the ego can buy.

In fact, finance and distance again need be no barrier to what, deep down, we may want to experience. As in deciding upon our break, we can simply select a cottage in some remote location, which offers a closeness and intimacy to nature, indeed, of course, to God. A tent or two by a stream in the middle of nowhere might do just as well.

Just so long as the place we have chosen provides the space and peace that our souls require to become silent and then go wandering off.

So that critically we have the opportunity to submit ourselves not just to the possibility of something entirely different, but to the possibility of something far more vital, the potential for a higher creativity, all of it flowing from deep within ourselves, from an extraordinary Source that even now is waiting for us, waiting to connect with us, to guide us back, to restore our inherent and deeper sense of unity to all.

Nevertheless, we may say, it is all very well immersing ourselves in all of that for a week or two, but what after that, what happens when we are re-submerged, yet again, back into the overwhelming ethos of the system?

It is specifically then that we must be absolutely alert to any signs of fear and negativity reasserting themselves by immediately putting into practice what we may have learned from our time away. So that we can maintain our healthy disconnection from that which would seek to reimpose its grip upon us.

With an agenda of our own that we may well have established during the visionary time we were away and which we must now be determined to live up to on a daily basis with God's help. As at last we insist upon persistent time in favor of experiencing who we really are in our lives, as opposed to tamely surrendering to who we are not.

By for example:

Responding to God's prompting to rise early each morning. So we can spend intimate and inspirational time with Him. Walking and meditating amidst His creation. Rather than simply slumping in front of the TV news.

So that at the outset of each day, we then find ourselves not just experiencing but giving expression to His loving and reassuring nature. Not just for our sakes, of course, but for the sakes of all those we come into contact with, all those we know, all those we love... but perhaps have not always expressed that love fully to.

Actions which, believe me, we shall very quickly see having a harmonizing effect once we are truly alive to He who is, after all, no less than our Divine Creator and guide.

Let us never forget that.

Nor ever underestimate it.

It is actually to God Himself who we are surrendering.

God Himself who we are opening our hearts to.

God Himself who is becoming alive within us.

God Himself who is voicing Himself through us.

As an expression of His all-loving nature.

Which, we now begin to see, is our nature.

Indeed the nature of each and every one of us.

Chapter 4

Addictive

Now this is where it can hurt. Most of us know that any addiction hurts when, in the end, we are compelled to face up to and withdraw from it. Whether through our own personal experiences, or watching family members, or when witnessing a friend's suffering. It hurts beyond any possible description.

And, as many of us are beginning to realize by now, despite many of the real benefits capitalism and globalization have helped to bring to our world, their underlying and all-pervasive traits are increasingly addictive and damaging in so many areas of our lives. As well as being the root cause of so many secondary addictions which keep us functioning and acquiescent within the system. Or our overall existence linked to it.

At the same time and crucially, they make it so hard for us to experience our genuinely healing and potentially transforming relationship with the Divine and the empowering effect that comes with that.

Now, of course, it is true that addiction can very often be an overused word nowadays. However, most people's definition of an addiction would be something we pursue compulsively or become psychologically dependent upon.

Crucially despite overwhelming evidence that it is both damaging to us – and even to our Earth.

Therefore very many of us would acknowledge that capitalism and globalization are addictions in so many ways for increasing numbers of us throughout our world. As we struggle in a whole variety of ways to emerge from the spiritually blocked and therefore deluded state within which we have become submerged.

A delusion and indeed a conflict that, for the most part,

does not seem to concern the rich and powerful and those who control the economic system, who will, of course, deny that they are in any way addicted. As yet again they focus (through ruthlessness and violence if necessary) on creating more and more unsustainable wealth for themselves with what is left of our earth's resources, never mind an artificial sense of need for the rest of us. As if that constitutes a perfectly sane approach to life on behalf of our world and its peoples today.

I think it's fair to say, however, that their views may not only be fundamentally warped, but largely unstable.

First and foremost because it is so hard for them even to glimpse and then embrace the eternal truth about themselves, which so many of us are beginning to do. Their obsession with profiteering and rampant materialism proving such tragic barriers to any authentic insight, especially when what is actually required is a total surrender of who they think they are to an entirely different dimension. Rather than clinging to the kudos and economic security they may crave as compensation for their deeper emptiness. To such a degree we may have some empathy with these words from Erich Fromm:

Satan is the representative of material consumption and of power over nature and man. Jesus is the representative of being, and of the idea that not-having is the premise for being. The world has followed Satan's principles since the time of the gospels.[7]

While some of us may struggle with the extreme nature of what Fromm says, we may still find it illuminating to reflect on how far he feels we have drifted from our essential and original 'not-having' awareness of who we really are. With the extraordinary understanding and indeed empowerment that is open to us when we reconnect with that awareness by literally letting go of our limited fear-driven identity.

The addiction to the accumulative way of existing is, of course, not restricted to the affluent and can become overpowering for all of us, especially when viewed from their blinkered perspective. So much so that there is little point in any of us merely attacking them for their greed and blindness when we may well be transfixed ourselves, to whatever degree.

What we must all increasingly accept in our daily turning to God is that whatever little empire we may set out to build for ourselves within this system is the absolute opposite of what He demands of us.

For what He demands in the end – which requires great courage, but which is extraordinarily liberating – is nothing less than our poverty.

Not primarily our financial poverty. Far deeper and more profound than that. Our increasingly terrified world, indoctrinated with the egotistical ethos of capitalism, has yet again got things extraordinarily twisted. For what God insists upon is:

A poverty that fully awakens us to our absolute fragility without Him.

A poverty that fully recognizes our utter dependency on Him.

A poverty that demands a turning away from selfish desires to others' needs.

A poverty that demands we act entirely according to His compassionate nature.

But how can the global rich and powerful or any of us awaken fully to this universal reality? If we allow our lives to be dominated by a system that is focused on entirely the opposite of this?

A system that sees poverty as absolute weakness.
A system that sees poverty as something abhorrent.

A system that sees poverty as something to flee from.

A system that is rooted in securing ourselves against our mortal terror.

Many of us are beginning to sense the truth of all this, however far-reaching it may still sound at times. No wonder, when we consider just how much our minds have been indoctrinated into obsessing in totally the opposite direction throughout our lives. And we are also starting to understand why it may be critical we not only acknowledge but also confront this poverty in order finally to shatter our addiction to the system.

For only by doing so will we be forced to rely on, in our precariousness and even despair, God's extraordinary presence at the heart of who we are. With God as the sole Creator and provider of all.

Not just now, but, in truth, we will soon begin to realize how He has always been there waiting for us, at whatever subconscious level. Right back to our birth when we come to think about it.

And now a voice in the wilderness calling us to turn back from our latest random and perhaps shortsighted decision. So He can help us deal with whatever dilemma or crisis is looming. Or whatever torment is tearing away at our souls wreaking some form of psychological havoc.

As, finally, we accept that there is really nowhere else to go for our ultimate reawakening, indeed our very sanity. In truth, for our absolute salvation when it comes down to the eternal reassurance which we all seek.

As, at long last, we courageously allow ourselves to be immersed in a nothingness and a silence, which, in the end, is vital to the unveiling of our true selves.

That is the journey of real poverty.

That is the journey of essential poverty.

Indeed a poverty, in the Christian faith, which finally makes sense of Christ's ultimate sacrifice for us. Otherwise there was absolutely no point to His crucifixion. If we merely persist doggedly under our own egocentric steam to some kind of personal 'saving,' with Jesus merely (if at all) acting as some kind of vague insurance cover.

Many though, I repeat, will still try to persuade us that it is possible to be both spiritually aware and an active capitalist. But that is a deception which conveniently ignores not only the very many inhuman and destructive consequences of the system, but also the reality, on a personal level, that our riches and savings are very often an indication of just where our hearts are. An addictive dependence upon which makes it impossible for us to free ourselves from fear and to trust entirely in God as the provider of all.

For, to put it bluntly, we cannot have one heart in the stock market and one heart in a spiritual market. We only have one heart, at the last count.

Trying to buy shares in both, especially the stock market's increasingly ruthless and more harmful ones, will only serve to perpetuate us in an agonizing conflict where our poverty will, in truth, be a pseudo-poverty. Where inevitably we will struggle desperately to accede to God's will while remaining compliant to the pressures of the system.

For example, as investors, we may finally decide to purchase some ethical bonds but, at the same time, fail to find the time to investigate the dubious activities of companies our banks keep investing our money in. Or as consumers, we may pay a little more for some items of fair trade clothing, but then not bother to notice that others we buy are only incredibly cheap because they were made at the expense of some poor, exploited people somewhere.

When, in truth, once we are awakened to God's vision and indeed power within us, we may find we are emboldened to be far more courageous with our money by investing it not just ethically but even altruistically, by offering medicines to hundreds, or restoring eyesight to thousands (depending on how much we have, of course).

As we discover that our journey to unveiling and expressing our true, more unified, selves in God does, at the end of the day, demand no less than our whole being. With our growing spiritual awareness raising us entirely beyond the increasingly self-centered values of the system, while, at the same time, energizing us to act radically with regards to it.

To such an extent that the poverty we now feel (I repeat, not merely financial) is not something that terrifies but frees us. As finally we begin to glimpse and even to recognize genuine wealth in the simple yet unifying life which this poverty affords. With our personal standing or circumstances, financial or otherwise, more and more not something that overly dominates our minds the more we feel secure in God as the Source of all. The more we actually act upon our surrender to Him and then experience His giving back to us in so many ways.

Indeed, all that we inevitably feel at this point is overwhelming gratitude for the extraordinary liberation that His presence brings. Rid as we are of any kind of reliance on this increasingly addictive existence we have left behind, which has held us back for so long.

But just how initially demanding it is to accept our essential poverty in this market capitalist world is emphasized by Laurence Freeman, leader of the World Community for Christian Meditation. He explains:

A materialistic society teaches us to deny the reality of human limitations, to avoid poverty and to see it as failure. Failure in our success-orientated society is an evil, something that always negates or diminishes life. The Christian version of poverty challenges that blurred view because its vision comes from Christ's perspective and has its focus set on the cross and the resurrection. With that focus we come to see failure quite differently. Not that we set out intentionally to be failures, but we come to see the poverty of life as part, one part but an essential part, of the mystery of life's unfolding, of its onward development and expansion.[8]

Indeed, over time, we finally begin to acknowledge that, in so many ways, this understanding has been at the heart of our life's journey for so many of us. Once we manage to see right through a dogma for living that may have been superficially and even temporarily rewarding, but has, in many ways, seen us conforming to so much that is inherently antagonistic to us and our true natures. Something that we may have sensed increasingly within:

Our stressful workloads.
Our pressurized personalities.
Our conditioned anxieties.
Our egotistical yearnings.
Our wholesale delusions.

All of this reflected in the profound sense of isolation and alienation that we may have felt so often and our desperation to reach beyond it to something far more harmonious.

A schism which – if we are not careful – can still find us searching for the kind of urgent relief that, needless to say, the system has always provided for, in all manner of ways, at its increasingly extravagant costs.

As its markets are, of course, our addictions.

Markets and sales that don't just numb us but then rearouse us for action on the work-play treadmill, with little care or compassion for the long-term consequences and the recurring turmoil for so many of us of ignoring what we actually feel deep down. As we continue to perform our dual role as workers/consumers, very often shelling out the money we earn even faster than we receive it to the delight of the credit companies.

With our pain even more acute if we become increasingly aware of what is actually happening to us, as it is actually happening, at whatever conscious level. Forced by the system, in our more realized state, into being who we are not, rather than who we are.

Until one day we finally wake up to the full consequences of this madcap existence and its side effects, and insist that enough really is enough. So much so, at long last, we determine to devote at least parts of each day to some peace and quiet, to a genuine discovery of who we really are. Even, yes, to our Spirit within.

As finally we start to feel that we prefer the honest acceptance of our poverty, whatever it truly means, wherever it may take us.

For at least it is a poverty that isn't a lie. Nor a poverty that keeps us enslaved in such a frenzied existence. And therefore, who knows, it may just rekindle some real meaning in our lives.

Even some enduring balance and sanity.

As it begins to ease our torment.

Without any craving for excess stimulation.

Or one last bargain off the Internet.

Not just for our own sakes, but, in time, we recognize, for the sake of all those who we are connected to, whoever they may be. Relationships that no longer have to suffer the debilitating effects of the pressures that can disengage and divide us all.

As well as the multi-various examples of compulsive behavior and consequent instability that have, for so long, condemned us to exist without an actual sense of our very being and the infinite peace that even now is available to us.

Helen and Paul's Story

My mum may be totally cracked but for some reason I can't quite walk out on her.

Most of my friends – especially the girls – say that if it was their mum they'd have had her sectioned a long time ago, locked away under some sort of mental health act. You can do that now they say.

"She's gross. A waste of space. She should be put down," is their verdict.

Maybe they're right. But something tells me it's not as simple as that. And it worries the hell out of me where it all might end... for the both of us.

A few months ago Mum asked me if it was OK if she changed her name. "Paul, what would you say if I called myself Helena?" I didn't see what was wrong with Helen, or why it was such a big deal to stick an 'a' on the end. But what do I know?

"Whatever makes you happy, Mum. Sounds kind of trendy, young," I said without really thinking.

She loved that. She suddenly went all kind of gushy and gave me a huge hug. Then kissed me – or more like smeared me – with that horrible glossy lipstick of hers.

When she came back a couple of hours later she'd bought me a £150 telescope. Don't get me wrong, I was really chuffed, but I didn't ask for it.

We're on the top floor and the night skies can be spectacular in the winter. The telescope I'd had since I was ten wasn't much good now. But I still didn't expect a new one just for saying she was trendy. But that's the way she is. That's the way she's increasingly become.

She wrapped it up in special paper like it was Christmas, instead of any old Saturday in November. My mum's the sort who'd love every day to be Christmas Day and not just because she dresses up like a Christmas tree even when she goes down to the supermarket for a bottle of wine. But because she is kind of like Christmas herself, all glitter and champagne, the fairy on top of the tree. Even if she is the mad, deranged fairy.

Anyway, she got dead excited and embarrassing while I was opening my present. "Go on, open it, open it!" Then when I went on the balcony to use it she just sighed and went to get changed again. "Have fun, darling. Explore the universe!"

She's like no other mum I know. Maybe it's not all to do with my dad walking out. But it's got to be a huge part. Plenty of other couples are splitting up around here and going nuts, though not as weird as my mum.

She was crazy about my dad. She still is. There are still pictures of him around the house, looking like some famous entrepreneur, which only he thinks he is. The pictures really irritate me and part of me wants to smash them up, but for some reason I don't. Maybe I sense it would drive her even closer to the edge. And me with her.

It's like, I don't know, she's... tormenting herself, still crying at night, even though it was a few years ago now. She even talks to his pictures, which is totally insane. "Les, do you remember when we did this and that?" or whatever.

It's so, so hard...

I've got to get out...

But I'm all she's got.

The first couple of years after they split up were hell. She drank so much and spent so much we had to leave the house he left her and move here. Whenever I saw her she was always in one of those dresses that look like an underskirt with a bottle in her hand. She hadn't got a clue whether it was time to get out of bed or time to go to bed. Not that she spent much time in bed.

More in the bath, still with her underskirt on. At first I thought it was her quick way of doing the washing, which I could have understood. Trouble was I could never get in the bathroom.

"Want to look at your stupid little acne in the mirror, do you?" she'd slur at me every time I knocked on the door to go to the loo. Something told me deep down that she didn't mean it – it wasn't really her somehow – but still she said it and I hated her for it. What the hell else was I supposed to feel?

Eventually, when she got out of the bath and put on another

underskirt, she'd say sorry over and over and slobber all over me, crying desperately.

"That was so horrible of me. I don't believe I said it. Please forgive me, Paul. I love you so much. You don't know how unhappy I am," she'd always say.

"Oh really, Mum, I never noticed," I felt like saying back. And eventually I did. I'm not a bloody saint.

I had to spend quite a few nights round at friends' houses during that time. I just had to take time out. But I was worried when I did. Worried about just how much of a sea creature she might turn herself into in the bath. How far under the water she might try to live.

Dad never phoned to check on her after a while. He became far too preoccupied with "managing his various commercial interests." In other words, with himself.

Looking back on it, he married her for her wildness and her... overwhelming love, Aunt Christina her sister told me. As well as the way she rebelled against much of her upbringing.

They had been childhood sweethearts, or whatever they call it, from different backgrounds. Hers a middle class, conservative, even religious one, which I find hard to believe – his a poor, abusive one – both tough in different ways, Aunt Christina said. They met when he was selling stuff on the streets outside the bookshop she was working in one summer.

In the end, even though she was talented and could have gone on to do something better, she was, more than anything, desperate to break out on her own. And so was he. Like a lot of people at that time. So they did, travelling the country in some camper van together, campaigning against everything. He was 20, she was only 18.

"We were footloose and fancy free," Mum said to me one day, with a glass in her hand.

In the evenings Dad used to run discos in various clubs and sometimes played his guitar with Mum singing in some purple dress she kept on about. She had been in the choir at school and had a beautiful voice apparently which blew Dad away when he first heard it.

In fact, Mum was beautiful full stop, judging by her photos, which she brings out now and again and which are… so tough to look at.

Whatever, the two of them felt they had it all way back then.

"We took one look at the way most people were living and decided there was no way we were going to live like that. We wanted something different. To do something that would make a difference," Mum said.

Until, in the end, Dad changed his mind and decided he did want to live like that. Not only that, he also needed to go up in the world, especially when he was offered a partnership in some nightclub by some "shrewd operator" called Mick and it all went to his head.

"Money talked and he forgot who we were, what we had planned together. Never mind who I was to him, who I still am, if only he could see it," Mum said, in tears of course, embarrassingly, yet still I can't help feeling for her. I don't know why, maybe, simply, because she is my mum. Or maybe, having lost my dad, I don't want to lose her too. God knows.

Anyway, suddenly Dad was out till all hours way past the time when Mum came back from the bar job he got her a couple of nights a week. And then she gradually turned into a "disgrace," according to him, as she kept trying to keep tabs on him.

"For hell's sake, Helen, just look at the state you've got yourself in," I can still hear him shouting over and over, waking me up, when he finally came home and found her slumped on the couch.

"I know, I'm sorry," was all she would mumble back.

After a while he didn't want her down at the nightclub at all. Claimed he was moving in higher circles and meeting important people. She was better off at home being a mother rather than making a scene with her drinking down there. Even though she was fast becoming incapable of looking after me.

Fortunately Aunt Christina came around as usual to help – to help look after Mum more like. Against the wishes of the rest of the family, who had cut her off. But Aunt Christina never gave up on her for some reason. She always loved her. Always saw a lot more in her. But she had... lost her way.

Something I could understand.

Whatever, in time Dad started coming home less and less. And then not at all.

You wouldn't believe the amount of money he raked in through the nightclub over the years, and through one or two shady operations on the side. Mum said – "Our lives were never supposed to be about that."

In time, he built a four-bedroomed place. "I've got to check on my mansion," he once said to me on the phone.

I thought he was joking. He couldn't understand why I was laughing.

"I've earned this!" he shouted.

I felt like he was threatening me. I was around 13 at the time.

I hated him then. What he did to her.

After a short while Mum called round at his lordship's. No doubt, imagining he had another woman around there, which surprise, surprise he did. Her reaction suddenly shifted from... desperation, as you would expect, to hysteria. I was terrified what would happen next. To try to keep her quiet, he gave her a job back at the nightclub. Even I was old enough to sense she should stay away.

"Where's your... self-respect, Mum?!" I shouted on her first night there, again feeling totally... humiliated, not just for me, but for her too. There was no way I could get through to her though. So I just got madder and madder.

She said she was going to wear the same purple dress the first night.

"Your dad and I are starting over, Paul. Don't worry. Everything'll be fine. We had a drink together. He's changed, thank God. He still loves me deep down. We're going back to what we had before. Being free. He's angry about the way things are in the world again. We're going to fight back. I still love him. It's who I... am. Being in love. I know he loves me really," Mum said.

I didn't know whether to laugh or cry.

Not only was it never going to last, needless to say, but it was never even going to start. All of it in her fantasy, escapist world like quite a few people I know today.

Meanwhile he was moving so fast in an entirely opposite direction nothing would get in his way. Except hopefully the dead end to which he was heading. He soon had interests in other nightclubs that went beyond drinking and dancing, someone told me.

While Mum just kept drinking and becoming wilder. Tried getting off with a couple of guests to make him jealous. One night he gave her a bin bag full of money from the night's takings and told her never to come back. Finally even she woke up.

"He's turned nasty, Paul, nasty, seedy and vicious."

She went even crazier after that. She got all kinds of jobs. To bring in more money. On top of what he sent her to keep her under control or out of guilt. She spent it on all sorts of incredible clothes. And drink, of course.

I was terrified just how bad things would get. We'd end up on the streets.

She carried on shopping whenever she was off work. She had to shop, almost like she was shopping instead of loving him. In love with shopping. Anything to stop her sitting in and thinking about him and the state into which her life had fallen. I didn't know what the hell to do. I was out of my depth, of course.

It was about that time that the spare bedroom became her dressing room. With three wardrobes in there. All of them full of stuff. She put on something different every night working in the pubs.

"What do you think, Paul, is this a little bit over the top?"

They were all over the top. The kind of dresses they probably wear at drag balls on Jupiter.

Everything soon became so flung all over her dressing room she got around by sprawling about in there rather than moving about.

I thought kids were supposed to be the ones with untidy rooms. I never had that luxury.

Some of my friends even questioned whether all Mum got up to at nights was working in bars. "She's too glammed up for just being a barmaid. She's just a slut," I overheard one of the girls saying. They really had it in for her.

But she couldn't do that, I felt. Sure she had one or two other men. But she's not like that. Something to do with the way she is... deep down. Why Aunt Christina doesn't give up on her maybe. Maybe to do with her upbringing. I'm not sure. I just feel somehow that that would finish her off. It would certainly finish me off...

Who knows, maybe she is simply out there still hoping to get a glimpse of Dad. It wouldn't surprise me. Whatever, even though part of me is still so close to my mum, I can't keep watch over her.

It just seems she's become a slave to who she is, and to him, Aunt Christina said. As well to her shopping. And to... selling herself short all the time.

"She should be so much more than this!" Aunt Christina said one night, almost in tears. Instead she seems to be permanently drunk... in a permanent daze deep down. Something she has to be to get through the days. And then the nights.

Something I can't see changing. How is it going to change? I don't want to be here when it all finally comes apart. Which it's bound to. So why the hell don't I walk straight out of the door now?

It's not just because I'm frightened of what might happen to her.

It's also... however stupid it sounds... because part of me can't help... loving her, almost... almost because of what she's become...

Why though? Why?

I know that sounds totally weird. It doesn't make any sense. But it's the only way I can describe what I feel right now.

Addictive 2

It's no wonder that it never occurs to many of us that we really could do with God, or a deeper spiritual sense of who we are, if we grow up seduced by the collective belief that everything we require for this life can be provided for by the capitalist system, irrespective of our particular status within it.

What's anything to do with God then?

How can He possibly help?

Equally, if we are all immersed within the system, it can be very difficult to recognize another person's dependency on it as having anything to do with us, especially if we see ourselves as above their particular perception of things.

"Oh, we're not like them. We don't need to keep making all the money they do to have what they want. We're perfectly content. We could do with a new kitchen and bathroom, of course, but we'll leave that to later in the year."

Or:

"At least we don't get more and more into debt the way they do. To pay for his drink and her spending. We can take it or leave it. Not that we're saying there's anything wrong with a good session or splashing out now and again."

Until some overwhelming crisis – personal, global or otherwise – finally blows right in on us too and, perhaps urgently, we are compelled to look at things in a deeply honest way. As we see just how reliant on the system – and even its addictions – we have, in truth, become in order to maintain our so-called 'quality of life' whatever that may be. Or our sense of who we think we are. Or simply to survive.

It is precisely then that it may just begin to dawn on us how random and fragile our existences actually are, fully open to the vagaries and excesses of such an inherently unstable system. As well as tragic, we begin to sense that we have allowed our actual gift of life to fall victim to this capitalist root of what we may gradually start to realize are agitated and even increasingly dysfunctional periods of behavior.

Where we may well have been initially dazzled by what has been on offer, indeed even exhilarated by its early impact, but, soon, forlorn at what we have ultimately felt at a deeper level, if we are honest.

Yet still adamant perhaps that any fundamental and even radical changes in the direction of our lives are not really necessary or possible, or they are simply too risky. Almost as if our overall basis for living, seemingly disconnected from God's spiritual presence, remains the only way forward.

With our absorption into it ensuring that all along it becomes increasingly hard to transform any difficulty or crisis to any enduring effect, cut off from the guiding influence of our actual Creator. From the omniscient, sustaining power of our loving Creator, who has, of course, always been there for us whether or not we were aware of Him.

Truths that daily are denied to us through the prevailing message that floods the airwaves and our working lives: "What are you talking about? Capitalism is the key to personal and global security. It is the only path to continued growth, prosperity and happiness."

A relentless, desperate and yes addictive message, which so many of us, and especially mounting numbers of the economically poor worldwide, are no longer seduced by.

For their overall experiences do not bear this out.

And haven't for so, so long.

Indeed many of our experiences at home do not bear this out.

For in spite of the many changes for the better.

So much else has been sacrificed.

So much else has been sucked out of us.

Especially about who we actually are.

Our inherently peaceful natures.

Our overwhelmingly empathetic natures.

For the benefits of the very few.

Something so many of us may well have sensed but now really can't ignore anymore as finally our circumstances tell us that we have nothing to lose by responding to the pleas of the voice from within.

A relentlessly caring voice which has been calling us to take radical action in line with the deeper vision that is now reemerging. Now that we have confronted the desperate sense of meaninglessness and even depression which we may have experienced for so long, seemingly apart from God's extraordinary intimacy and love.

A desolation which we must continue to face up to in silent surrender so that the spiritual can be awakened within us more and more, and at long last we fully understand what was meant in the New Testament book of Corinthians by:

My grace is sufficient for you, for my power is made perfect in weakness.[9]

Indeed, God only works through us if we do not resist what this world sees as our human failure while we courageously undergo our time of personal renewal, as Laurence Freeman tells us. For there really is no alternative to putting aside our temporary addictions and confronting absolutely the "failure of the human spirit to move beyond itself, its mortal frontiers, by its own resources."

If we do resist it and deny it, we are claiming falsely that we ourselves can do something about it and that yet again God is not at the heart of us. Freeman goes on to explain:

> If we want to understand poverty of spirit we have to accept it as the reaching of the boundaries of our being and our capacity, and finding we are unable to go further by ourselves. Yet we know that we do go further. We know the cross stretches out into the limitless expanse of the resurrection. Beyond our frontier is the realm of God.[10]

This is our ultimate destiny. The destiny of finally letting go and allowing ourselves to feel God stirring within more and more, at the same time realizing that it is Him which we are actually experiencing.

As we go on to fulfill our unique potential through Him by thinking and then acting at one with His and our true nature. Instinctively drawing on His inspiration, His presence and His power in every situation we encounter. Now that our past ordeals and future dreads have at long last been nailed to the Cross in the Christian faith.

At the same time, we should never underestimate, and keep alert to, the scale of deceit that we will continue to face from a mentality to which the statement, "we are unable to go further by ourselves," is completely nonsensical. As every day the system persists in propagating its frightened, egotistical road to salvation.

Therefore, every morning and evening, I cannot emphasize enough, we must start anew and ensure that we direct our entire sense of who we are in silence towards God, to challenge its mass manipulation of us. So that our spiritual Father can guide our thinking and bolster our resolve to make the positive, bold choices we need to make.

As we become fully alive to the extraordinary consequences of us making these choices, not just for ourselves individually, but ultimately for our loved ones and, yes, even for communities and our world.

So that growing numbers of us are then freed to reject the debilitating excesses of this economic order, as together we counter its assimilation of us and indeed humankind into some kind of terrified and monopolized think tank.

As we emerge from what has been nothing less than a battle for our souls, however conscious we may have been of it as that. A battle which has demanded enormous levels of courage and resilience and, of course, God's wonderful grace that we now realize was so tragically blocked off from us for reasons which are now much clearer to us.

Now we have seen an alternative vision, which we have uncovered through going in exactly the opposite direction from the one we have been circling in for as long as we can remember. In exactly the opposite direction from the one we may even have felt we have been sleepwalking in.

Until finally we woke up to the poverty of that exhausting existence.

That was never really going to fulfill us.

But merely delude and deny us.

By keeping us enslaved in our anxieties and 'needs.'

In our torments and addictions.

Limiting or wasting our lives.

Even forcing us to live them destructively.

Very often as someone else's minion.

As mere functionaries within some desperate collective.

As mere followers of some misdirected and frantic ideology.

Subservient to fixations and fads.

That could never reflect our real life's purpose.

For we are far, far more than that.

Each and every one of us.

Capable of experiencing God's extraordinary presence within us, whoever we are, wherever we come from.

So that we can finally move forward with real surety, meaning and therefore renewed energy in what is, less we forget, a miraculous opportunity to express our unique and eternal lives. And above all to express God's loving nature.

Helen and Paul's Story 2

Mum eventually ran short of money one day she was spending it so fast. But that, needless to say, didn't stop her shopping. Not having money or a valid credit card may have been inconvenient, but it was never going to be the end of her daily trips into town. As she tried to steal a red dress one morning that made her look like Santa's wife. I never said my mum had taste.

She was caught, of course. Partly because she was hopeless at shoplifting. But also because she was actually wearing the dress, the miss-me-if-you-can dress, as she walked out of the shop. The neon red lights on it were probably even flashing when she went through the security gates. Who knows, maybe because she was desperate to get noticed or she may have even fancied the security guard.

Or just maybe, as Aunt Christina said, she really wanted to get caught.

An overwhelming cry for help, she said.

All of this only a week after she had apparently taken a pile of her clothes over to the local charity shop. A one-woman conveyor belt from the shopping mall to the charity shops. Her insane idea of saving the world. As I said, who knows?

Just about everything was falling in on her at that time. And therefore, surprise, surprise, on me, because I couldn't leave her. She was the most drunk, the most unstable, the most weird she had ever been.

Goodness knows why, but she even pleaded to see a priest when she appeared in court. Probably just another desperate, hysterical move that was bound to fail. There didn't seem any way out for her.

The judge was trying to decide how many hours of community service to give her. But Mum just kept demanding, "I must see a priest. Please! I must see a priest."

"Please, please be quiet for once in your life," I kept muttering under my breath.

OK, her gran had taken her and Aunt Christina to church when they were girls, my aunt said, but I didn't know where this was coming from. There wasn't much evidence of God in her life up to now. Except her ridiculous attempts to tell me about it now and again, which made no impact, of course.

Anyway, someone or other in court must have thought she was genuine or took pity on her. Because he suggested a Father Jameson. The social worker suggested Father MacPhail.

Father Jameson told Mum on the phone to come to his service the following Sunday. She said she felt naked throughout it even though the dress she wore was respectable by her standards. No one was really welcoming or friendly, she said, although who knows with her. Whatever, she described the whole thing as "deadly dull" and said God certainly wasn't there. Though goodness knows how she would know.

As for Father Jameson's sermon, she said it made her feel like there was only one place she was heading after she died. And it wasn't somewhere where they wore wild and wonderful clothes.

In the end, Father Jameson didn't phone back like he said he would. And that seemed to be that. "I'm probably just a tart to him," she said, in her typically melodramatic way.

Soon after she tried Father MacPhail and he invited her around for a cup of tea in his kitchen which suited Mum more. Even though the dress was a lot brighter. And shorter.

"He sounded younger," she said.

"Mum, he's a priest!" I replied.

"So…" she laughed kind of anxiously.

She didn't bother changing whatever I said, of course. Another… excruciating moment that left me banging my head against the wall.

Whatever, to my amazement, Mum liked Father MacPhail.

"What did he say?" I asked, highly dubious about the whole thing.

"Not a lot," she said. "He just let me go on and on. It felt OK to talk to him. That's one thing I'm good at… talking to people… when I feel… comfortable with a person."

At least I didn't sense Mum had fallen in love with him, which was something. She had fallen in love with her new therapist, Rio, who had been married twice and wasn't looking for a third wife.

Father MacPhail asked Mum why she had wanted to talk to him.

"Because, I need to know… I mean, I know God cannot possibly love me after the way I've lived my life… compared to what other good people do… but is it possible… is it just possible He may not have given up on me… completely… even if it's just some of the time? What do you think?" Mum asked.

She repeated what she had said to him almost as if he was still in the room, excitably, urgently and… ridiculously.

He demanded to know whether she had really chosen to live her life the way she had.

"Think for a few moments before you answer that question, Helen," he said to her. "And tell me the absolute truth, as far as you can see it."

She answered that she had chosen to end her life on quite a few occasions but had never quite drunk enough. That was almost certainly true.

"But did you yourself choose to live that way!" he insisted.

"Well, I had a choice. Of… of course, I had a choice. And I thought I was making the right choice at the time… well, most of the time. Trying to live… according to what I believed… we believed. But then everything seemed to get in the way… and stopped us… stopped us living it. We got lost. I got lost. Terribly lost. And I became desperate to… escape… whatever it took," she replied. "But if you're asking me who is to blame for what's happened to me, of course it's me. Who else is to blame?"

"But in the end have the circumstances and people around you really been dictating the direction of your life, or have you?" he wanted to know. "Have you missed God as much as He has missed you in helping you make the important decisions in your life? Have you missed someone you could really trust at the heart of your life? Someone who, even now, if you turned back to Him, with everything you are and everything you have become, would love you even more, like you have never been loved before, and help you start over if you followed Him?"

Mum was breathless and in tears repeating all he said. Part of me was sure she was going way over the top again, but then part of me also felt that she sounded… genuine.

"But God couldn't love me that much, could he?" she replied. "He couldn't love anyone like me that much. Let alone me. I have only told you a bit of what I have done. God knows it all," she said to the Father, which all seemed true enough.

"You may not realize it yet," Father MacPhail responded, "but if you turn to Him utterly in despair at the direction you have gone in or been led in, you will become closer to Him than many of us. Precisely because of what you have gone through and what you now feel. Nor are you alone, believe it or not. For, in the end, we are all trying to get back to Him. We are all… victims, I believe, of so much. And desperate to discover what is really at the heart of our lives."

My mum was… transfixed telling me all of this despite her saying she found it so hard to believe. It seemed to… I don't know… connect with her… somehow… even if she thought it was impossible.

Whatever, her meeting and the meetings that followed with Father MacPhail did begin, I noticed very slowly, to give her some new... sense of hope... and therefore peace, I suppose.

For instance, soon after she started visiting him, I occasionally caught her in her wardrobe room, just sitting quietly on top of her clothes for a few moments, looking out of the window. Even though she still went out to the bars she worked in, of course, wearing her dresses.

She also finally began to start drinking a little less around this time and her moods that went way up and then down weren't so... unstable. OK, these were all small changes, but they were changes that made things just a bit easier for both of us. Even though there was so much that still worried and frightened me. She was still, for the most part, off her head.

I also felt... battered and bruised, I suppose, from all that happened over so many years. And I still hadn't got a clue where it would all end.

After an initial couple of meetings with Father MacPhail, Mum then began to meet other people who were being helped by him, all of which encouraged her more. "I feel like I'm not all alone anymore, Paul," she told me. "I have been lonely for so long... except for you, of course, darling," she quickly added, which also seemed weird, considering she always seemed to have people around her.

During one meeting together, Father MacPhail told Mum he felt "very close to her." As did the others. Whether she realized it or not, she was very quickly giving so much to the whole group, the Father said. Father MacPhail thought Mum was a "special person."

She was both bewildered and, at the same time... thrilled with this, even though I couldn't really understand it.

Especially as she was still the same a lot of the time at home. Still acting wildly at times. And my friends were still certain she needed to be sectioned. But the big difference, according to Aunt Christina, was that she was no longer... what did she say... "solely focused on what was happening to her."

After a month or so, Mum and the other folk she shared her experiences with began to have private masses with Father MacPhail early on Saturday evening before she went to work. It was timed to coincide with a difficult time for alcoholics and other addicts, she said. Though, as far as I could see, every night had been difficult for her.

Whatever, she asked him if it was all right if she came in her glamorous dresses to save going home and getting changed for work. "I'll be delighted to see you in whatever you come in," he said.

So were Bob, Rita and Jack, and a few of the other people I heard Mum mention, who also attended these meetings, which I could see were good for her. Eventually they all became close friends, except for Jack, who's struggling a bit, she said.

He has a gambling addiction, but he did give her a tip on a horse called Jam Doughnut, a complete outsider, which brought Mum a spectacular win. She went straight out of the bookies into the high street and bought a Tahitian dress or something. An incredibly over-the-top number, even by her standards.

Father MacPhail loved it and said if he wasn't a priest he'd like to wear it. Or so Mum said. Whatever, he didn't feel the Catholic Church was quite up to its priesthood wearing Tahitian dresses just yet, which seemed fair enough.

He did, however, drop in early one Friday night at one of the bars she works in. He had gone to ask Mum – incredibly – to lead one of their sessions while he was away.

He came round to visit us soon after and told me he couldn't get to speak to Mum for ten minutes because there were so many people chatting to her. So he just watched from the side.

"I could see that people really warm to her. Quite naturally. So do I every time I meet her. She's so... open... always there for folk.

"I spoke to some of them in the bar that night. They all seem to know about her life. And about what she's done with it, or not done with it. But also the way she has come through it all, they said. And the way she still goes on.

"How she's able to give more of herself now. Not trying to hide what she feels despite how she felt about being... rejected in her life. The kind of rejection many of them have suffered too, they told me. So they feel able to share what they have been through with her. Because they know she won't judge them. And they seem to... love her for that. For the understanding... and the genuine concern she shows them, one of them said.

"The understanding that comes from facing up to herself. With why things happened in the way they did. So she can begin to forgive herself. To... accept herself. Even to... love herself. For who she is. So her life can become a little easier and move forward. According to what's inside her. That's all I have been able to do for her, I think. Finally make your mum realize just how much she is loved by God and by everyone. So she can really be herself."

I couldn't believe it. To hear a man of God like him talking about my mum like that. When I had seen her slumped in a bath of booze, with a drink in one hand and a cigarette in the other. I couldn't really understand it.

And yet maybe... what he said began to make... at least some kind of sense with what I had... felt about her for a long time now. And with what Aunt Christina had told me about her.

And it made me somehow feel even closer to her. It meant something, as weird and as embarrassing as she still was so often. I also grew closer to Father MacPhail in all of this. I like him if I am honest. There's no bullshit about him. He's good to talk to. So much so I began to think of him as someone I was always pleased to see, whatever anyone says.

He gives Mum a huge hug when he arrives at our flat. You

can see he's genuinely happy to see her.

"He goes through a lot. It's not easy being a priest nowadays," my mum said.

"He once called our flat a sanctuary to him. Having a cup of coffee up here with me. Would you believe that? Just like the… the bar can be for me sometimes, I suppose, especially now I am drinking far less. Maybe it's where I feel most comfortable for some reason," Mum said.

Something that sounded as mad as usual. But then it was my mum saying it.

Meditation

We struggle to wake up one Saturday morning feeling bloated and hung over, not just with food and drink, but perhaps, we are beginning to wonder, with our overall existence.

Yesterday we had worked all day, at the end of another hard week, only pausing to do a little shopping at lunchtime. We had picked up the kids on the way home, quickly changed one into her party dress and the other into his football gear before dropping them off. We then raced back to the house, before showering and getting changed for a night out with friends at an Italian restaurant, which we really could have done without.

On the way to collecting the kids again, we had stopped to pick up "Granny," who had been asked to babysit, only to be told that her online shopping hadn't worked properly (again!), and that her carrots were "wooden" and her bran flakes and air freshener hadn't turned up at all.

We felt like saying that there were plenty of things that went missing in our childhood, and they still are, but it's not possible to raise those, of course.

So we were forced to take another detour to the supermarket, scouring in and around the aisles in record time, before tearing off to the football pitches.

On the way, Granny became Granny, warning that our driving had become even more erratic and "why hadn't we got anything to say?"

Before, finally, we pick up our daughter, trying unsuccessfully to extract her from the party before the birthday cake candles had been blown out. While waiting we absent-mindedly gobbled a few sausage rolls and some disgusting brown sauce-crisps before smiling gruesomely as we frog marched our little darling out to the car.

Granny and the kids were then virtually bundled out when we got back home, with our partner running past them in the driveway, demanding to know why we were late. Our language then began to deteriorate, before he reversed out and tore off to the restaurant with both of us feeling about as stressed as it is possible to feel.

Ah well, at least we had the Italian Pizza and Pasta Night to look forward to.

Needless to say, the first two glasses of wine went down in five minutes and we proceeded to overeat by about two platefuls, but then it was one of those 'eat-as-much-as-you-can' evenings. The effects of which we noticed very quickly when going straight to bed at 2am, gripping the extra three pounds around our waists in the mirror on the way. "Ugh! Disgusting."

Indeed, throughout the very short night that followed our stomachs felt like hot air balloons with heartburn and raging indigestion. So much so they were still stretched to the limit the following morning when we couldn't even summon a burp.

That didn't prevent Granny proceeding to offer bacon, fried bread and eggs, of course, which she is cooking for the kids ("Nothing wrong with a good cooked breakfast"), but which we find infuriating. Our partner somehow manages a plateful of this but the stench of the fat drives us frantically outside.

We grab a bottle of water en route, telling the rest of the

family we don't want to be disturbed, despite Granny's pleas that she needs a lift to her new gentleman friend, Arthur, who is 74 and "creepy" according to our children. For once we agree.

Fortunately, our partner is taking the kids swimming today and he will drop Granny off on the way. She still looks disappointed. Despite everything, she still wants to talk to us, but unfortunately we've not much left to give right now.

So we go into our new garden house for almost the very first time. We still haven't managed to buy any furniture for it yet, so we sit on a cushion on the floor, our back against the wall. It is tucked away in the corner of our lawn. The sun shines directly into it most of the day and already it is getting warm.

We sigh very, very deeply. It is such a release simply to be relaxing here, gently sipping water, allowing yesterday's mishmash of work, food and general mayhem to digest right out of our system, and we're sitting here till it's done, we've decided.

For an hour or so, we try to allow this day, which we really did not need on top of so much, to float out of our consciousness.

Our final conversation with our partner before bed incidentally had been a row about the cost of this one day, which comfortably ran into four figures all in, including shopping, filling up the car with petrol, the meal and a couple of hefty bills.

Finally, in that momentary peace before sleep, we insisted "never, never again," although we know we probably will, as soon as next weekend looking at the diary, because of the way we live our lives. We are supposed to enjoy eating out, it's meant to be some compensation for all the madness, but we have begun to question whether it really is lately. More and more it merely seems to be part of it.

Whatever, for now, in this garden haven, we at least feel like we are in some kind of recovery. After another half hour or so, we managed to unleash our first belch, which sounds more like one of our partner's and echoes like an impending natural disaster around the neighborhood. We leave the door of the house open as it begins to get hot through the glass and we sip more water.

We sense that we have been wanting to experience a morning like this for a long time now, a morning that is... empty of everything, as we breathe in smells and even hear sounds from the garden that we realize we haven't been conscious of for years.

Until our thoughts are suddenly invaded by conflictive doubts about whether we remembered to do "this or that with the advertising department yesterday," not to mention taking action to amend so and so's report. Closer to home, we can also feel a deeply frustrating and inevitable guilt over Granny coming through.

After our first toilet trip around mid-morning, we begin to feel the pressure not only to do something but extraordinarily enough, in the kitchen on the way back, to eat something! Perhaps just a healthy snack, such as a piece of fruit – that wouldn't do any harm, would it? It may even help.

But then something suddenly says to us, "Hang on a minute, you've been enjoying this morning, haven't you? Did you enjoy much about yesterday? And will you enjoy this afternoon if you start eating again? Or will you be disappointed and depressed with yourself? For goodness sake, what is the matter with you?"

We return slowly to the summer house, our still-expanded stomach now making groaning sounds, more probably because it's still working through yesterday's pile. We sip some water and sit once more, needing absolutely nothing, we realize, except to be empty and still.

After a while, as we manage to relax our minds again by letting these conflictive thoughts pass, we discover that we are, to however small a degree, opening ourselves up to feelings that we haven't felt for a very long time. To something that, we sense, may even involve more than simply wanting to be at peace that we recall from long ago.

But then we begin to get increasingly anxious that we may

have just heard the front door bell. Other concerns pour in on us: a tax-related phone call we need to make, an insurance letter that must be written, a new carpet that needs to be ordered, so much so that in time we almost feel as if we need to take our minds right out of our heads in order to find some peace! Maybe we do...

"Please help!" we almost plead into space.

It continues, at times, to be a desperate struggle, but the more that we remain still and accept this isolation, the more we realize just how the deep breathing of today may just be far more beneficial than the hyperventilating of yesterday.

So we become determined to breathe even more slowly and deeply.

As, at last (a big breakthrough!), we suddenly feel that we now have a place to which we can go, not just now but, who knows, regularly in the months ahead to find some peace, away from that which makes us so tense so much of the time.

If only we can find the time though.

Which we seemed to have when we were younger.

And which we just must make again now.

By insisting upon the changes in our lives that we need.

Not just for ourselves.

But... yes, even for the benefit of our whole family.

There even seems a certain sanity to what we are realizing and saying to ourselves now, compared to so much that isn't.

As we now close our eyes, almost as if we are closing down nothing less than our total... yes... our total sense of who we are in order to be entirely still.

Immersed as we are in a silence that is, it almost seems, trying to... yes, it is trying to help us, indeed to be with us, maybe... even... to say something to us. A silence which... if we are honest... we almost feel able to... to fall right into... as it calms us over and over.

How... amazing this all is, it suddenly dawns on us.

What a relief it all is.

The more we simply allow ourselves to experience it.

Experience something that is...

... not just trying to connect with us...

... but, yes...

.. yes... even to love us.

Part II

Liberation: Discovering Who We Actually Are

Chapter 5

Confronting Death

Queen Elizabeth II, Sovereign of the United Kingdom and one of the pillars of the established order, also recognizes, feels and clearly yearns for the truth about who we all ultimately are. Many of us may have forgotten her Christmas address at the beginning of the new Millennium when she said:

> Whether we believe in God or not, I think most of us have a sense of the spiritual, that recognition of a deeper meaning and purpose in our lives, and I believe that this sense flourishes despite the pressures of the world.[11]

But what led her to think that? Is it something she felt she ought to say as head of the church in her kingdom? Or has this spiritual sense come directly from God in connection to her own life's experience?

The Queen is in some ways, of course, just like the rest of us when it comes down to it, in the sense that her personal life has had to face up to all the joys and tragedies that so move all our lives, and her suffering has, I'm sure, at times, sent her plummeting to the depths of despair, just like the rest of us.

Wealth and privilege offer no sanctuary when those who we love are in torment or dying. The comforts they provide can help but, in the end, we all confront death not just penniless, but, more critically, finally facing up to the truth about our ultimate identity.

So perhaps, like many of us, the Queen has been genuinely driven to God in those moments of despair, in those moments of utter poverty that tear into our structured lives and provide opportune moments to bring ourselves urgently and yet intimately before Him. And her developing relationship with Him at these points has led her to put to one side so much of what is ultimately illusory and focus on the "deeper meaning and purpose in our lives," which she clearly feels most of us sense.

It was perhaps an unexpectedly open, even extraordinary, address in the context of our increasingly secular world, governed and controlled by the powers and pressures of capitalism and globalization, bearing in mind what she is supposed to represent. But then is it that surprising when you consider just how much we have glimpsed of not only her humanity, but also her vulnerability over recent years?

I am certainly inclined to take what she said far more as a heartfelt spiritual appeal to us all as fellow human beings, rather than as some kind of platitude from the head of the institutional church to her subjects.

The relatively illusory economic order we live under *is* the antithesis not just of the dominant Christian religion in Western capitalist countries, but also of our wider universal spirituality.

It is crucial for our own ultimate reawakening that we recognize and face up to that truth.

And face up to the reality that it will always – due to its roots in our faithlessness and fear, seemingly apart from God – focus primarily on our financial and materialistic security as our basis for being alive on this earth. Thereby indoctrinating and coercing us into somehow trusting in all that for our salvation rather than focusing on our eternal and therefore spiritually empowering sense of who we really are.

We also have to confront the inescapable truth that, by its relentless and insatiable nature, it will make it increasingly difficult for the vast majority of us to find the frequent silent time that is essential to take the attention off our egotistical selves and reconnect more profoundly with our Higher identity.

That said we really do not have to be this system's victims.

And increasing numbers of us aren't.

As finally, in the midst of whatever difficult or even traumatic period of our lives, many of us feel compelled to face up to our relationship with God rather than with the desperate, prevailing fixations of this age. Almost as if they are more important than life itself.

"Hey, we need to take out an insurance policy on the life assurance policy we've got, just in case the life assurance policy we've got doesn't pay up, in the unlikely event one of us should die, which we won't, but just in case we do."

No. All these anxieties and pressures can, at long last, be put to one side. Once we finally face up to that which we feel most vulnerable about, that which keeps us enchained within this terrified system – our sense of being ultimately nothing because we have no sense of being primarily spiritual.

In other words, our sense of death or oblivion.

A sense which many societies, especially in the West, reflect so little on, talk so little about and therefore have so much difficulty dealing with, even though from a very early age many of us may have to experience it, through the loss of grandparents or other members of our family. Perhaps even immediate ones.

An avoidance and perhaps painful denial of this subject merely, of course, serves to intensify our enduring dread and even terror about it. Like so many things that we block out because they involve an apparent unknown that doesn't, in reality, have to remain unknown. Because, all the while, given a more honest perspective, inspired from within, we can begin to tackle it head-on and then to see right through to the other side.

To see beyond the darkness of our wretched fear to the reality of our God within.

To see beyond our separate, illusory world to the unity of the spiritual within.

To see beyond what we have turned this life into to what our eternal life truly offers us.

To see beyond Christ's sense of desolation to His realization of the Kingdom of God.

As finally we begin to put who we really are right at the heart of our whole life experience. By giving full expression to our Divine consciousness, as an expression of the natural rhythm and indeed wonder of life that is continuously available through all that God gives us. A full appreciation and acceptance of which really does begin to transform us.

So much so that when, in time, we come face to face with the ageing of those we love, perhaps with regards to our own parents, or we look back on photos from when we ourselves were younger, we do so with a sense of fulfillment at the journey we have all been on. Reflective of increasingly aware lives – lived first and foremost by individual spirits – with our full potential gradually revealed and then expressed.

Rather than to view ourselves simply as sad old people who, sooner rather than later, are merely awaiting our departures from this perplexing world into some vague hope of an afterlife.

Especially when it never had to be that way. For we all have the opportunity right now to experience the spiritual consciousness that is within each of us as a force that will never dim.

Because, less we forget, if our spiritual God is infinite then so, through His eternal presence, are we.

Indeed, of course, we may well find that, the older we become, our intimacy within this presence stirs an even greater sense of surety and empowerment, as we act far more wisely and effectively in dealing with whatever situation comes before us. With our daily lives lived far more in harmony, rather than in conflict, with who we are, to the benefit of all those we come into contact with and our world.

A confrontation with our ageing and even possible death at any age therefore can, in the end, be an extraordinary opportunity. For by beginning to contemplate that which we cannot avoid, we can not only begin to liberate ourselves from our infatuation with saving ourselves, but we can find ourselves opened up to life as it was always meant to be for us, at one with God's selfless and limitless vision.

Something that begins the moment we stare straight into a sense of nothingness that isn't, in reality, a nothingness at all.

But a release from feeling bound by a fear of death and therefore of life.

A fear that merely incites us to enslave our hearts and souls in a relentless struggle for security. As if that is more essential than actually being alive.

The folly of all that.

Of always worrying about what lies ahead.

Of always being anxious that we haven't got enough.

When our lives are so precious right now.

And the end just may be closer than we think.

We can miss out on so much if we are not alive to this.

The chance to reveal God's extraordinary grace and love.

Especially to those who are closest to us.

But also to those who we may meet at any time, who feel little or none at all.

Most critically of all, we could even be missing out on the opportunity to transform and empower people with the sense of eternal surety that we now have. Inspiring them with deeper and lasting insights that they may well have been seeking for so long.

For that is now the most vital vocation in our world today, the vocation of being at one with God's nature, which is our nature, wherever we go. Offering His extraordinary spiritual peace and compassion which radiates a level of awareness way beyond our understanding.

As more and more of us finally wake up fully to the fragmented signs of our age and embrace right now this urgent opportunity for change that is waiting to be revealed through us all.

By, at long last, acting upon our true identity which stands way above this compulsive existence, and is far more reflective of who we really are. Through our listening to a deeper voice within that is forever trying to speak to our weary and at times bewildered souls. Uttering words of guidance amidst the sometimes hysterical goings-on in our daily lives. Seeking to pierce the terrified din with a way forward if we can only take heed and be silent.

In the end what it comes down to is that we must trust this spiritual consciousness for what it is – our own true and ultimate consciousness – and listen to it reassuring us that our physical deaths really aren't the end for any of us, and with that reassurance we can launch ourselves into free and exceptional lives that express our Divine potential. If we can finally calm our mortal terror and stop insisting that we are in control.

When we are so clearly not.

Indeed, the days of our ego-led existences are coming to an end.

It is only a matter of time.

So many of us sense and know this.

So much of our world even yearns for this.

We simply cannot go on and on like this.

Things inevitably are coming to a head.

So why don't we face up to this reality?

Why don't we move beyond our self-absorption right now?

Let us surrender without delay.

As we finally give expression to our Higher selves.

Rachel and Ruth's Story

"Molly, I've got something quickly to tell you before I go to work. Mummy... Mummy may be going away... for a little while... even a long while... do you understand what that means, sweetie?"

No, of course, I didn't say that to her. She's only just three. What would be the point of trying to tell a three year old that? Especially when it's not true anyway.

My husband Steve mopes around the house every waking minute, cuddling Molly, as well as Katie, all the time. Making it obvious something may be up. Even though it isn't. Causing so much chaos in the house!

As if I haven't got enough to deal with at the moment with all that's going on at work. Still though, he keeps telling me to speak to the girls. As if what he is suggesting is somehow easy, never mind necessary.

"OK, you try. You try if you think it's so simple!" I yelled at him racing out of the door one day.

I was rushing, needless to say, because I was late as usual. One of the few days recently that I've actually felt fit enough to work, so I've got to make the most of it. I must have time to consult with my solicitor before the talks begin with Darrow. That's what's important right now.

"Make sure Molly's on time for nursery today and especially Katie for school. And make sure you pick Katie up from Karen's. Oh, and don't forget my dry cleaning," I shouted at Steve. Sophie, their nanny, has Fridays off.

What is the point? What is the point to anything? Being brought up. Getting educated. Getting a good job. Being married. Getting a nice house. Having children. Getting a better job. Running my own business. Getting a bigger house. Expanding the business. What is the point to any of it, if I am just going to... if I am just going to die? Which I am not. When I've got it all.

Why me? I know everyone feels this. But so what? I'm me. And I can't bear it. I can't! I want everything back to normal. I don't want even to think about the possibility of being dead. Even if it is just a possibility. Which it isn't. Not that I'm scared of dying. I am genuinely not. I just don't want to be dead. That's fair enough, isn't it! I've so got much to live for.

Just look at the business that I've built up. All my work. Who will run it without me? Danielle and Natalie couldn't run a burger stall.

I want my life back just as it was. My business. My family. My children. I'll even put up with Sophie despite her nattering all over the house. At least the kids like her and she somehow manages to keep on top of things.

Do you know what Molly said to me the other evening? "I love you so much, Mummy, I don't know what to do." Can you believe that? Of course it was sweet, but it was horrible. I'm not insensitive. I love her too. It's just I'm incredibly busy. I can't face it. I shouldn't have to!

I must stop all this ridiculous imagining. That's the worst thing. Especially with this vital meeting coming up. Darrow is a small, outdated travel company but it has a good customer base. Once fully modernized and specialized with tailor-made itineraries and eco credentials it will be an excellent acquisition. I must be absolutely focused. And, above all, not start throwing up. Especially over Patricia Darrow. Whatever I might think of her personally.

Please don't let me throw up, God. All right, be a bastard and threaten my life. But don't let me throw up. Otherwise I really will wonder what kind of torturous God you are.

Feelings I revealed to my oldest friend Ruth the other night in our house. And got back one of her inane... pained stares in return.

"God is trying to kill me, you do understand that! He's deciding whether He should take my life away. Not that I will let Him. I won't!" I almost shouted.

No response, of course. Almost as if there is nothing actually switched on inside her, whatever I say. Taking sides with Steve because I haven't told the girls.

"Nothing to say, nothing to help me? Can't you speak? I thought I was the one who was supposed to be ill," I suggested without response.

Still nothing. As dumb and docile as ever. Which I refuse to be like whatever is happening to me. I never have been and never will be like that. I will go on and on, striving as hard as I can, like most people. Especially now with such crucial negotiations going on.

"My life isn't over yet! Nowhere near yet," I feel like screaming at her, even though I don't because I don't need to and I can't be bothered.

How can she be like that... my oldest friend? It's so easy for her who is healthy. Not that she's lived any kind of life up to now. Single, in a part-time job, stuck in that couscous café stroke bookshop, with no kind of a social life. Pretending to save the world by doing nothing.

I'm not being horrible. I know she's been through a lot lately and been a wreck at times, but I'm the one who's lived a full life with my career. And my family, of course. She's just retreated instead of fighting back and meeting it head-on. So who is she to be insinuating I might be dying when I'm not?

"I'm your best friend... since we were five," she said sickeningly to me recently, as if she was making some grand statement.

Well, she won't be my best friend much longer if she keeps glaring at me like that. Except I don't bother going there. Because I haven't got time to argue.

And also, because I still feel for her, who came home to find a note out of the blue from her partner, Gary, saying he was leaving her after nine years and was starting a new job down south on his own. Well, that was what his message said. As well as the thoughtful, "Our relationship has become boring."

After Ruth stupidly let herself love him too much. And then she fell totally apart. Gave up a promising career in land surveying, sold the house at a loss, everything gone. Went back to live with her family for a while. Back to square one. Now here.

All of which was crazy in my view, but not as crazy as this strange, deep outlook on life she now has, which mostly involves trying to be calm and is just a little difficult to accept. Especially with me up to my eyes in acquisitions and death threats.

But what was especially difficult to take from her was what happened next. Suddenly, one evening, she started to become all sort of emotional with me after we'd had a couple of glasses of wine. We were reminiscing about when we were younger, and as I got up to walk out of the room, she tried to hug me. I didn't mind the chat or even the hug to a degree, but then she even started to... cry.

I pulled away instantly. "For hell's sake, Ruth, what's the matter with you? There's nothing really wrong with me. I'm still living if you hadn't noticed. Pull yourself together."

I hated her reaction to that. Yet another pained sigh, followed by yet another agonized expression, before she finally managed to summon the energy to say,

"Rachel... do... you... know what is affecting me the most?"

"Goodness knows," I replied.

"It is... actually facing up to the reality about just what it means when our lives... mine, yours, everyone's... all we have ever done and experienced over so long... when they actually come to an end on this earth and we have to move on..."

"What are you talking about?" I interrupted.

"Do we really appreciate the full consequences not just for us... but for everyone in our lives... our friends, our families... and especially our children?" she asked.

"What? Of course we do!" I yelled back.

"That we will no longer... see... what... becomes of them. Who... they will marry. Their... children. Being close to them... with them... during all the important moments in their lives. It's all so... amazing... so... heartbreaking," she carried on.

"I never thought much about this before. Not until everything I went through last year when Gary walked out... cutting himself off entirely from me. Dying, I suppose, in my life... something I am... going through again right now... with you," Ruth concluded, before bowing her head, almost in exhaustion.

Suddenly the utterly matter-of-fact, utterly cruel way she said that imploded within me like... I don't know... like a block of ice on a cavity. I couldn't for the life of me understand why she was saying it. Why she was being so... brutal?

As much as I hated her at that moment, I knew she just wasn't like that.

I was desperate to let out my fury, but somehow, I just couldn't. Something... inside was tearing away at me and I couldn't stop it. As she started up again...

"It has taken me so long to face up to this separation, this loneliness that maybe we all face at some point, Rachel. To face up to it and somehow move beyond it. By learning to cherish every moment we have with those we love, even though we know that, in the end, we all have to say goodbye to each other, in this world at least."

Finally, I managed to respond. "Why are you saying all this to me now? Why... why are you being so heartless? It's not actually helping me, believe it or not! Especially when I'm not anywhere near dead! You're not standing over my grave, you know."

I moved away from her. "I'm going back to the office. There are some important documents that I have to pick up that I forgot. Steve'll be back any minute."

But she wouldn't leave it there. And, for the life of me, I couldn't understand why. It was taking so much out of her, never mind me.

"Stop following me around, will you?" I bellowed. "Look, I really have to go back to work. I've got my meeting tomorrow. You can stay and keep an eye on the children, can't you? You haven't got anything urgent or vital, have you...?"

"You know I will always keep an eye on your children..."

I really didn't like what she inferred, by that. But I had finally made it outside. And I was just desperate to get away from her. But, unbelievably, she stepped uncertainly in front of me. Suffocating me.

"What are you doing?"

"Rachel, please, you really have got to face up to..."

"To what?" I shouted.

"You know what..."

"Look, Ruth, I told you, I need to get to the office!"

"Things are getting totally out of hand here..."

"Please get out of my way!"

"Katie and Molly have to be told..."

"Move!"

"Steve can't..."

"Steve can't cope with anything! And nor can you!"

"Rachel, you've got to..."

"Get to work! Let me go!"

And I pushed her aside as she tried to block my path again because I really had had enough. She stumbled over either accidentally or more likely melodramatically.

Just then, of course, true to the day I was having, Katie and Molly came out of the front door. They claimed they were frightened by our shouting. They began asking a whole lot of awkward questions.

"I have to go back to work just for a few minutes, girls. Mummy won't be long. Daddy is on his way home. Ruth is staying till then," I said and drove off.

Katie and Molly's... terrified eyes haunted me over the next few days.

What did everyone expect of me?!

If Ruth was right, which she wasn't, I was the one with little time. And I was the one who was buying a company, for goodness sake! Our future! Their future!

Why couldn't everyone keep their emotions under control?

Yet they couldn't. So it even began to affect me. I lost it myself later that evening, running out into the back garden later on, screaming, "I can't deal with this!" even though I am still not sure I have anything to deal with.

Ruth rushed out, overreacting and panicking as usual, which quickly made me pull myself together. She sat down panting, staring at me.

"What's the matter with you? Can't I even yell now and again," I protested. She went back inside. I thought she was supposed to be helping. But how could she? She'd never experienced the kind of pressures I was experiencing.

Despite everything that was going on between us, she had started coming over every day after work to help out with the kids, which I suppose was good of her. Not that I was arriving home that late or was that unwell. But we needed her because incredibly Sophie had left for some reason that she would only tell Steve.

Why was everything changing so much all of a sudden?

Why was everything so uncertain so much of the time!

Whatever, I started going into work a little earlier in the morning. Because I decided throwing myself into the company was the best way to deal with my so-called death sentence. I wasn't feeling any worse some days despite them warning me about doing too much. All I was was just tired and sick sometimes with the treatment and the piles of medication I was on. So I got on and worked. And occasionally had a short nap in the middle of the day. Danielle and Natalie weren't so useless they couldn't wake me up.

It also avoided all the chaos and tears in the house in the morning. Steve was better at dealing with that. Nor did he need to be in so early. He was on flexi-time. In fact, his whole life was on flexi-time as far as I could see.

The only problem was he didn't really deal with it. Katie and Molly had both started being very naughty with him in control, or rather not in control. So when I had to come home early some days, because I was exhausted, there was mayhem around the house. The girls were cheeky to me, especially Katie. They screamed that they missed Sophie. But they didn't realize what I had to put up with, with her non-stop nattering.

Then there was Ruth with that saintly look. Supposedly helping. She was lucky she didn't have a real job, shared a house and only ate lettuce. Some of us have bigger overheads.

At least Steve was just silent and got on with it, in his own inefficient way. But I could tell Ruth still wasn't going to let things rest with me. My dearest friend! Things blew up again one night:

"Steve and the girls, Rachel, they have... virtually stopped talking. They're very frightened..."

"What, about me? Do you think this is easy for me? With this acquisition still in question? Missing virtually the whole of last week? Do you think it's easy for me not being able to do everything I usually do?" I replied.

Unbelievably, she looked amazed at my response.

I had had enough. It was incredible what she was saying to me. What did she expect me to do with the girls? Spend all the time I supposedly had left telling them how I might be going to die, even though I wasn't? What was the point in that? I had to focus on what was important. What I could still do for my business. And for them through it. So I could leave them some legacy if the worse did come to the worse, which I was still convinced it wouldn't.

I shouted all this at her and then added, "Why can't you understand what I am saying to you?"

"Rachel, they need you right now. Not when it is too late," she pleaded incessantly. "This time is critical!"

"And that is precisely why I am trying so hard right now! I am worth nothing dead. My business could be worth a small fortune. I have someone in mind who could run it after I go. If I go. If only I can make this deal. It's who I am right now. Why can't you see this?"

But I could tell from her expression that yet again she just couldn't grasp it. She just couldn't get it whatever I said to her.

Confronting Death 2

Eventually... eventually when we are confronted with the mortality of those we love, or even, in the end, ourselves, we may feel so broken that we become compelled to give up on our own egos, not to mention our ultimately frail bodies and minds, as the source of our salvation.

Depending on whether we can summon the courage to face up to our desperate predicament for exactly what it is and then give ourselves boldly and exclusively to God in the silence of His reassuring presence.

A silence that may initially feel like an absolute nothingness but in time we realize is filled with His all-enveloping spirit that gradually becalms our fears and inspires an altogether Higher and more harmonious awareness of who we are.

Lifting us way beyond the agonizing sense of separation we will continue to endure if we keep turning to what the capitalist world offers for some kind of solace. Where more and more we feel that our lives are enclosed in some kind of ghetto of perpetual deceit and therefore anguish. That for so long has made it so difficult for us to see up to and beyond such a terrified and limited perspective.

To see that there is and always was something inherently extraordinary and even miraculous about our time on this earth, which we have been kept so tragically from. Something inherently sacred and primarily loving beyond the values of this economic order, which have been predominantly conditioned by.

This order which continues to propagate its competitive and aggressive messages of need and greed, poverty and profit, failure and success, for ourselves and humankind. In direct contrast to the Divine nature that is reflected in our far more contented, assured and harmonious selves.

A schism that is reflected in our obsession with what we ourselves strive for on a daily basis compared to what God can accomplish through us to far greater effect.

Until, finally, we respond to our instincts and search for:

Something far more liberating in a world of such prescribed fear.

Something far more visionary in a world of such blinkered ideas.

Something far more intimate in a world of such fractured relations.

With our vision beginning to change dramatically.

Through our regular surrender to His spiritual consciousness.

Through our inspired reaction to His daily promptings.

And through our absolute reliance on His infinite grace.

With our God and Creator, now no longer in tears at so many of the wrong turnings that we have ended up taking, at so many different stages of our lives. But rejoicing in the courage we have shown in returning to our true and original natures in Him. Having finally accepted that nothing less than the actual death of our egotistical selves will suffice. With any vestiges of our old yearnings for personal security or even kudos consigned to a past to which we shall never return.

As we understand that:

Facing the absolute dissolution of who we once were opens us up to life as it should be.

To an eternal life that embraces us all.

To a unique life that gives meaning to us all.

To an unfettered, exciting life that risks all.

For the love of all.

Reflecting the ultimate life that, at the same time, fills us with gratitude for all that we have already been given and then seek actively to pass on.

Now that we have finally and urgently faced up to our

mortality and seen how, in the end, such courage can restore us to our authentic state, to a realization of our actual being in God beyond birth, death and body. In this world, yet also not of this world, as the Christ of the Gospels told us.

With our values now no longer driven by those perpetuating such a desperate order, but with us wholly liberated, we are able to lay genuine seeds of hope and renewal wherever we go. Indeed the essence of who we are now begins to overflow with Divine inspiration and compassion.

A state of being we become passionate to pursue once we don't just sense but know that we are acting in absolute harmony with who we really are. Exhilarated that our lives are at last genuinely alive to all that is both within and around us. The more we respond to our spiritual voice urging us to let go of and to die to any preconditioned fears that may be trying to resurface and instead we turn resolutely each and every day to who we truly are.

Whatever situation presents itself.

However difficult it may prove to be.

However even perilous it may even seem.

Indeed especially in such situations.

We must be utterly committed.

To the awakened presence in our lives.

So that over and over we experience God's reassurance and enlightenment affecting all that we do. At the same time making us awake to the many extraordinary opportunities that will come our way.

For they will come our way.

With God guiding our every action.

His voice urging a leap of faith.

His grace providing a way forward.

Through a whole new vision alive within us.

What a blessing this is for us.

What a transformation it offers to us.

A transformation from death to a fullness of life.

From fear of death to an urgency for life.

Indeed to an expression of the Kingdom of Life.

Something that is a tragedy to continue to deny.

Something that is an agony to continue to deny.

Something that we will no longer continue to deny.

Rachel and Ruth's Story 2

Rachel finally died exactly two weeks ago today.

I'd been expecting it to be one of the most unbearable deaths I could watch anyone suffer. Hanging on in sheer terror. Even more in terror than in pain. Until finally it killed her. With little sign of her being able to let go at all.

Of course, I too had initially been terrified of what was to come. I now realize that was one of the reasons I was so... horrible to her, my closest friend. I needed her to face up to what was happening to her for my sake too, not just the girls'. And somehow ease the intensity of my grief as well as hers.

I am not a strong person. I have always been a frightened person, I suppose. I don't know why. Maybe that's why I made the mistake of relying on someone like Gary so much, who I can now see was always liable to take off when the time was right.

Rachel's frantic struggle to avoid the inevitability of her death was... to a large part, of course, because of her inability to contemplate something after life. As a result, I knew that I would have to be with her right to the end, whatever we were to go through.

Especially after all that came out in those final terrible weeks. When things finally began to... unravel completely.

That we had no idea about, Steve or I. That at first I absolutely refused to believe. And couldn't even begin to deal with. But now weeks later, the desperate signs are there, if only I'd been more aware.

I never, ever imagined Rachel was having some kind of an

affair. I know the TV and the newspapers hark on about affairs as if every second person is having them. But the majority of ordinary people aren't. They just go on. In love, in friendship, or neither, I suppose.

So when you suddenly discover someone very close to you has actually taken that desperate step, especially someone with young children, it is an incredible shock.

None of us could cope with the fallout. As if we weren't dealing with enough already.

To us, Rachel was Katie and Molly's mum as well as Steve's wife.

She was not someone else's affair.

No wonder she was so stressed when she came home every night.

She wasn't just dying.

She wasn't just saying goodbye to her children and husband forever.

She wasn't just running her precious company like some mad woman.

She was also racked with the guilt of her terrified affair.

With her personality becoming more and more... unstable.

Of course, she blamed herself totally for all that had happened. "I can't bear myself. I knew exactly what I was doing. It all started at the end of another horrendous day. And I just... Ruth, I'm evil. Doing that with what Steve and the kids are going through. Be... betraying my family. The Darrow acquisition collapsing too."

The affair was, I guess, just some kind of relief from the pressure she was under, something I tried to tell her. Probably some kind of... frantic attempt to... hang onto life. To feel... still alive.

"Please don't be so hard on yourself," I said, not really knowing what to say. The words by now just sort of... tumbling out, uncertain of whether they were making any impact.

In hindsight, the affair may well have accelerated her decline even quicker. So much bearing down on her every moment of every day.

Her whole desperate, frantic existence killing her just as fast as her illness was.

Certainly, she couldn't escape anywhere. Home was no longer an escape. Work certainly wasn't an escape, whatever she felt. And her failing body and tortured mind were, of course, no escape either.

He, whoever he was, became the escape.

"It's no excuse, Ruth, but I just needed some kind of… secret… separate existence," she told me. "Into which I could lose myself for a short time. Before having to face everything again."

It went on intermittently over three months. Only I would ever know the extent of it. As I decided there was no point in anyone else being aware of it.

The whole thing only came to light because Rachel told the man she was simply suffering from some virus which wouldn't go away. Yet another deception. And when he found out the truth, he responded without thinking and burst round to the house. Katie answered the door. It was obvious from how upset he was that he wasn't just some work associate from another company.

"Is it true? Is it true?" he kept asking Steve and I. "I could see she wasn't that well."

Though part of me was desperate just to shut him up and send him on his way, part of me somehow felt deeply for him. It was obvious that he loved Rachel.

I tried to convince Steve otherwise. "They're just good friends," I said, putting my arm around him. Though part of me felt that what I said was a waste of time.

Steve was already living in a shell. Occasionally, popping his head out. He didn't pop it out anymore. Fortunately, I was able to make up some story so the girls didn't realize who the man was. But I knew, during the desperate time I spent with Steve, that he could not hold it back from Rachel completely. I didn't ask him to. It was too much, having to lock that inside.

However, all he said to her was, "The man you've been having an affair with came round today. Your daughter answered the door." Then he walked out. The courage and willpower it must have taken to limit his response to that was enormous.

The revelation of the affair broke Rachel utterly. Deep down, I knew she had been devoted to Steve and her children. But other things had got in the way, particularly in the last few years. Her wholesale absorption into her business really took off with all the new technology she had introduced and had to pay for. Then onto the re-marketing of the company and the takeover plans.

She seemed to become hooked on it all and therefore became... I don't know... increasingly uptight... and, at times, even unbalanced, it appeared to me. She needed, above all, to slow down, not... not intensify everything. Although she would completely disagree, of course.

"I do love Steve really, you know. And Katie and Molly," she kept saying over and over one horrendous night, when the drugs were taking effect. There was little holding back of anything by then. "But somehow I just felt so... restless and frustrated so much of the time for some reason. Like... like something was continually getting under my skin. Do you know what I mean?"

By this time I felt I'd reached way beyond what I could deal with, coming on top of what I had gone through with Gary. But somehow from somewhere I managed to get myself up each day and start afresh.

By evening time I was... emotionally drained again... but was still being sustained through it all while at the same time being stretched to new limits.

After managing to struggle on for a long while, Rachel grew noticeably weaker fairly quickly. Work became out of the question even for her. Her bouts of pain and increasing sickness wore her down. She was not helped, of course, by panic attacks over her fate and the circumstances in which she was leaving Katie, Molly and Steve behind. It was all suddenly hitting home very hard now that she was simply having to lie down with nothing to occupy her mind.

The people at my work were understanding as usual and gave me holiday time and then some unpaid leave. And somehow... despite my overall sense of helplessness... I did begin to wonder whether I was somehow... just meant to be there, even though I constantly wanted to run straight out of the door.

Meanwhile, Steve continued to go to work and the girls to school and the playgroup. Rachel was in and out of hospital. Until, finally, she came home, not to die, but to cling on. The Macmillan nurses, who are wonderful, came around to help.

My increasing faith in... and sense of something beyond this life, which I had discovered in my own... isolation at losing someone I had loved... grew even more intense during some of the days that followed. Which was just as well as Rachel's torment occasionally became incessant. And took both of us, of course, way beyond anything we had ever experienced.

But this was not about me. This was about her. Imagine, from her perspective... staring into an abyss of... of death and annihilation, rather than being comforted by at least some hope... some faith in an... eternal life, if only she could have felt it. Something I have glimpsed from time to time and now hung onto desperately.

Quite a few times, I pleaded with Rachel to open her heart to at least the possibility of our life here being a... a passing journey for all of us... before going onto something else... however much part of me felt I was wasting my breath.

In truth, though, Rachel simply became obsessed with the guilt and even failure of her life towards the end. "Patricia Darrow is now running my company. I cannot believe she of all people has taken it over. And she got it for a pittance. All because of this! She knew I had to sell," she kept on... and on.

So much so, I believe, she died, at times, reliving the most painful failures, the very worst acts and... I suppose in the final days, the most dreaded fears of her life.

What on earth made her do that?

What blinded her to so much of the good within her?

Because, believe it or not, she had been a good person. A... funny, rebellious, even radical friend when she was younger. A... concerned and caring human being before she was married... and, yes, a... a deeply loving mum and wife.

Only in her later years had she... lost her way. Somehow struggling to sense what... what her life was... truly about anymore. Frantically torn this way and then that all the time. Trying to hang onto who she had been.

As for myself, with so much time spent simply sitting and waiting during this period, I read and reflected even more than I had done before in the last couple of years. As much to keep me sane as anything. During all of this I came across some words from the American psychiatrist, M. Scott Peck, two weeks before Rachel died:

> Our unconscious is God. God within us... We are born that we might become, as a conscious individual, a new life form of God... If we can identify our mature free will with that of God, we will then have become one form of the grace of God.[12]

I didn't fully... appreciate, of course, the full meaning of these words when I first read them. The impact they can have. On all of us. And as for putting them into practice...

But something about them meant something and affected me during that intense time with Rachel. Offering me some understanding with what I sensed about her – that not only was she really an instinctively good person, but something prevented her living as a fully… 'conscious' form of God's grace in the later years of her life.

That, to me, was the tragedy of her life.

The tragedy, maybe, of so many of our lives.

At the right time, I would try to share these words in a positive way with her even though they may have had little impact. I would also try to share them with Steve and eventually with Katie and Molly in relation to their own lives. For I would never lose contact with the three of them, I knew, because they were now my only earthly link to my oldest friend. And I loved them dearly, especially after all we had been through. Just like I had loved her.

Steve and Rachel were, in fact, reconciled a little close to her death. Maybe, I have to admit, because I felt something compelling me to draw them together, despite my doubts and fears that I might make the situation worse. But at least, I suppose, it meant that Rachel could summon a simple, "Steve, I'm so, so sorry," which may be important for him in the years to come. And they were able to hold hands and embrace in silence for a moment… one agonizing yet, I think, essential moment together.

Perhaps, in time, I hoped… they would even inspire memories for Steve of what they had once shared. Although that may have been hoping for too much. I don't know. Whatever, I did feel he loved her despite that final act of desperation. He always had. Her natural… exuberance had given so much joy to his… his deep-rooted conservatism in the earlier part of their relationship.

It wasn't, however, during Rachel's final days with Steve or indeed with me that something suddenly began to change a little within her. It all began to happen, unsurprisingly, during her time with her young children, Katie and Molly. With whom her… aching heart was always liable to break apart, I suppose, at what life… in the end, had thrown at her with her premature and, even… unprepared death.

I have no children. Maybe I will never have. I don't know anymore. But at least I can sense how a mother's maternal instincts can only possibly scream aloud at the utter desolation she will feel at the prospect of a lifelong separation from her young ones.

When she is so desperate to protect them, but in the end cannot protect them. And when, of course, she is so desperate to love them, but cannot be there to love them. At least not in this world.

Amidst all this... something... God... nature... call it what you want, at the end of the day, seemed through Rachel's children... to try to wrestle her free from... what felt to me like... some kind of relentless state of... resistance.

Until, after so much struggling to stay in control, she finally began to accept that... everything was really out of her control. As she finally broke down with her daughters on consecutive nights and at last seemed to recognize just how little she could do about what was really important when it came down to it. All of which, in the end, just maybe enabled her to feel a small degree of... peace in her suffering.

It all happened when Katie and Molly were coloring pictures for her on the edge of her bed and Katie plucked up the courage to ask, "Do you like my picture, Mum?"

I could see that Rachel was at last at ease enough to put aside her anxieties and stresses, and look in detail at what her elder daughter, now eight years old, had offered her. "It's for you, Mum. To keep," said Katie, trying so, so hard.

Initially Rachel had sought to stop her tears flooding out in front of her children. But eventually the... force that gradually seemed to be stirring within her from time to time now, which I so wanted to be with her right to the end, released her to express her grief in sobs and hugs that lasted a little longer each time.

In truth, and I again plead guilty to this, I had again somehow felt compelled to put Katie and Molly up to this. Not that they were entirely unwilling. Nor, I believe, deep down was Rachel.

Part of her, I believe, sensed what I was doing, and had perhaps really wanted to face up to more of what was happening now, given the urgency of everything. And the memories for her children would, I felt, in time, be important. Perhaps... who knows, even awakening their own instincts about the... natural connection between their lives on this earth and what is beyond.

It was the only thing I felt able to give Rachel with regards to her future on this earth. As, at last, I began to wonder whether, somehow, I, in fact, may just have been having some small impact on her after all... despite how futile my efforts had always seemed at the time.

Having some impact... by somehow responding instinctively to what I felt was... stirring more and more inside me. For in truth, I know I could not have gone on without this stirring, as everything was all so unrelenting and so... raw at that stage.

Rachel had deserved at least to be at peace with her children and Steve. And to a degree she discovered that at the end. But, of course, tragically, she still felt it less with regards to herself. Time was too short for that. The... horrors of her guilt and critically the... remnants of her fear clearly ran too deep. And involved too much. Who knows, maybe there was still too much fear within me to help release her.

Whatever, something within me demanded one final embrace with her during the night on which she, in fact, died. Oxygen mask or not, I insisted upon it. To tell her what I really felt about her. Even though she responded, with a joke that couldn't conceal her anxiety, that "the hug might kill me."

I whispered simply in her ear. "You have been a good person. You really have." In the deep emotion of that moment I felt that the truth just had to be stated, however much she may have denied it.

All that night and indeed the early morning that followed she continued to struggle on for hours refusing to be taken from this world as we held hands. Until eventually it was I who fell asleep first, in absolute exhaustion at so much.

Fell asleep inevitably into a very deep... dream... I suppose is what you would call it. Although I had never experienced being so awake or even... so conscious in any dream... at the same time feeling like I was being touched by some kind of... yes, some kind of presence... so close to me... even within me... which simply whispered the words, "Thank you"... nothing more, nothing less, so powerful and yet so clear.

When I awoke, I was so completely caught up for an instant by what I had just experienced that I failed to react to my situation until I quickly snapped back into being aware of just where I was.

And, without even looking to see, somehow knew, of course, exactly what I was about to witness. As with her eyes closed and her head to one side, I discovered that Rachel had finally departed this world, to the peace that, I really do believe, somehow exists beyond this life and beyond all she had struggled with and experienced so deeply here.

Meditation

In the end, as many of us have realized, we not only have to see beyond capitalism's overbearing and ultimately limited and illusory concept of who we are, but then we have to do whatever it takes to break free and experience living at one with our inner spirituality, so that it can express something altogether deeper which emanates from God.

Otherwise we could find, if our time on this earth is suddenly and tragically cut short, that we may have only glimpsed but not felt and realized our eternal link to the Divine, and the vast understanding that it can bring to us in this world and beyond. That's if we have glimpsed it at all.

The intensity of our separate, egotistical image is such a formidable barrier to overcome, and no wonder, as it is very often ingrained since childhood. Since a time when, very quickly, we sought to feel secure after being born into such a seemingly divisive and therefore vulnerable existence. When unfortunately those who cared for us may well have felt so agitated and anxious themselves that their inherent capacity to love us unconditionally may just have been compromised.

Now, I am not intending to be morbid when I ask you to visit a graveyard with regards to the practice of the following meditation. In fact, the opposite, as you will see, is the intention, as the aura it creates within us, because of the nature of the place, is very important.

On arriving there, and after walking for a time amongst the gravestones, reading what has been engraved and allowing ourselves to be affected by the words of grief and faith, and also the silence and peace that surrounds us, we should find a spot on a bench and gradually, and even courageously for many of us, begin to contemplate and confront our own imagined physical 'deaths.' Drawing perhaps on memories of medical scares we have suffered in our lives or scares affecting our loved ones. We may even have experienced losing a loved one.

We should recall any poignant feelings regarding the fragility and indeed urgency of life from that period, and also how we may have felt unfulfilled up to then. Perhaps we even pleaded to God to give us more time.

Especially when we examine how the conditioning we may have endured, we can now see, forced us to act apart from who we instinctively felt we were. Whether towards our loved ones, our families, our relationships with friends – even our lack of participation in our communities, or our failure to campaign wholeheartedly against the great injustices in our world.

However, we should not seek a solution of our own from our reflections on our lives to this point. But merely look to surrender them all utterly to God. And then to be silent.

We may well then find, the more we are able let go and even

instinctively weep at whatever may have gone before, God, in the present moment of our meditation, offering comfort, reassurance and, in time, insights into the nature of His eternal Spirit within us. And into just what He can bring to our lives.

So much so that, little by little, we may well feel ourselves yearning to enter over and over into this deeper, ultimate state of awareness within Him. As finally we realize and accept that we are entering into nothing less than an abandonment of our old selves and the summoning of our true being. A state which will offer us a great sense of intimacy, as well as vitality and fearlessness the more we return to it.

But first, what we must do is face up to our mortality here on earth.

All our lives here will, of course, end at whatever age, at some time or another. The same goes for the lives of those who are closest to us. We are all vulnerable and transient.

Unlike many cultures, as I have said, we very often run away from these apparent truths in terror, a denial that can negate the urgency and immediacy of life as it can and should be lived.

For, given our eternal spiritual state, they really are free and miraculous opportunities which we must embrace and cherish in order to become fully conscious of who we really are. Thereby allowing God to animate His extraordinary presence within us for the good of all. As finally we ensure that the relatively superficial image the capitalist system has made of us up to now is at long last subservient to our Higher selves.

So let us leave the tiresome nature of these former existences behind in the graveyard right now. Let us rise above them, almost as if we are looking down on our old lives from our now reawakened spiritual perspective.

Let us commit ourselves to being ready each day to live vitally and without fear, determined not to waste any more of our time on this earth.

And, above all, resolved, through our Divine consciousness,

to live according to God's true calling for us and therefore our unique potential.

Chapter 6

Leap of Faith

Certainly it demands honesty...

Certainly it requires endurance...

And certainly it calls for Divine inspiration...

... but in the end we must take nothing less than a leap of faith in order to escape from the desperate seduction of this capitalist world towards an infinite sense of just who we are.

For when crunch time is reached, we all have to be brave enough to jump clean off the sinking ship of our innermost illusions within the system and to keep swimming away until we are clear of it.

True, we may initially be desperate to cling to some sort of debris too close to the ship and risk getting sucked down with it. We may even want to stay with others who are too close because we feel afraid of venturing further out alone. But not until the fantasies of the debris or the misguided beliefs of other people as our salvation have actually gone down in our own minds and hearts will we have submitted absolutely to what we are being called to do.

Saying as we swim away, "Help! I believe you are out here. I know there has to be some Higher purpose to my life. Some deeper, even eternal, meaning. Something that will bring some genuine understanding and happiness. So please show me. Please help!" however absurd, never mind out of control, we may feel at first.

Whatever, we must keep saying it, because the more we do, in our growing acknowledgment of the vulnerable nature of our time on this earth, the more intensely we will be embraced by God's loving and indeed empowering presence, which ironically is already within waiting to respond. Indeed waiting to respond to all of us who are willing to go that bit further.

For certain, as I have said, it is much easier to find some temporary comfort for our insecurity in this capitalist world by fearfully working away all hours and then constantly typing in our credit card numbers on our laptops. Allowing our lives to be controlled forevermore, blind to any need for genuinely radical and lasting change.

But then we are merely surrendering to addictions which are driven by the ultimate addiction. And perpetuating our torment by ignoring something deep down that we may sense is not only true about ourselves, but which alone will really satisfy us.

Something that we cannot initially see and therefore fully appreciate. Something which may even seem beyond reason and even appear to be sheer lunacy, but, which in time, we begin to appreciate is and always has been the fount of who we really are. That spiritual something that all along has been calling for us to accept what it offers, not just with regards to our lives on this earth, but way beyond that.

It will though, at times, be a desperate and seemingly ceaseless struggle, which many of us are going through right now in so many different ways. For once we set off on our quest towards what is a realization of our Divine identity no less, the greater will be the turbulence inside us.

As we start to question many habitual thoughts and actions that we pursued without a second thought when we were immersed solely in our hypnotic materialistic existence, and which will still entrap us if we allow our minds to wallow in past mindsets and future anxieties.

It is at times like these that we must turn consciously and consistently to God in order to break these habits. Making the time to be with Him resolutely and silently almost without thinking. Not just at regular periods during the day, but as a recurring counter to our distracted and therefore fractured vision. So we can build up our intimacy and affinity with His very nature, which, lest we forget, is ours too.

A nature that we really will begin to feel impacting on our daily lives.

So much so that increasingly we will find that we want to say no to so much of what is offered that keeps us compliant within the system because there is now something inside us that can't bear being in any way deluded, hyped-up or even half-blotto on a fairly regular basis. When all we truly yearn to be is fully alive to this transformation.

Something we may put into practice by, for example, living according to what we now sense is right for us, by modifying our consumption and purchasing to the requirements of our basic needs, or by the regular periods of meditation and exercise we take each morning, which set us up inspirationally for the day ahead.

As our focus becomes centered on expressing who we are as spiritual beings, with our greater potential now emerging subtly and gradually from the growing time we spend with the true Source of life. That Source which has never wanted to stop us from enjoying ourselves, as capitalism's cheerleaders in the media have maintained, but has always been far more interested in fulfilling us at our most profound and joyous level. Whenever we allow Him a spare or silent moment to connect with us and to live actively through us.

So that He can rouse us to make the positive, vital changes He wants us to make (and we need to make) to our lives. That help us to grow in confidence with our sense of who we really are.

Until finally, through His growing presence, we experience not just intermittent moments, but whole parts of our day when we feel genuinely exhilarated and at one with what is happening through us and deeply grateful for its impact both on ourselves and potentially all those we come into contact with.

As our leap of faith finally becomes a leap into what seems like a whole new, yet in the end, familiar consciousness. Indeed a unifying consciousness.

But first we may even have to reach rock bottom, and languish for a while at rock bottom. Until we get so sick and tired of all the mayhem and the whole masquerade that suddenly it dawns on us that we really have got nothing to lose.

That we really can give up on whatever constitutes our life to this point because it really is not working. It really does not reflect what we feel in our hearts. We really do need, not just help, but a whole new sense of... being alive if we want to stop going round in circles avoiding the deeper truths about who we really are, about our real nature.

That just may be connected to a sense of presence and assurance which we have clung onto from our childhood. Something that was a deeply caring influence in our childhood that touched and affected us and somehow still resonates within us. That exuded and expressed love and... yes, loved us.

Is it really as simple as that though, we may wonder?

How can it be as simple as that?

What have we done to be worthy of such love?

But then is it really anything to do with 'worthy'?

If love is already our very nature?

And love is God's nature?

Yet how do we grasp this love?

Or again is it anything to do with 'grasping'?

Or more to do with giving everything up?

And saying simply, 'Let Thy will be done'?

Surrendering our soul back to this love.

That gave me Life in the first place.

This is why nothing less than a leap of faith will do if we hope to experience such a spiritual renewal, and why we must be absolutely resolute in shutting out the fear-rooted, collective thinking of our age.

Until finally, we become so passionate about the transformation we are going through that we realize that simply 'having to' obey this vague and distant icon, as we perhaps once thought of our relationship with God, was never merely some dutiful or nonsensical act. Now that we have witnessed a whole new vision of Him as the ultimate liberator of ourselves and of all people. Rather than the disconnected figure that such a deluded existence so often painted of Him.

A realization that emboldens us to go out and joyfully give expression to this relationship as often as we can each day. As we confidently confront whoever and whatever situation we face through His enlightened perspective. For the less egotistically burdened we are ourselves, the more, through God's grace, we will discover the situation being resolved according to His Divine will.

As we learn to listen to, to understand and to empathize with all that may plague others. While at the same time being intuitively aware:

Through our silence and their silence.
Through the silence we share in God.
Through our compassion and their compassion.
Through the compassion that emerges from God.
Through our love and their love.
Through the love that unifies us all in God.

As we go on to affect each other subtly yet perceptively, perhaps even touching one another deeply, way beyond any preconceptions, words and thinking that may have lingered from our previously anxious and limited lives.

As if they could possibly reflect not just who we really are, but what we can accomplish through God to our fullest potential.

For that, ultimately, is where this initial leap of faith takes us, into a total revolution of who we are and can become through the awakening of our true spiritual identity. Through our awakening to what increasingly we feel God had always planned for us.

This revolution would, of course, be too overpowering in its intensity if it weren't gradual; but transformed we are being and we will continue to be by our resolve to move closer and closer to this experience of God. And not to resist Him at all.

As finally the continuously grating sound of the capitalist machinery becomes increasingly unbearable for more and more of us to be anywhere near.

Ed's Story

I'm not sure why I first noticed Jo Fitzgerald because I wasn't noticing much at that point.

It was in the swimming pool of the hotel where we were staying near Fort William, on the west coast of Scotland. Maybe it was because of the way she dived in and floated effortlessly underwater its full length. Before resurfacing and lifting herself out, all in one movement. The ripples of the water quickly disappeared.

You'd almost wonder if she had actually been in there.

I have never had that impact on a pool, of course. Or anything else for that matter. If I jump in, it's always like high tide, with the waves crashing everywhere, sending everyone scurrying for cover. And that's with me trying to relax.

Illustrating one of the major differences between us that I increasingly realized: she who, on first impressions, seemed to go through life almost on autopilot, gliding through it to some effect. While I have always battered my way through it to little... or even destructive effect.

Why though?

Why have I always been like that?

I am so tired of it.

Jo had originally, I soon discovered, become a household face in her home country, New Zealand. She was generally considered to be one of the most promising and, needless to say, attractive of reporters on one of the main network's TV news.

Her life didn't change just because she drove her car into the side of a truck one morning on some dual carriageway just outside Auckland. Burning herself so much the plastic surgeons could only do their best. "There is a limit to what can be done," the consultant told her bluntly.

Her life also changed, she told me, because she woke up to the insanity that had made her drive at nearly 90mph, not just on that morning, but regularly. Finally, the insanity caught up with her. She should have died, aged 34.

"How did you... I mean, does it bother you talking about it?" I enquired first, having blundered in as usual over a beer.

"Not really," she said. "It's... part of me now. I mean, I should be dead. Which makes my life... different, I suppose..."

The scars are prominent down the left side of her face. Continuing down the same side of her body.

"I was checking on a story for the evening bulletin the following night. It was a feel-good story about a pet monkey, can you believe? You know, the closing item after you've spent 25 minutes depressing people.

"Yes, a story about a chimp nearly cost me my life. I was very good at my job. Well, I thought so at any rate. I was young, shallow, rich, and ignorant. And used, of course. You know, riding the pressure, breathing it all in, until I went on fire," she said, recalling it with a slight tremor of her beer bottle.

Her obviously... vulnerable but at the same time... uninhibited honesty, I suppose, was another of the things that... drew me to her, even in my generally depressed... done-in state. It was something she strangely was at the same time.

"I've wasted enough of my life with all the nonsense. Haven't we all?" she said. Instead, she now focuses, for the most part, on everything that isn't that. Or so she claims. Hell knows how she does that. Filled with so much... regret and even anger as she must be.

The day after we met, I laughed at her invitation to get up

early to go for a walk. We had moved onto the Island of Mull and her plan, ridiculously, was to go on some epic hike for miles down to somewhere called Fionnphort. The place, apparently, where the ferry leaves for the neighboring island of Iona, made famous by St. Columba and the ecumenical community that now resides there. Jo told me the Abbey on Iona had apparently got an "extraordinary atmosphere" – or so her father claimed following some visit in the 80s.

"Look upon it as a pilgrimage..." she said, trying unsuccessfully to raise some enthusiasm in me for some reason.

Anyway, I told her plainly that I did not get up at 7:30am to go anywhere, except back to bed, especially on my holidays. My sleep had, in fact, been erratic for months, even years in truth.

Even though it was the only place I seemed to get any peace away from... from the constant... turbulence raging in my head and... I suppose, the consequences of so much of my life.

Still, Jo kept nagging me that she'd start her walk via my guesthouse from where she was camping, and if I was awake I was awake and if I wasn't I wasn't, which was fine because there's no way I would be.

However, when it came to it, I heard her pacing around underneath my window for what seemed like hours, which then forced me to get out of bed to shout down to her. But before I could say anything, she yelled up, "Ah, you're up, Ed! Great. It's a lovely morning. See you in a minute," and went out of sight. All of which irritated me like hell, especially her... infuriating enthusiasm.

Though in truth, I have to admit, some miniscule part of me was still intrigued by her and not totally disappointed she had turned up. Something I couldn't fully explain. Whatever, when I went down I was somehow persuaded to go with her.

A decision I regretted very quickly when the "pilgrimage" we were on quickly turned off-track through endless heather and bog across what seemed like half of Mull. Jo, of course, reckoned it was a "stroll." But then she's originally from the South Island of New Zealand and is used to going on five-day treks into nowhere with her brother.

My clapped-out trainers weren't the only sign of my being out of my depth. Though something made me determined to plough on reluctantly now I was up. If only to keep up with her and curse her under my breath every step of the way.

Panting doesn't even begin to describe my physical reaction to this assault on my overweight body. A warm summer's day was building. Most sub-editors I know tend not to be the fittest people. I do that for a living by the way.

"I thought you'd prefer to walk during the cool of the morning," she said, enjoying herself, I sensed, with a faint grin. Increasingly, I wasn't in the frame of mind to grin back when I had a permanent grimace ground into my face.

One hour, twenty minutes into the walk, we paused for a rest. One hour after I'd hoped to.

Every part of me was aching by now, especially my head. I wasn't even sure I was going to survive this. Maybe a massive brain hemorrhage was the answer to so much. To everything that just kept repeating itself over and over in my life with little sign of change. Nothing... decent ever lasting, in truth. With me... something inside me... always seeming to incite some kind of breakup with whomever I was involved.

However, at least Jo resisted what I thought might be the immediate, "Right, let's get on," as I almost drained one of the bottles of water we had in one go. Hardly surprisingly, as most of it missed my mouth. And her sympathetic smile seemed to accept me for who I was, especially when I said I'd have traded the water for a pint even at this time of the day.

After about another half an hour, Jo went further off the vague track we were walking on to climb a small hill. "I could do without anymore bloody detours," I murmured.

I finally caught up with her and woke up to the incredible

panorama that even I noticed encircling us. The beautiful colors of sea, sky and hills, and the incredibly clear air, which I vaguely recalled from yet another fractious, angry family holiday, where my dad sought some kind of peace that he would never get off my malicious, malignant mother.

Jo stood silently, taking it all in. There was a very gentle breeze blowing. And a real sense of… calm. Something that seemed… strangely to be both… all around… and even… I sensed, within her…

Jo was celebrating being still alive, she claimed, by travelling across the world, her entire journey being some kind of pilgrimage. She picked up any kind of work she could on the way

"It's the best way to get to know people." It wasn't all waitressing either. She even spent some time as a walking guide in Western Australia and as a minibus driver in Sri Lanka, which suggested she was slightly mad.

The network had offered Jo a research position after her accident. There had been an "agonizing debate" within the studio about her future apparently. But her bosses felt her scars would only "distract from the viewers' ability to focus on the content of the news, which is what we are all about."

So she flew out of Auckland within three months. Seven months ago now. Most of the time she has been living out of a small tent and cooking on a gas fire. Occasionally when finances have allowed she has splashed out on a night in something more up market to have a bath.

"So you must spend a lot of time on your own then…" I suggested.

"Not necessarily. People are normally drawn to you more when you're on your own. But then I've got this which keeps some of them away," she said, indicating her face with an awkward smile. "What about you?" she asked. "Are you on your own much?"

"Me? No... not much. Why?" I replied.

"It's a pretty essential part of living," she suggested.

"Is it? Thanks for letting me intrude on your living then," I said, somewhat irritated again.

"Why not? I wanted you to come," she said, with a smile, her honesty again surprising... and frustrating me somehow. "It's good to share these moments. There'll never be another one exactly like it, that's for sure."

"That's one way of looking at it," I said. "A pretty intense way. You always this intense?"

"I suppose it's just the way I see things sometimes. I'm lucky. I have met some special people. Recently a lovely French woman, Monique, for example. I stayed with her near a Buddhist monastery in Kandy. People like her change you."

Ah... Buddhism... religion... maybe I should have guessed that was coming. Up to now, Jo's honest assessment of who she was, what had happened to her... seeing through all the rubbish... I could go along with all of that. But religion... I wondered if that might crop up.

Anyway, I had to let it pass because she was up and off again. Though hell knows why I got up to follow so quickly. OK, maybe there was something about her, which seemed... I don't know... to be genuinely interested in me... but that didn't mean it would lead anywhere.

Especially for me who has finally got so sick and tired of always doing what other people told me. People who talked about nothing of real value, who did nothing of real value, except the same old thing over and over, which didn't lead anywhere, except to the same old problems. I mean what is real anymore?

I know that's to a degree why I've taken time off to come away. The chance of something different. Of change. A friend had been over to this west coast of Scotland and said there was something special about it.

"What?" I asked him.

"See for yourself," was his helpful reply.

So finally on the first day of a holiday I mostly felt forced to take, I woke up, tossed and turned till noon, and finally thought, "Hell, why not, at least they like a few drinks there."

To be honest, my partner Anna told me she needed some time on her own, surprise, surprise.

That's always the way it ends for with me, who's always been part-time in full-time commitments. And I'm almost 50 now. With about 50 part-time relationships in that time.

Instant relationships. The way, I suppose, I've always done everything in my life... drunk my coffee... flicked through the TV channels and... even gone for walks! Dragging Anna's ridiculous rat-like dog, Reg, round the block as fast as I could.

Well, that's what it has always felt like. Never giving myself time to do anything except... dip in and dip out. Nothing permanent or everlasting. Almost like I'm not... really experiencing anything for some reason.

Just racing round in some kind of... continuous daze so much of the time. Desperately trying to satisfy some... screaming urge inside me... that's been going on for so long. It seems all my life. But not even getting close.

For once I managed to catch up with Jo as she paused to look all around again. We walked on as she spoke.

"Do you know, for all the things that have changed within me since the accident – and so much has changed – I still find myself thinking like I used to, at least some of the time," she said, shaking her head.

"All the crap just comes in on me, even out here, looking out over all this. Until I quickly see beyond it. While guessing its next pathetic move to drag me back again. And not to allow me to focus on who I really am. Which is essentially free, of course."

Free.

Now that was a word or... concept that I did like. But there was no freedom in most of what I did, that was for sure. Or in what anyone else I knew did, as far as I could see. Except the superrich, of course. I've earned barrel-loads of money already, working all kinds of insane hours, but it's never been enough to be free like them.

What is there without it? No escape from this constant throb in my head. And almost every part of my existence. A throb of thrill and then throw up. Which always seems to reach some kind of desperate climax at the end of each day. Like a hangover that just won't go away. Even if I stick my head in a bucket of iced water.

Where's the originality in all that? It's all about as original as a long session in a bar. I'd do anything to stop it. To stop me strutting and storming about in this state that even seems to infect those I work with, and the hangovers they affect me with. It's so predictable.

Infecting too those who I really care about for once, who aren't many, except Anna... as well her two boys, or I like to think are... our two boys, Jason and Stevie, aged just six and four. A proper family to me. Who I've grown fond of to my total amazement, considering I've never really even thought about having kids up to now for some reason...

But kids who are now starting to act like me. The other great side effect. Of me and my life. With something, whatever the hell it is, making me the way I am. Me, of course. Who the hell else is to blame?

But there's no time to do anything about it, is there? What can I do? I'm desperate to. But I can't. Even times like... this... out here... hardly ever exist. So I just seem to go round in circles, so often just thinking about altering my life to stop what is happening from happening over and over. But not coming up with anything different. Who the hell am I to come up with anything different?

So, in the end, the only conclusion I make is that this... is... it. This is as good as it gets.

Or is it?

"How the hell are any of us free?" I suddenly blurted out, still tramping after Jo. "I mean, how are you free? How!"

Jo paused at my outburst and stared back, reflecting calmly for a moment.

"I didn't say I was free. I said who I really am is free. Something that... all along I may have felt, I suppose, and then very suddenly... very suddenly one day knew, of course."

"What...!" I felt totally exasperated by her answer.

But she moved on again and was quickly too far ahead of me to respond. So I had to pant on and on for nearly another half an hour with sweat pouring off me by now.

But somehow I was frantic to keep up with her now, to argue it out with her. Finally, I rose high enough to see right over the Sound of Mull to Iona. Still miles away but at least it was there. I couldn't help gazing around in... astonishment, I suppose, despite my almost total exhaustion and frustration.

I was desperate for some more water. Jo, who was out of sight for a minute, suddenly reappeared with some from a burn. "Ed, you're keeping up..." she said, with ironic surprise.

"Of course, no problem," I replied, talking and gulping liquid down all at the same time.

"Nearly at the ferry now. You OK?"

"No, I'm nearly dead. But don't worry about it."

She laughed but then before I even had time to say anything more she moved off again.

"Hey...!" I yelled, still swallowing the water, quickly slogging after her, shouting at her on the way, "Hey! Hey!" She paused momentarily. "By the way," I appealed, "how exactly do you 'very suddenly' realize you're free... if you don't go through what you went through? Not many of us go through that. Well! How?"

"You wouldn't even be screaming, Ed, if you weren't going through something yourself too. If you hadn't... begun to see through some of it too. Use that honesty to help you," she said.

She then stared intensely at me. "Find the courage to face up to whatever you're going through and explore it. Stare right at it. Feel it. It was more than about one car accident for me as bad as it was," she explained.

"Be entirely honest about what you keep feeling. Asking, why? Why am I going through this? What is really behind it? Right now or in my past? With no fixed idea of what the answer will be. Not seeking an answer. Staying totally silent. Letting the answer come to you. Not denying or rejecting the truth of it when it comes."

She marched off again but continued.

"Then start asking, just who am I in all of this? What has made me the way I am? Is this all I am, what happens to me day after day? Or am I something more? Again, don't seek an answer to the question yourself. But let the response come to you. Silently facing up to any pain you may feel as over and over you reject what you may begin to see as all the lies in your life.

"And keep on asking these questions and keep on reading books that ask these questions until you begin to attract different... insights about yourself, of who you really are in this life from what you've ever known before."

She paused again.

"Believe me, Ed, they'll come, they'll come if you're genuine and... and passionate enough. However impossible it may seem right now. They did for me. Whatever you do, stick at it, day in, day out. Never ever give up. The alternative is to keep getting screwed."

I couldn't keep up anymore. She was off up and over another hillock. I'd catch her when I caught her if she didn't wait for me which I felt she would. The bluntness and honesty of her language again surprised but drew me. Compared to so much that, for so long, had been irrelevant. Yet, I just couldn't really understand it. However increasingly desperate I was.

"The alternative is to keep getting screwed."

One thing for sure, for as long as I could remember, I felt I had been screwed enough.

Leap of Faith 2

So, just how difficult is it to take this leap of faith and launch ourselves into a spiritual transformation of who we are within a society that, in general, assumes our happiness and yes, even our overall identity to be judged primarily by our economic and materialistic security?

Just how difficult is it to act on any glimpses of a truly radical alternative immersed as most of us are in largely rational and finite minds that insist we control our own destinies?

Just how difficult is it to confront the underlying fear and vulnerability prevalent throughout society with the courage, time and space we require for such a journey?

Is it really possible in the end to wake up to and to remain connected to the inherently spiritual beings that we are under such conditions, so that at long last the eternal force within us can inspire the full blossoming of our Higher natures? And potentially all those we connect with?

For so long now, so many of us have never tired of identifying with the timeless philosophy and words of inspired people such as Indian leader, Mohandas Gandhi, who at the time of independence from Britain insisted on a society which would give priority to a spiritual way of life, calling for India's new government to rule with a self-denying sense of humility. He recognized that mass British or Western industrialization was totally out of place in his country, whereas the freedom to follow personal truth was intrinsic to it.

He was emphasizing a reality about who we all are, which has for so long, of course, been incomprehensible to the minds of those in power in the West. But it is not now incomprehensible to more and more of us, who, through our yearning for what we sense is innate within us – whether or not we may realize the true source of our stirring – are growing frustrated and rebellious in so many different ways against what keeps us from it.

Particularly the more we become aware that it is capitalism, driven by its aggressive and insatiable nature, which works directly against this liberating expression of our deeper identity. As it denies us not only the opportunities to offer ourselves regularly and silently to our higher selves in God, but prevents His peaceful, loving presence flourishing fearlessly and selflessly within us for the good of all.

To such an extent that many of us end up feeling torn apart as we vainly seek for some kind of deeper meaning to all that is happening to us during our everyday functions or dysfunctions.

Something that could be explored far easier in a society where the demands of work, growth and consumerism play a part but not such an overwhelming part of our daily life. In a society where patience, frugality and inner contentment are allowed to prosper as essential, integrated aspects of what happens to us every day. With what we do being far more reflective of our true natures, rather than leaving us tormented by a deep and baffling sense of disconnection.

In a report entitled "The Danger of Losing the New Testament Pattern of Simple Life-style," Mesulame Nainoca from Fiji has no doubt what is at stake with regards to the threat to his particular culture and just where it is coming from. Many of us, in our daily exhaustion and turmoil, can, I am sure, identify deeply with these words:

> The issue of a simple Pacific life-style is too precious a treasure to lose. It is not only part of our culture, but more importantly it is the Christian culture of the New Testament. The greatest challenge facing the Pacific churches... is, "How can the Pacific churches counter the influence of western culture in the Pacific?"[13]

This is the challenge, of course, which many are trying to bring to the forefront of local, national and international debate in so many different ways, in and way beyond the West. Such is the ever-increasing and all-pervading scale of the fallout from capitalism and globalization both on so many increasingly hectic, manic and fractured lives and even more critically, of course, on our submerged spiritual instincts.

The term "simple" incidentally, which Mesulame Nainoca links specifically to the Christian culture of the New Testament, is one which some in the West, especially the powerful, often disparage, whether directly or not. As they associate "simple" with being backward, and if they hate to be thought of anything, of course, it is backward. They, who mostly think of themselves as highly developed and, needless to say, technologically advanced.

Part of the dictionary definition of "simple," however, is enlightening. It is described as "not affected" but "unassuming" or "unpretentious"; as "not guileful" or "deceitful" but "sincere," and as being "without embellishment" and "not elaborate, elegant or luxurious."

Being "simple," therefore, often has little to do with being a simpleton.

It offers often hidden, unstated and altogether more subtle virtues.

Globalization's leaders, as I have maintained, however, continue, in their deep-rooted fear and arrogance, to judge so-called "simple" societies almost exclusively according to their economic and materialistic status. With their profound sense-of-community, sense-of-culture, sense-of-environment and sense-of-legacy, linked very often to their heightened spiritual awareness, not considered of value and therefore not applicable.

Increasing numbers of us in the West, however, and, of course, throughout the world, no longer accept these shallow, small-minded judgments as we respond to our instinctive feelings about just what is more beneficial and harmonious for all of us. That very often are reflective not only of the natural empathy we may have built up for these cultures, but also our yearning to explore how differently we may wish to live our own lives. As an alternative to the overriding sense of emptiness and antipathy we may increasingly feel towards aspects of our agitated home existence.

So much so that instead of insisting on pursuing the excesses and artificial needs of the economic system, we may feel inspired to take daily leaps of faith ourselves that somehow involve us in living and acting in simpler, more mindful, less accumulative ways. Even, believe it or not, in ways which bring us a genuine sense of happiness and fulfillment.

For example, by regularly finding the time each day to be aware of so much of what is already within and before us, which gradually helps to induce a vital sense of calm assurance and even gratitude. Indeed we may well then begin to notice this sense of peace and humility leading us to have a more positive impact in all we say and do rather than sporadically making little or no impact. All of this flowing from our growing relationship and even intimacy with the Source of our spiritual being and the more we devote ourselves to act in ways that are a direct response to what we feel genuinely called to do.

We may even go on to reflect on and then alter the very expectations and structure of our lives, which may possibly involve us in lifestyle, vocational or location changes, the more focused we continue to become on living first and foremost from the basis of who we are and not who we are not.

A development that we may then begin to recognize in other individual lives around us, amongst folk who too are enjoying the liberation of breaking out of the collective thinking of our day. Some of whom, we may suddenly appreciate, are actually inspiring us to go further in the direction we are heading.

To such an extent that, at this point, we will feel that there really can be no turning back for us. Why would we possibly want to turn back and therefore deny this extraordinary awakening and transformation within us just because our 'advanced' society says our spiritual lives are too nebulous or indefinite to bother with when we know that that simply isn't the case?

When our hearts tells us this is no longer the case.

When God's voice within tells us this is no longer the case.

Offering us insights and inspirations we never thought possible.

Offering us a genuine daily impact we never thought possible.

That has sparked critical changes in perception, priority and attitude in our lives.

Changes that are coming from the very core of our being.

Leading us from economic enslavement to Divine deliverance.

From ego dependency to spiritual empowerment.

From what is very often predictable in our lives to what can be wonderfully unpredictable.

All of this originating, lest we forget, from that initial leap of faith.

When we finally decided we simply could not go on anymore without reacting to what we instinctively ached for, to what we may well have felt was eating us up inside.

And we took what may initially have felt like blind or even futile steps into a bizarre nothingness or silence that at least calmed us and then, very gradually, seemed to clarify our way forward inch by inch. Until we began to realize that these steps were filled with God's grace and therefore illuminated by a profoundly creative energy.

Something, increasingly we recognize, is indicative of a wider reawakening that is stirring everywhere and is gathering pace. As the system of indoctrination begins to unravel in so many lives now that more and more people are no longer prepared to be squeezed tighter and tighter but are determined to be freed so they can live according to their true natures.

Reflected in the hundreds of thousands of popular organizations that are emerging far and wide to vent a louder international voice. Not just against the obscene divisions in wealth, for example, that globalization insists upon the world over, nor just against the increasingly destructive war that it continues to wage on our earth's resources, but also against the suffocating effects of this overall existence on what should be our primary sense of who we are.

Many of the organizations are, of course, not openly rooted in their spiritual awareness, but many are, led by alliances drawn from community groups, human rights workers, environmental organizations, trade unions and religious folk, as well as various other bodies. Each filled with people stirred by their deeper selves into discovering a greater meaning, justice and freedom that they are determined to cherish.

All part of a movement that will, of course, gain even more momentum the more these groups are able to focus on what unites them in their passion to act rather than on what separates them. The more they recognize the actual origins of their desire to act, a voice within that never relents and convinces us of the absolute validity as well as infinite potential of what so many are feeling called to do.

A call that is, of course, not necessarily a response to a religious call from courageous leaders of whatever faith, but is primarily a spiritual call sent urgently to our very souls, that awakens both who we really are and then our life's direction if we will only but surrender to its will.

Reflective of the approach of the mystical, contemplative traditions of these religions, with their emphasis on each of us being empowered by our actual experience of our Higher selves for the genuine benefit of all.

An approach that the wider religious hierarchies would do well to take on board at this critical time, with the consequent impact on the overall movement, which would, of course, gain even greater momentum if it was assisted by a challenge from within the established capitalist order itself. Especially at its heart in the West. So that, crucially, the very nature of the transformation so many of us seek and what evolves from it is actually rooted in our spirituality.

That is why the Western churches, for the most part being seen as being an integral part of the establishment, must finally find it within themselves to express what is at the heart of Christ's message, the mystical heart of His message, and find a common voice on these great issues of our time with the other religions of our world.

For that is surely something that they can all unite peacefully on. At the same time expanding the spiritual force that will confront these global dangers.

As more and more aware people everywhere no longer persist in merely protesting about what is happening, but instead, and together, take a worldwide leap of faith which demands that who we all ultimately are, as a reflection of our far more selfless, all-loving selves, genuinely determines the way we now live.

Rather than the fearful, accumulative way we live being allowed to determine the approach to our faith. Or lack of it altogether.

For a revolt without a spiritual heart will only send us spiraling into evermore desperate capitalist circles reflective of its nature, as we merely, and at best, try to modify a system that must be altered at its core.

Indeed what else, when you think about it, can truly transform us other than a global reawakening of our actual relationship with our Creator no less? Through the intimate presence of He who alone must guide us in all we do, as an expression of His Divine nature, that, in time, we realize to be our Divine nature?

A revolution that was never merely open to those residing in some monastery, ashram or other sacred retreat, but was always open to each and every one of us. Indeed, we can now see, it is absolutely essential to each and every one of us.

So that love, unity and the welfare of all, and not just the few, becomes our instinctive demand. With basic sustenance, shelter and education for all, and genuine care of our planet, whatever simplified and liberated (yes, liberated, as it will reflect our true natures) lifestyle this affords us. All inspired by the greater time, space and opportunity which is laid aside to nurture our critical inner reflection and renewal.

As, at the same time, we put an end to this divisive existence which has plagued us for so long. The more we become increasingly secure in our Higher, eternal rather than limited, egotistical destiny, and can then begin to accept the supreme paradox of this earthly life, as here described by Laurence Freeman:

> It is the paradox of loving life passionately, being able to say with every fibre of one's being, "Yes, of course, I want to live," while being with equal intensity ready to let go whenever the moment comes.[14]

For that is what our true and inspired lives, in the end, become to us: gifts of life, offered by God, which are extraordinary, empowering opportunities. Indeed the lives He always intended for us.

That embolden us to live with a fearlessness, a grace and, yes, even with a genuine celebration of life we never thought or had forgotten was possible. Even though we know, at the same time, that we may have to relinquish them at any given moment back to God.

What a wonderful opportunity that provides for us.

What a startling urgency it creates within us.

Being open to whatever God yearns within us.

Being alive to whatever God expresses through us.

Being alert to whenever God intervenes as us.

Without any trepidation on our part.

But enthused by His spirit to act.

Out of His boundless love.

Until the drawing of our very last breath.

Ed's Story 2

The heat of the day grew intense. "Can this really be Scotland?" I thought. By now I was moving so slowly I felt like a couple of slugs crept past me. Jo seemed to be getting more elusive all the time. Though somehow I felt she wasn't too far away.

Surely the island of Iona and the ferry across must be close now. Though they had gone out of view again and, needless to say, I had trouble keeping to the track she said was a track. It looked like a sheep's track, which even the sheep had got lost on.

Out here my mind felt like it was being pounded not just by the usual... storm of things that had always gone wrong in my life, but especially by what was happening right now with my... family, Anna, Jason and Stevie.

For some reason it was really breaking me apart this time, as yet again I seemed completely unable to prevent what was going to happen from happening.

Unlike me, Anna had already been married and had another long-term relationship even before I came on the scene. Now even more family explosions for the two boys to deal with.

Do you know what really worries me, what really frightens me the most – is just how this next generation is supposed to react to this supreme example of exactly how not to live?

Never mind my generation still dealing with my parents' generation. Me dealing with my mother's generation. Me dealing with her righteous judgment, never mind all the constant criticism my dad had to put up with.

As her tension and anger became my tension and anger, and my tension and anger becomes my kids' tension and anger. We just can't seem to find the time to stop ourselves. Or to confront what is really going on. As instead we just buy another monthly rail pass to work and get on with it, as if it'll miraculously get better somehow.

But how the hell can it when everything's all... breaking apart so much?!

Why isn't there even some hint of... something genuinely different that I can see?

The full horror of it all was really coming in on me out here. With so much time to think about it in this wilderness. I was desperate to switch everything off but simply couldn't.

I don't know why but something about these particular boys had somehow got to me. No other woman's kids had. The reality, for whatever reason, was that I... did feel for these two. They deserved some kind of chance to have some kind of start to life, whatever that meant anymore. So much so that my role as Daddy number 3 had become... I don't know... important to me.

OK, I know, by the time they're older, they'll probably survive in some kind of... state. Like the majority of other kids. I mean, if they manage to survive the war zone of today's school playground, they'll probably survive anything. But that doesn't make it right.

Every time they asked me to play or to read something to them, I immediately regretted the arguing they'd had to endure between their mum and I. And I knew deep down that I hated myself for the fear I'd brought to their eyes. Just like I hated the fear that I had to endure in my own poisonous childhood.

But in spite of that I realize that these boys love me despite everything. So... I suppose... they love me unconditionally. Which is all way beyond me. Why would they do that? When they're not even my boys?

Finally, I just had to sit down. The heat was almost making me delirious with the intensity of all this. And I was sober, far, far too sober.

I looked out for Jo. I couldn't see her for a moment. Something about her really did irritate me. But in another way, I felt that, despite the fact I knew so little about her, she was maybe someone who, I don't know, had some kind of... genuine insight into all of this. Some... deeper understanding. Very occasionally I have come across people like her. Out of the blue. People who seem to be... in touch with something worthwhile for a change.

"Face up to whatever you're facing and explore it."

"Stay silent, not seeking an answer."

"The alternative is to..."

Whatever the hell any of that really meant.

It was all jumbling around in my food blender of a head.

I was too exhausted to think. Even more exhausted than I've been lately, which is saying something. So I fell back into the heather. And very quickly in and out of sleep. Initially I was trying to keep myself awake. Then I wasn't sure whether I was dreaming I was trying to keep myself awake or that I was actually trying to wake myself up. Whatever, it was all totally seismic. Until finally, I came up with my usual solution to everything lately and said to myself,

"To hell with it, just fall asleep." So I did.

But I awoke abruptly as usual to the conflict still raging inside me. With no peace at all due to how aware I had become of the total bankruptcy of my life. That despite the 'success' of my career and my large bank account that keeps emptying as fast as it fills up had not fulfilled me... meaningfully, passionately, creatively... in the way I thought it might a long time ago now.

My relationships too... locked into the same cycle of love blossoming, but then feeling such pressure... squeezing it out of me, on to its inevitable disintegration. Even as I was aware of it happening. Yet unable to do anything about it. So busy and agitated.

All the while my job constantly on the line like most people's. Like Anna's. She's hardly been on a go-slow ever since we met. All to pay for the huge mortgage, the extortionate council tax, the endless bills, the large loans, running the cars, never mind the VAT on everything except breathing.

If only we could earn even more so we could slow down for a second!

I stood up and this time saw Jo in the distance walking into Fionnphort. Yet, however much I was drawn to her, I couldn't just believe in what she believed in especially if it simply came down to God, religion and all that nonsense.

To me, that was all gibberish after all the *Onward, Christian Soldiers* nonsense my mother insisted I experience at school, never mind the hypocrisy that has gone on ever since.

So, I don't know, maybe, at the end of it all, it was really up to me to try to sort things out myself. By going back at the end of the week and facing the music. Even though Anna made it absolutely clear that it was over if I didn't change. That I was "too irritable and... closed" to be around.

"I am trying to be more open!" I told her over and over. Hoping against hope that I won't lose someone I love yet again especially with what I feel about her. Never mind Jason and Stevie. Because I really can't go back to being on my own again. Not anymore.

Not now.

Not at my...!

In truth, we've been going through a trial separation for a while now. The first Sunday seeing the boys had been a disaster. They'd seen Daddy number 1 on Saturday morning. And he was late. Then Daddy 2 on Saturday afternoon. And he had to leave early, which was just as well as he seemed half-pissed apparently.

So when Daddy 3 also turned up late and hassled, their faces said it all. So did Anna's. Then, of course, I had to tear around in the short time we had together and I even started swearing at the traffic on the way back, screeching to a halt in front of her. "No, Ed's not been swearing, Mum," Jason stuck up for me when we got back.

A six year old who loves me for no reason lying for me.

Jo was now staring back up the track towards me to see when I was coming. I saw the ferry starting back from the Iona side. She was now in the heart of the village and slowly turned and wandered down towards the pier. I quickly moved on to catch up with her.

But suddenly I was not even sure which way to go I felt so… exhausted with everything. Suddenly I thought about going back the other way if I could find the road to walk back along. And catch a bus maybe.

Back to my guesthouse. A shower. A couple of drinks. A lie down. Hell. I'm on holiday. Where was Jo really going anyway? It dawned on me that maybe Iona was just some tourist place for all I know. With some old building you pay to get into. With, who knows, not much else.

OK, I did like Jo. There was something about her that I sensed I wanted get to know more. That made me want to walk on. But the reality was that… that… I don't know… there was also something about her that was maybe a bit vague and… uncertain. Just at a time when I needed to be absolutely certain. Not going on some mysterious wild goose chase when I really needed to deal with everything once and for all!

But how the hell was I going to do that?

Why the hell am I so useless?

I reached the road. It was actually quite close. I looked both ways. Now which way should I go? On down into Fionnphort and the ferry to Iona. Or back. Deep down, I knew this moment had been coming for a long while.

I tried to look for Jo again. To see if she was still looking back. Where was she?! I couldn't see her. Who knows where she is now? Is that her? No, I'm not sure. Not positive, anyway.

Just then someone drove up. "Do you want a lift back up the road?" he offered. I hesitated, almost panicking, now really unsure what to do. "Hey?" he repeated.

"Uh..." I prevaricated for what seemed like an eternity.

Then, finally, under pressure, I agreed.

Soon after he started driving I very nearly asked him to stop so I could get out. But I didn't. Instead, absurdly, I put up with some part of me telling me I was going the wrong way the whole way back, while another tried to assure me that I wasn't.

In time though, I began to sense just which part I should be listening to as I grew almost frantic the further away from Iona I got. As I was forced to face the truth... that for whatever reason, I really did miss... really did miss being with Jo just now, however crazy that seemed, whatever it meant.

In fact, during the evening in the bar, I even became desperate to see her again, imagining, ridiculously, that she would walk in through the door at any moment, even though she probably stayed the night on Iona. None of it made sense. It was not like it had been some amorous infatuation. I have had enough of those to recognize them! It's just that I was really worried that I might miss her and never see her again. I even stayed awake half the night.

What the hell is the matter with me, I kept asking myself?

I finally fell asleep in the early hours of the morning and didn't wake up till late. I quickly jumped up, ran out and managed to find where she was camping. There were only two tents there and neither of them were hers. Then she suddenly walked up, carrying her packed rucksack.

"Hi, Ed. Where did you get to yesterday?" she said.

"I... uh..."

"The Abbey is amazing. Very special. You should go and see it."

"Oh..."

"It might even cheer you up..." she said, with a grin.

"Hey?" I replied, puzzled.

"Anyway, I'm heading off now. It was good to meet you."

"What! I mean, why? Where...?"

"I'm not sure. Up the north west coast, maybe. It's meant to be very wild. Anyway, thanks for sharing the walk as far as we did."

She held out her hand. I didn't know what to do. Except to stop time. To stop her moving forward out of my life. I know that sounds melodramatic. And ridiculous. But it was what I felt. I was desperate to bring back yesterday. I just couldn't let her go like this.

But she was going. Still she held out her hand but I ignored it and suddenly stumbled forward into her, hugging her, feeling totally out of control.

"I'm sorry," I said. "I..."

She seemed understanding, even smiling considerately.

"So what... what happened on Iona yesterday?" I suddenly asked, somehow trying to hold her up, as she lifted her rucksack onto her back.

Again she smiled, almost as if she hadn't heard, although she must have done. Whatever, she simply said, "Take care, Ed, and do visit the Abbey," before calmly walking away.

I wanted to run after her. I was desperate to run after her. But, for some reason, I felt I couldn't. I just had to let her go. I just had to watch her go.

The pain of loss I felt over the next seconds, minutes and hours was extraordinary. I couldn't understand its intensity. But the reality was that I could not bear the thought that I might never ever talk to this human being again.

I had to admit, she seemed to sense and understand something about me. And she seemed to... share something... meaningful with me. I don't know, she even seemed to give me a sense of... hope... where there had been none for so long... for as long as I could remember.

Exactly how though? What was it about her?

Whatever, I found it impossible to accept her leaving my life forever. Indeed, I became so desperate after an hour that I went off searching for her, hitching a lift up the west coast, looking inside cars she may have caught a lift in, inside buses. Before I caught a bus myself back down to the ferry terminal because I thought she may have changed her mind and be about to leave the island. All the while my imagination was running riot about where I would bump into her and what we would say. I even became angry with her again. Very angry.

But I never ever found Jo.

And I would never ever meet her again.

Something I finally realized back at the bar later that afternoon.

In a despair that it is almost impossible to describe.

My God, there have been some dark moments in the last couple of years when I have looked back on experiences in my life... choices in my life... insane decisions in my life... and somehow I kept making them... even though... I sensed that part of me never really wanted me to... but I could never manage to... stop myself and do anything truly different.

All of it... somehow... leading to this point, this time in my life, right now... where with my drink untouched in front of me... I finally felt like I had absolutely nowhere left to go... nor energy to do it and no reason even to try anymore.

Because everything seemed to be drained right out of me.

For sure, my heart may have still been beating, but I... in some ways had just stopped altogether. Sitting in a kind of... blind stupor, with absolutely no desire to emerge from this state.

Why should I, I thought?

As I almost seemed to will this... nothingness upon myself.

So deep did I feel a sense of... worthlessness... and... and incredible loneliness, I suppose.

That went on for a seemingly endless period of time.

Until, eventually... suddenly from nowhere... I wondered whether I had anything to lose by maybe going on the ferry to visit Iona, however late in the day, as Jo had suggested.

At first I rejected this out of hand, mostly because I couldn't be bothered to, but the more the thought persisted, part of me, in time, wondered what else I was going to do.

Especially as, in truth, I was still desperate to feel close to Jo somehow. In the vague hope of easing the overriding torment that was still pulsating away inside me. However much I was certain that the whole venture would lead absolutely nowhere.

Whatever, I set off almost in spite of myself, and once I had taken a local taxi and crossed on the ferry, I walked around a little of the island, had a pint and a bar snack and then finally crept uncertainly into the Abbey and waited for an evening service which was to take place under candlelight.

I couldn't remember the last time I was in a church, let alone a place like this, aside of a couple of weddings and dreadful funerals, especially my father's, after my mother finally drove him into an early grave. Incredibly she chose *Onward, Christian Soldiers*.

Whatever... in time, a long time, I slowly began to feel a little more at ease as I simply sat back and waited for what seemed like an eternity, and gazed around silently after the totally bewildering couple of days I had just endured.

The emerging congregation, over time, did little to disturb my slow recuperation until eventually we began with a period of silence, a couple of songs and a reading. Then, absurdly, some small strips of paper and pencils were handed out, and we were all invited to write down something in our lives which we apparently wanted God to help us with, or release us from, or something. We were all to go forward and to pin our folded papers to a large wooden Cross that had been placed between the central two aisles.

"Fat chance," was my reaction to all that, of course.

For a time, nobody went forward. But then a trickle of people surprisingly developed into a queue to my amazement. Suddenly feeling a little self-conscious, with people young and old all writing around me, I quickly pretended to jot something down.

But then what I was thinking about myself was overtaken by the deepening atmosphere that was building up, as a few people appeared close to tears, either attempting to find the right words or to go forward and pin their papers to the Cross.

However cynical you are – and I'm right up there in the top bracket – you couldn't fail to be moved by what they were clearly going through.

As meaningless as I felt the whole business was, I had to accept that this wasn't some kind of fake crusade. It was all very genuine and very personal, with real people sweating blood over real... agonies in their lives, or so it seemed. Even though there was absolutely no pressure on them to come forward at all. It was all about them and down to them, as they tried to deal with whatever was clearly... tormenting them in many cases.

And, as far as I could see, none of them were running out of the place. They were facing up to what they wanted... help with. A couple of them around me were even trembling.

I suddenly felt a slight sense of shame when I compared their sincerity with my pretense at writing something down. I then asked myself what harm could it do to write down the names of Anna, Jason and Stevie, which I then did. Though I was certainly not about to go forward and pin the paper to the Cross.

I mean, however worthy these people were and therefore how justified in going forward – I knew I certainly wasn't. Even if I had the courage to, which I didn't.

I then noticed one or two still wrestling with their bits of paper, which reassured me. Especially as the number of people going forward began to dwindle.

However, a small part of me then started to feel like I did when I accepted the lift away from Iona and away from Jo the previous day. Again, I began to think that just maybe this was some kind of strange opportunity, whatever it was. The second in two days.

At least... somehow to see things, I don't know, in a... different... kind of light. Something I would again feel regret over if I didn't take it. Even though I knew nothing would happen if I did, of course.

I really hated these feelings of regret and... I don't know... anxiety, I suppose, if I'm honest. Indeed, I... sensed more than ever now that these two emotions somehow seemed to sum up my entire existence... in so many ways.

Whatever, I did feel convinced about the authenticity of this place and what was happening here. I even felt for the people because it really was all down to them. And most of them seemed desperate to respond.

I looked at the names Anna, Jason and Stevie that I had written on the paper. And it suddenly dawned on me that that wasn't even true. That wasn't what I needed help with, or certainly released from. I couldn't even get that right.

But there was no way I was going to write anything else down. Or certainly to take it forward.

The number of people going forward was now down to the odd one or two. Even though there still wasn't any attempt to rush anybody.

I thought of Jo for about the 2,000th time that day and wondered whether she attended something like this yesterday. "To stop being screwed" is what she might have written on her bit of paper, at least at one time. Maybe it's what millions of us should write in our different ways.

But a young woman behind me wasn't going to write it. She wasn't going to write anything. She suddenly chucked her bit of paper away and walked out looking totally distraught. What the hell had brought her to that? At least, however selfishly, it made me feel better. Well... part of me maybe. Especially when I noticed that there was no one left at the Cross. And that part of me hoped they would finally call time, or whatever they did.

But then, to my irritation, a bedraggled old man to the side of me slowly levered himself up on a stick and stumbled forward, looking like he was terrified he would miss out. He paused for what seemed like an eternity before pinning up his strip of paper. He then turned and returned very slowly to his seat, head bowed, tears trickling down his cheeks.

I stared at his face, which suddenly seemed... I don't know, to reflect something about the whole... aura of this Abbey. And then I looked around at many of the others who had gone forward and at their faces and something almost seemed to... to cave in within me.

As I sensed that just maybe these people, whoever they were, whatever they had gone through, were not, in fact, very different from me. Many of them even looked and maybe felt like I did.

Looking at that old man's face, utterly... broken, stirred those agonizing pangs of regret inside me again, which were now coming thick and fast. I now felt that what I was walking away from wasn't really about Jo. Maybe it wasn't even about this place.

Maybe it was about what both of them represented... I don't know... the... hope, at least, of... of some kind of... change... at long last... from so much of what had gone before... over such a long, long time.

Isn't that what I should be writing on this bit of paper? And pinning it up like everyone else? However worthless an act it would prove to be.

OK, I didn't believe in God, religion and all that mumbo jumbo, but what had I got to lose? I had to do something. So why not try? If it goes on like this I'll be on my own... again. Never mind the fact I'll upset even more people. Children this time. Children who I've never really wanted for some reason. But children who now somehow love me!

And maybe I wanted to... to love back... if I'm honest.

God knows what would happen to them if everything broke

down again!

I couldn't bear that.

I've never been able to bear that...

Look, I said to myself, if all these people who walked up to this Cross didn't feel humiliated about exposing what they felt in such a public way, why should you? They were all... I don't know, humble enough to be honest about themselves.

Again, there was no one at the Cross. Now it was my hands that were trembling.

For goodness sake, all you're asking for is help.

What is wrong with that?

Why is this such a big deal?

Just go forward for goodness sake...

OK, I suddenly said to myself.

And I scribbled down what I genuinely felt I wanted help with.

Or to be released from.

And I lurched forward quickly.

Before I even had a chance to think.

And I pinned the paper to the Cross.

I then turned and looked all around.

To accept my public humiliation.

There was not a sole looking at me.

Most of them had their heads bowed in prayer.

They *were* utterly genuine.

It was an extraordinary moment at an extraordinary time.

And somehow I felt... that I would never ever forget that moment... whatever it really meant.

As I looked back at the Cross with all the small bits of paper on it, including mine, and simply uttered the word, "Sorry," because I genuinely felt sorry. Very, very sorry. Ultimately about so much.

Before I returned to my seat to sit in exhausted silence for a long time.

A long, long time.

So much so I barely noticed the closing of the service as I continued to be completely overwhelmed by the whole experience.

At the same time... strangely... and extraordinarily relieved at all that had happened.

Strangely and extraordinarily... at peace for the first time for so long. Though still trying to work out just what it had all been about.

Until, finally, all alone, and goodness knows how much later, I slowly got up to leave, first wandering down the central aisle toward the Cross, while taking in the rest of this amazing, ancient, utterly silent Abbey en route.

In time, after reading a few of the anonymous, moving notes on the Cross, I became aware of, among many other things, a very large notice board in one corner of the Abbey. It was almost completely covered, for the most part, in prayers for different countries, different conflicts and also for so many different people.

Concerned, caring and clearly, the more I read of them, deeply felt prayers. Something that... well, yes, I suppose it amazed me, the sheer scale of it. The sheer... selfless... sincerity of it.

So much to pray for, so many names... including... including... to my astonishment... my very own, right in the corner, on a small piece of red paper.

What on earth was my name doing there?!

My name?

But then, I began to wonder, was it really so astonishing, in view of all I had experienced over the past couple of days? In view of the extraordinary... intensity of all I had experienced because of this chance meeting with one particular person over the last couple of days?

Whatever else I felt in the emotion of that moment, I felt that, at the very least, it was actually genuine. That someone,

someone that I hardly knew, felt that I... belonged there, with all these other names, even if... to a large degree, I didn't.

And it filled me with... that... strange sense of hope, again. A hope... that I had not felt for such a long time. Since I could barely remember, in truth. A hope that I was... desperate not to let go of.

In a place to which I never ever imagined I would happily return. Just as so many of my friends – from as far back as I could remember – had never returned.

Meditation

Situations arise when we are given glimpses that combined with an open mind, an acute ear and a receptive heart tell us that there really is some greater truth about our reality out there waiting to fulfill us, however much we may have doubted and even struggled against it all along.

A truth that, in time, we realize is a spiritual, eternal and unifying truth, which through God's grace finally enables us to experience who we really are beyond our apparently superficial, separate and even self-centered selves. Beyond perhaps our years of underlying faithlessness, fear and agitation. Even beyond faith itself, once we have opened ourselves entirely up to it.

As I have said, we will most likely find it when we consciously take time out somewhere, somewhere totally different where we are entirely still. At the same time, reading something entirely fresh, listening to someone entirely different and opening ourselves up to a whole new, yet, in time, inherently familiar plane of being and living.

Or... in contrast to that, we can continue to exist in this world of collective illusion where, as Shakespeare wrote, "All the world's a stage, and all the men and women merely players," where we all survive very often behind masks not just of fear but therefore of egotism, fully absorbed into a system which doesn't just manipulate and control but continually makes demands and threats, and therefore places wholesale pressures onto its servants.

So much so it very often takes great and persistent courage to rip off these masks. The kind of courage that so many of us may have been trying to summon for so long now. Until after much painful procrastination, we finally move out of our often tormented minds and beyond our false sense of who we are.

By relinquishing control of our lives entirely to an initially silent, inner presence that we may have continuously denied but no longer do. As we thrust aside thoughts that may doubt the very logic and even sanity of our actions. By insisting on taking a leap of faith, whatever it involves.

For not to take it is ultimately to yield to a mass deception, which we cannot possibly do anymore.

When something vital inside us really is insisting on drastic change.

Through an awakening to its role as the heartbeat of who we are.

And a commitment to its presence as the very soul of who we are.

Something we now practice in this particular meditation.

Which demands we already live as if we are at one with this Divine perspective. And therefore have absolutely nothing to fear. For we don't just hope and pray, we now expect God to act.

For it is His nature to act.

It is His nature to give.

According to His will for us.

Whatever our situation.

As finally we take this leap of faith we are committed to right now.

Aware that it is all part of His plan for us.

He has been preparing us for this moment.

To this leap of faith that tells us that nothing is beyond His power.

No transformation, no fulfillment, no Higher purpose.

We are all inspired by His nature.

That is now our assured nature.

There is nothing that He cannot change within us.

There is nothing that He cannot change through us.

If we let go entirely and give ourselves back to Him.

Who really is alongside us right now.

For example in confronting whatever we sense we need to confront most in our lives. Indeed, we may well have imagined facing up to this moment for years.

Well, let's not imagine facing up to it anymore.

Let's not even think about.

Let's just tackle it.

First meditating silently on it.

Meditating repeatedly on it.

Meditating positively on it.

Dissolving the fear that it contains.

Dissolving any negativity that has built up around it.

By simply offering whatever it is up to God.

To His outcome.

To His will.

Which we feel increasingly secure in.

Then we go on to confront it and to deal with it.

Let's consider the effects of our actions afterwards and on just how far God has brought us with regards to our boldness and courage.

Reflect also on just how different we feel now and on just how much He might go on to accomplish through us.

Chapter 7

Empowerment

I had placed my life in the hands of a power which was infinitely beyond me and I knew from this time that the sole purpose of my life must be to leave myself in those hands and to allow my soul to be governed by that will.[15]

This may well reflect the stage many of us are now experiencing, as revealed by Bede Griffiths, the Benedictine monk, who created a prayer center by the sacred River Cauvery in India for people of different religious traditions to seek the ultimate truth.

Finally, at long last, for perhaps the first time since childhood, after which we became separated from our spiritual instincts by our increasingly faithless, fraught and blinkered society, reflected ultimately in the all-pervasive influences of the economic order, many of us have emerged from years of struggle to reignite our extraordinary relationship with our loving Creator.

Indeed we may have felt compelled to by the various periods of desperation and desolation that we endured, before surrendering, oh so urgently and even longingly, to the calling of our original and true being in God.

Along the way, of course, we may well have continued to go through turbulent periods, still partially immersed in the values of this agitated world, as it persisted in trying to entice us back. But deep down we could at last see the torment it drew us into, seemingly apart from who we really are, and many of us decided we had put up with that for long enough.

So much so we resolved to let go of it more and more, and owned up, not just to our superficial identity, but ultimately to our absolute frailty, even nothingness without a full awareness of God's presence, which we now knew was the only way forward.

Indeed, this reawakening, we could now see, had all along been our primary purpose in life, with our new direction now diametrically opposed to our previously terrified perspective of self-preservation within the system:

The one disempowering us through an illusory existence that disconnected us from the unity of the eternal spirit within, therefore denying us the opportunity to unlock the depth of our unlimited potential amidst this transient, mortal life.

The other empowering us by helping us realize that our spiritual reality is indeed embodied in the form gifted to us by God, and the more we accept Him unconditionally as our fount of everlasting life and therefore as our Savior, He literally begins to live through us, guiding us in all we say and do from His ultimate perspective.

Indeed, at this point, and increasingly, there is only His Divine presence living inspirationally and dynamically within each one of us for the good of all, including ourselves.

Now that we are free, at long last, of any underlying sense of being abandoned.

Of relying on our own egotistical efforts within the economic and material.

Of being conditioned by the fearful and functionary.

But instead filled with a growing sense of instinctive peace, understanding and insight, which the capitalist world has been at the forefront in denying to so many of us, because of the dread of death and extinction that engulfs its chief advocates and their tragic failure to confront it in depth.

And their desperation, no matter what the cost to millions and millions, to preserve themselves, even if it has meant compelling so many of us, especially across our wider world, to exist like scarecrows in some windswept field. Fully open to the elements of the market but then very often to the ravaging of the crows if we became superfluous to its needs. Leaving us conditioned to exist apparently separate from the God who, it always inferred, we never needed.

Our ultimate delusion.

And their ultimate delusion.

For we have never needed God more.

Indeed so very many of us now know.

That we and our world literally cannot go on without Him.

So why on earth should we even try to resist Him?

The very Source of all life.

The very Source of life as it should be lived.

A Source who alone can transform not just our vision but actually involve Himself in all that we do. A relationship that is essential to challenge all those in power, who go on blindly committing so many self-seeking and ultimately self-destructive acts aimed at increasing what they 'have.' At whatever insatiable and unsustainable cost not just to ourselves and our planet, but to the basic rights of whole societies and populations, even our very own. As well as to the inherent harmony within each one of us.

But not anymore. With God's influence, we will simply not permit them to continue controlling our lives with airwaves of propaganda that ignore what is so palpably going on. Nor, at the same time, allow them to impose more restrictions on people's rights to protest peacefully and speak freely so they can carry on regardless, increasingly in an age of mass, indiscriminate surveillance.

As more and more of us finally wake up to the reality that so much is being sacrificed, in these desperate, disorientated days out of fear, with the fallacious justification that it is all being done to fight those who would seek to undermine our 'free and democratic' way of life, the bedrock of which is these very same human rights.

Indeed, we can now see quite clearly how those in power – if they remain locked into the system's shortsighted perspective – will merely carry on denying the link between their relentless policies and what will inevitably result if no primary and lasting changes are actually put into effect. If critically who we all are as ultimately spiritual beings is not allowed to guide the way we conduct our lives.

Something more and more of us increasingly recognize, now that we are actually experiencing and not just voicing our faith in God as the essence of who we are. Our God, who has been waiting so patiently for us to take the time to surrender to His eternal vision that breaks through the illusions of this capitalist order.

So that He can fulfill His natural purpose for us by expressing His loving and giving nature through us – the natural rhythm and flow, indeed the very pulse of life being awakened and transmitted through us. Indeed, as I keep maintaining, what else would a loving Creator possibly do?

Other than to offer all that He is to renew us all. In order to sustain us all. Not just for our benefit. But for the benefit of all those we share this life with. So that we can live this life as we were meant to live it.

A prospect that galvanizes so many of us each morning in our urgency to be filled and empowered with His presence. In order to transform our perspective both at home, at work and in our communities, as well as globally. To enable us to act and lead others in ways beyond anything we previously thought possible, however pie-in-the-sky such a vision may initially seem.

For what is the alternative we can now see?

We only have to turn on the daily news or read a newspaper.

Indeed watch a week of it or read a week of them.

Even allowing for the obsessively negative and debilitating emphasis, we now know that we cannot continue to deny the overall direction of where we are heading and claim we are still in control.

Especially when we reflect upon the world of our parents during crises in their lives, our grandparents even. International wars, dictatorial ruthlessness, economic exploitation, family sufferings and personal hardships certainly. But obsessive greed, wars over resources, global mass poverty, environmental disintegration, social fragmentation, population displacement, individual isolation and psychological disorder on this scale?

Realities which may even lead some to ask, has totalitarianism really gone away, or does it just wear a more subtle, corporate guise?

All of it rooted in our futile insistence that our own terrified and self-serving strategies apart from God, apart from His instinctive guidance, are the only strategies available to us.

Our God, who in our childhood innocence and simplicity we may have sensed as both innate and integral to who we are, and finally again have got our heads around as a constantly-accessible force for good alive within us at all times. Indeed, the ultimate spiritual Force.

Now that we are past this lengthy period of trying to let go and of accepting, finally, that, on our own, we cannot control everything. We simply can't work or sort it all out. Indeed we, our egos, should never have even tried to direct or redirect things, we can now see.

But instead acknowledged all along that God and God alone (or our Higher presence within) is in control of whatever situation we find ourselves in, or whatever predicaments our society finds itself in. As we turn everything over to Him at so many critical moments, rather than up to our random and sometimes reckless judgments.

What a massive adjustment that has always been to make though.

What a total shift in emphasis.

Letting go completely until we became a focus purely for Divine will, by moving forward – very often in blindness and sometimes in terror – from goodness knows whatever situation life threw at us.

Pleading for extraordinary reserves of courage from Him on our road to who knows where (or so it may have seemed at the time). While trying desperately to keep our hearts and senses wide open to whatever insights were freely given on our way.

And they were given, we can now see.

However much we may have failed to spot them at the time.

Amidst the agitation and even pain of those often tempestuous times.

When the peace of God was frequently drowned out of our lives.

Making us feel so relieved, in the end, that we somehow survived and made it through what must have felt like an unrelenting conflict. That, more than likely, both brought us right to our knees and yet, at long last, very gradually saw us healed.

Redefining not just our lives but our very sense of who we are. Liberating us to fulfill the distinct purpose that, we can now see, God always had for us. Indeed for each one of us.

We who are now so willingly shaped by the hand that both created us and breathes fresh life into us each and every day.

So intimate with us, so loving towards us, so actively involved with us, so at one with us, whatever we go through.

As, with increasing trust, we access all that God provides for us, all that He feels we need, way beyond the vagaries and wild fluctuations of our previously unstable existence.

Alison's Story

Another Sunday I dread when I am struggling to get up without work to force me. When, as usual, within seconds of waking and beginning to think, I feel overwhelmed and straightaway things go rapidly downhill.

Another Sunday, above all, when I want to feel absolutely nothing at all. But instead I am forever... engulfed with that one overpowering emotion... tied to that one overpowering image inside our... car... what remained of our car... that will forever be with me.

If only I could work seven days a week. Twenty-four hours a day. Every minute of every week. To keep it away.

But, for the most part, I can't. And on top I have to deal with that voice that keeps pestering me all the time, forever telling me that just maybe today can be different.

Ridiculous, I know, because there have been so many... false dawns, so many... futile moments, so many... exhausting days outside the distraction of work.

But still I keep being told that things will really change today if I can simply go out and walk... and walk... and keep on walking.

A... nonsensical thing to do, I know. But one nevertheless which this small part of me still insists I must do if I really want to jolt my existence back into anything worthwhile at all.

Which I do, of course!

But I simply can't.

For how can I? When I feel totally adrift in a life that is almost totally disconnected from the one I used to live... someone called Alison, aged 34, a primary school teacher, a Sunday school teacher, a wife, a... mother... an unspectacular... life.

Just who was that person?

She is like someone I once knew. Someone whose life is permanently on hold, still waiting for news... news of a recovery that, I know, is coming. But still having to wait so long...

Frozen almost... routinely now in my own personal... emptiness, while at the same time facing up to these incessant calls to go out and walk not just this day, but even on into the next!

"But why should I? What is the point? What about my work? For goodness sake, leave me alone!"

Still, crazily, almost in spite of myself, I find myself getting out of bed, getting dressed and packing my rucksack yet again.

Making the same monumental effort for no good reason.

Don't stop at the front door, nor at the gate, nor even at the start of the path, I am told. You've done that so often before. Just keep walking, breathing slowly and deeply. And you will go further.

No... I won't! How can I? It's impossible. I know what will happen. Because I have been through it so many times before. I mean, just how much more can any one person take!

Remember, don't look back, the voice persists. You'll soon be right out over the coast. The clifftop with the... raw intensity of the fresh sea air blowing in. Whatever you do, keep going, keep going further... so, stupidly, I do.

Badgered and badgered even though all that is happening is a... terrible... intensification of what I am going through already until I reach an inevitable dead end, the... brick wall that I knew I would...

And I scream aloud that I can't possibly go any further! I must go back. I am going back! Why shouldn't I? It is my choice. My life! To do with what I want! I'd rather be back at my new job. Making telephone calls all day. Absurdly. But at least anonymously.

The prospect of which eases the pressure temporarily... especially when I remind myself that my work takes me closer to where I most need to be, of course...

Waiting for news at the hospital just around the corner.

Waiting for news that I know is coming...

It is, of course, impossible to remember exactly all the days, hours and minutes I walked Ellie along this path.

I mean, there were all the years with her in the backpack, from just about the time when she could hold her head up in it. With me pointing out absolutely everything on the way. Heaven knows what she made of me chattering on. But it was all communication, all sharing together... and I really did treasure every single moment... I hope... I pray...

Then, after I went back to school, we moved onto all the very, very slow walks at weekends when she investigated every little thing in minute detail herself and this time I was the responsive one. When absolutely everything had to be touched, smelt and listened to.

And occasionally I used to say under my breath, "Ellie, why can't you hurry up just a little bit?" Even though I tried very hard not to.

Oh no! My reminiscing has started again! It always starts out here.

So I quickly head back to my old house. Because it really is OK for me to... to find some slight relief from this torment, which I know I can always get back there...

Yet that something deep inside still keeps harassing me, "No, don't turn back, stop thinking, keep walking forward."

So I end up rooted to the spot once more, panting deeply, not knowing what on earth to do.

I look out at the scene around me, almost beside myself, until, in time, some words I read somewhere suddenly come to me:

"The empty spaces of the very moment. Don't fill them with anything."

Whatever that really means! I have read so much, spoken to so many people, but I find it so hard to put anything into practice.

Then... without knowing what I am really doing... I start moving forward again... even though I know that all that is ahead is an even greater suffering than what I have already gone through.

A suffering, which, such is its force, has even led me to question not just who I really am but who are any of us? Other than some lost souls bound up in some lost and increasingly traumatic way of life.

With our relationship with any kind of god, when it comes down to it, no more than some naive and desperate yearning, which we finally see through at the times when we most need

Him in our lives... and He isn't there... when I most needed Him in my life, and He wasn't there.

I should have known it was too much to ask for.

I now know that it was.

Hoping against hope, amidst it all, for some kind of understanding that would answer so many questions. And give some sense of meaning. But no. Nothing.

Reflections and... recriminations I then carried on in my garden especially. My sounding board in the months that followed. So much time digging furiously in my border, bellowing at my plants... as my emotions entirely got the better of me... while I still waited for the good news about Ellie, of course. Ignoring the stares of occasional passersby, who can only have determined that I was a mad woman.

Most of them, needless to say, just walked away awkwardly, which, I suppose, is fair enough – pain is so hard to confront.

But then one particular afternoon... to my increasing irritation... a single man paused and glanced across at me for a time... and kept glancing when I... momentarily returned his look. And as much as I then tried to ignore him, he persisted with a concerned expression that... I suppose, I can now see, tried to make me feel that I was not alone.

A concern that didn't, fortunately enough, ask or demand anything of me. Because I had absolutely nothing to give in response. It was just his reaction to what, no doubt, he may have... sensed in me.

He came past a second and then a third time over days, lingering for a few moments on each occasion, until finally, hesitantly, I struggled forward to say a few words to him, if only to tell him to leave me alone. But, in fact, he merely listened and, in time, asked simple questions that seem to connect with... I suppose, exactly where my heart was. Indeed, after a while, I found myself eager, somehow even desperate, to answer him, just as long as he was there to... respond.

Hanif was not some priest or... mullah... doctor or therapist. I'm not sure who he was. He never really answered me the few times I asked. Maybe he was about 30 years older than me in his late 60s. Above all... he seemed to care. That's all that mattered. He seemed to care and indeed, I suppose, he showed he cared.

And gave me something without asking anything in return. And then kept on giving me something every time he stopped. It was as simple and yet as... profound as that.

A complete stranger... who would come to have an influence on my life.

Back on my walk I finally reach the coast after managing to struggle through some of the most... emotional parts where Ellie and I used to stop for picnics and games. And I come face to face with so much wide open space. Feeling, of course, extraordinarily... fragile, as I knew I would. My mind, of course... the excruciating image... so intense... especially out here.

Why on earth are you putting yourself through all of this, a voice within again tells me.

While another voice, just as persistent, insists I keep walking forward, slowly. Staying focused...

Focused on what though? There's nothing to focus on!

I have only recently just begun to stop the torment of my imagination going over and over what might have happened on another day... how Ellie might have been... a little less seriously injured. Blaming people less, especially Ellie's dad, Craig, my... husband... and myself, of course.

It's so... so unfair, knowing right from the start you will go over it all again and again, to absolutely no purpose, and there's nothing you can do about it!

Isn't it enough to have experienced it in the first place?!

It has taken me months and months and months just to reach this stage, whatever stage this is. But then, I suppose... my heart had to be... cut right out of the wreckage of that car...

Whatever, I was finally able to apologize and tell Craig over and over that he was not in any way responsible. I mean, it's not as if he was to blame. And, one day, I felt, he just might be able to forgive me.

The mind is a killer. It has nearly killed me. It is an instrument of torture when it is so alone and so in pain. How could any kind of god have possibly left me so abandoned? A god, supposedly, of love and compassion. Why couldn't He have been there alongside me that day, at least to... to absorb some of the... anguish Himself?

Why isn't He even here now!

Especially as I've come to a complete stop again... thinking about all of this! Not knowing whether to keep walking forward into this wide open space or to... to... go back...

"This isn't fair, it's too much! Way too much!" I plead. "Especially when I should be at the hospital, waiting... waiting for news of Ellie... "

"Let me go to work, let me go home!" I beg, desperate to return to somewhere familiar... anything familiar...

Instead though I begin walking quicker. In time, jogging even. After a short while, extraordinarily, running as fast as I can, despite having my rucksack on my back, stumbling everywhere, veering off ridiculously, in who knows what direction, just as long as I keep moving, For I have had enough of standing still. Especially when I discover that the trauma of my exertion and exhaustion is actually beginning to help me drive out the anguish of what I am feeling inside, however temporarily.

On and on. With nothing to stop me. Because I am now desperate not to stop. Running for I don't know how long. As long as I can keep going. Way beyond anywhere I have ever run. Until, over time, I literally run myself right into the ground, falling to my knees, panting like I have never panted before... as if I am going to die of the heart failure I almost wish for...

Dying and yet...

I suddenly realize…

And suddenly take in…

Incredibly alive…

Even amidst all this.

Though there doesn't seem to be any way my galloping heart will slow down. I don't know how many breaths it took. But eventually they become slower and deeper and, in fact, so deep that I, at last, start feeling a touch calmer and then even more aware of the… the slight respite that my wild escapade had created in my tortured thoughts.

A respite and feeling that, for some reason, left me reflecting on something Hanif once said to me, which I, needless to say, failed to comprehend at the time.

Eventually he dropped by more regularly. And while I was sitting on my garden wall one day, with him simply listening to all that I was still pouring out, as well as my hopes that Ellie would eventually… he again seemed to… to sense something within me.

"Alison, I think you are beginning to realize that while your pain is completely natural, as well as in so many ways… necessary, you are also starting to… glimpse something else beyond your mind that may actually be trying to help you," he said.

"What? I'm not glimpsing or feeling anything!" I replied.

"Believe me, from what all you have said, you clearly are, however quietly you may be experiencing it whispering to you," he said calmly.

But I wasn't. I felt sure. For nothing was really changing, especially with Ellie just the same in hospital. And that despite all the understandings and insights that may have been helping some people like Hanif, they were clearly not helping me! It was all way beyond me.

Indeed, in spite of the lull in my anguish brought on by my mad running just now, I quickly know that I had only created a temporary gap in my stream of thoughts and the image I know I will always keep seeing.

For this, clearly, is my destiny. I will simply have to go on and on enduring it. Seeing myself flung around in an instant from the front of our car and forced to gaze at my little daughter in the back... without me even being able to reach out to her... and to touch her...

To cuddle her warm body.

So that all I have left is my hopes that she will...

I can see her right now, in fact...

Hoping very soon that she will...

I can see her up close...

Hoping against hope that she will...

I can see her in the back of our car now...

Trying to reach out to her now...

I should be helping her now...

But increasingly she is lost in the flickering light of our car...

Our once warm... secure... family car...

Now somehow crushed into some metal barrier...

Our possessions...

Our bits and pieces...

All tangled and compressed...

Now suddenly not even any sounds from the splashing puddles on the road...

Nor any flashing lights from passing vehicles...

Even the thumping of our windscreen wipers has stopped...

All is very abruptly and very finally still...

Even Ellie has stopped moaning...

She is barely stirring...

Both of us trapped and...

... and seemingly interred...

With me not able to do a thing!

She is actually...

Ellie might actually be...

She might actually be unconscious...

... I think...

No...

No...

... surely she is not...

She can't be dead, can she?

Yes... yes... she is dead, I can suddenly see.

I... know she is dead.

I can see her at last.

A death that I have long since craved for myself since the accident, of course...

But never ever for her!

Never ever for her...!

I have no idea exactly how long I continued to lie there. Almost like part of me wasn't even there. All I sense, when I finally become more conscious, is that my life has finally come to a resounding halt... and so, however temporarily, I eventually realize, has the... incessant, furious struggle that has been going on inside me.

As I find myself sitting up, clinging to my rucksack, which is somehow off my back. My mouth is so dry I take a few sips of water and then look up and realize I am at a point of the path that I don't recognize at all...

Managing though, at long last and however vaguely, to begin to glimpse at least some of the truth about what has actually happened to my family and I... while simply gazing at the broom that is everywhere, the endless fields, and up to the... remorseless sky, which all appear so dull and inconsequential as usual.

But at least I feel a slight, if eerie, sense of silence emanating from them all.

A sense that stays with me a little while longer, in my numbed reaction to all that has happened to me, until inexplicably and all of a sudden, the whole scene I experienced before, the broom, the fields and the sky, everything I initially took in, I now see it all... I am now seeing it all almost as if I am seeing it for the very first time... blossoming broom, rich, green grass and perfect blue, near cloudless sky.

No longer is any of it merely dull and inconsequential.

And an extraordinary sense of... of I'm not sure what... utter peace, I suppose... passes right through me just for one split second, no more. A sense of peace that tells me simply but emphatically that everything will somehow... yes, it will somehow all be alright.

Contrary to so much of what I have felt for so, so long. Indeed the peace is even accompanied by a sense of... yes, a sense of... wonder, I suppose... which is somehow connected to all that is both all around... and strangely even within me. That's the only way I can describe that one split second.

All of it certainly astonishing... but also unmistakably clear.

And very quickly after this, I also suddenly realize that this is a moment I may have been waiting for... not just a long time... but in truth, I quickly recognize, all of my life.

Not just since Ellie's death, or her birth even, but, yes, since... since my very own.

Since anything I have ever known or ever experienced in this life.

Empowerment 2

So much of our suffering, not just personal and family-rooted, but even national or international for that matter, has been locked not just into past ordeals or torments, but our often frightened and rigid mindsets. Exacerbated, of course, by the ceaselessly pressurized nature of our modern-day existence, which has blocked out the time and space that is required for the unveiling of our developing relationship with the Divine. And therefore the entirely fresh perception and, in time, potential healing, as well as liberation that comes with that.

All of this reflecting a tragic denial of who we are because in the end very many of us have ended up not truly living at all, or not as it was intended for us.

For the eternal spiritual life-force within us was always there to break through so much of our preconceived conditioning and anguish, just as soon as we could surrender ourselves silently to it. Allowing it to express itself through an intimate daily counseling that transforms the way our lives can be lived.

For so long, we have believed that only we and our individualistic striving could possibly lift us out of the despair of whatever situation or crisis we have fallen into. Even though we can now see that what we really required was what so many of us, in the end, have received – entirely new illuminations, coming from a far higher level of awareness.

Even with regard to our prayers (that is if we have prayed at all), it was perhaps a long time before some of us finally perceived them as being a mere imitation of others' often babbling requests, as very often we endeavored to manipulate our 'separate' God to our own ends.

Instead of simply yet courageously leaving our whole circumstances silently and courageously up to Him. By allowing His consciousness to become our very own. Thereby leading us fearlessly in whatever direction He sought to take us for the ultimate benefit not just of ourselves, but of all.

With any question of religious doctrine being no more but also no less than a pointer on our way to definitive truth and we didn't merely end up replacing one form of prescribed or habitual thinking with another. Or following another set of man's interpretations or rules.

Rather than allowing the innate sense of the spiritual to flow forth from our total awakening, from our humble and direct relationship with our abundant God and His all-giving nature. A relationship which, I cannot emphasize enough, we must keep breathing fresh awareness into just as soon as we awaken each day. And then as often as we can throughout that day.

Not just in order to remain conscious of who we truly are but also in order to grow in confidence in this renewed identity, to become entirely reliant on it, to feel entirely assured about it.

As it:

Heals us with spiritual compassion.
Fills us with spiritual presence.
And inspires us with spiritual energy.

So that we can then rise above the inevitable distractions that will still come our way, by seeing them for what they really are, mere obstacles in the way of the full expression of our true being.

Then, and only then, will we remain fully open to the extraordinary impact that God can always have on our lives as we feel a whole new vitality in all that we think and do, and critically in what we attract to ourselves through Him. Indeed, in what we come to expect through Him.

As we move closer and closer to the full realization of our higher potential and the unique role each of us is to play for the good of all, however improbable all this may have seemed prior to this.

This same dedicated approach also helps to highlight the deep sense of harmony we increasingly feel uniting each and every one of us in God, as we start to perceive more and more people we meet with overwhelming feelings of empathy and compassion.

People with whom we now share a sense of connection to the Sacred, which we go on to express, rather than focusing on what we previously assumed was separating us.

It also follows, with regards to the way we view our environment, that we start to experience ourselves as being increasingly at one with and therefore receptive of its essence.

Indeed, everywhere we begin to look and are genuinely alive, we experience our spiritual energy connecting us with the spiritual energy that is out there all around us, if we genuinely give it a chance.

As the Divine within us inevitably tunes into the Divine the world over. Making it impossible therefore for us to exploit it continuously. But only to nurture, sustain and to love it. For the good of us all.

How tragic, as well as destructive, it then becomes clear to us.

To have existed, for so long, apart from such insights and understanding.

To have existed apart from such vision and clarity.

A tragedy that has not only enslaved and endangered us.

But also denied us access to life as it actually is.

And could always have been for us.

As so many of us allowed our innate spirituality in God, our 'detached' God, to be downgraded to a bystander's role or no role at all. Or even worse accepted the grotesquely distorted image of Him, which some have painted: an image of a primarily judgmental, conflictive and even vengeful God, who inflicts pain on us. When His overriding nature has always been overflowing with compassion, as daily He seeks to fulfill all our unique, earthly needs as He sees them.

Our God, therefore, who has never in any way been some mirror image of our increasingly frightened, agitated and therefore aggressive world, but who has always sought to reflect His loving, eternal nature – His all-giving, all-sharing, all-sustaining nature – through each one of us.

Crucially, as soon as we choose to be silent and allow Him.

As soon as we choose to grow in humility and accept Him.

Making Him, therefore, so appealing to so many lost, unloved and even desolate souls – to so many of us, whatever we have endured – if finally we could all be presented with this vision of Him. And maintain this liberating image in our hearts and minds.

As finally He fulfills all our yearnings to be embraced and to feel entirely secure in who we are. So that we then realize our true calling.

By going out and taking this revitalizing presence into our relationships, our families, our communities, our workplaces and into campaigning situations everywhere, in order to confront the reality that the problems we all face are rooted first and foremost in the spiritual alienation of our times. And yet there is nothing that cannot be transformed to any lasting effect once we reactivate the infinite power within each of us that has been denied to us for so long.

A power, which, when truly alive, we begin to sense more and more, concentrates its attention through each of us wherever it most needs to be concentrated, so that more and more lives can then reflect this journey of poverty and renewal. As the love and power of God reaches out and touches everyone along the increasingly confident path we now take.

Indeed the term 'leadership' begins to take on a whole new meaning through us.

A leadership that does not seek to rule but to liberate.

A leadership that does not seek to restrain but to rekindle.

Through our instinct to listen so that all can be heard and cared for.

As we each learn to react to the depth of silence that stirs all our souls.

So we can respond intuitively, indeed unconditionally to whatever is asked of us.

However broken, wretched, even torn apart, in this desperately fragile society, we may have felt at some point in our lives.

For none of us are beyond His rescue and redemption.

Whether leader or listener.

None of us are beyond His renewal and resurgence.

Through finally acknowledging our poverty and dependency.
Before handing our very lives back to Him.
Who even now is ready to reawaken us:

To the grace and miracle of who we really are right now.
To the vast, rich life we are all offered in God right now.
To the energy and vision that can inspire us right now.
To God living passionately through us forevermore.

Once everything about who we are finally falls into His hands.

Making us feel wholly relieved and deeply grateful that at long last we have embraced what we have always needed to embrace in life. Rather than continuing to sense at whatever level that we have merely been floundering upon the waves of sheer fate, undermined by our habitual sense of economic, materialistic or even mortal anxiety.

But not now we are genuinely alive in God. So much so, at times, we almost begin to feel as if we are a spectator over and above this life and yet still immersed in it. So that everyone we meet and every situation that confronts us is now seen from a whole new, understanding and bold outlook. Indeed an outlook with infinite possibilities.

So that any new initiative is now possible, any family reconciliation, any work resolution, even any international poverty resolution, ecological agreement or ceasefire settlement.

Even any new vision regarding the global economic system that has ruled over us for so long, which could in time be viewed from a whole fresh perspective, free of all the wretched fear, self-obsession, greed and recklessness that precipitated the financial crisis of 2007-8 and threatens even more international turbulence in the future.

Once we finally begin to see a far greater percentage of money and precious resources being used on behalf of all in our world and not just the few. Being shared out sustainably and proportionately to all in our world and not just the few.

With a rise in endeavors that are increasingly geared at social and just rather than purely profit-making objectives. Whether they be connected to community banking, shared risk enterprises, fair trade, local food projects or whatever. With these ventures ensuring that basic human needs, as well as rights, are enshrined far more comprehensively through a sense of joint responsibility, with the consequent reassurance and reduction in personal stress that can flow from mutual cooperations.

Investment, too, could well be viewed not just from an ethical point of view, but even more courageously and harmoniously, through a focus on what actually promotes our well-being to a greater extent rather than simply on what doesn't harm us, or, of course, others across our world. With more and more emphasis on the long-term rather than on the short-term, on slow capital rather than on venture capital, and especially on a low-carbon economy rather than on one that continues to be obsessed with propping up the financial system at all costs.

Indeed, with God's vision altering ours so radically increasing numbers of us may well begin to view the entire concept of prosperity and what it means to be wealthy in very different ways.

With our emerging sensitivity to the fate of the whole of humankind leading us to work to secure a fairer, less growth-obsessed, simpler, sustainable life for all. With a focus now on consumption levels that are indicative of our needs, not our greed, never mind on what is sustainable for our fragile earth. Above all, our global institutions must be required to reflect this whole new perspective and approach, as we all prepare for the world of fewer resources that is coming.

At the same time, this emphasis on a selfless quality of life rather than a desperate quantity will induce a greater sense of meaning to all that we do, as well as an extraordinary appreciation for all that we already have.

In truth, what other direction are we likely to go in with God guiding us all so assuredly? With Him encouraging us to share what He gives to us on a daily basis? For that is how things work with His nature alive within us.

So much so we could never go back to being so enslaved by being so predominantly focused on our ego-driven selves as we may well have been before. Or so in denial of what is palpably happening before our eyes brought on by the wretched fear that so many of us feel.

Indeed, we may now even begin to question whether we really wanted to be that survival-at-all-costs person deep down if we ever were. Now that we have experienced the peace and surety in God that was so tragically kept from us before. Now that we have surrendered to and become alive to our true and unique inheritance on this earth and beyond.

With each of us living anew from now on.

Each of us living according to our ultimate purpose.

According to God's Higher purpose for us.

United in our resolve for each other.

In our resolve to protect our planet.

Now that we have all been freed.

By actually knowing –

And not just having faith –

That through God's grace,

We all live forevermore.

Alison's Story 2

The first evening of the course was always going to be difficult. With guests coming from all sorts of situations, of course, and bringing all kinds of... turbulent baggage with them. So, I became very conscious of trying to spend as much time chatting to everyone in the lounge as I could. Together with Anne, who is a friend, as well as a counselor. In order to make them all feel at ease.

However, it is very obvious straightaway that to some my

big, isolated house, high up near the coast with gales blowing in from the west today, is not helping matters. Indeed, when there is a pause in the conversation, the howls of the wind and the… groans of the old place are all that they hear. And some are looking very uneasy… nervous even.

At least, they appear to like their accommodation for the week across in the converted old cowshed, although who knows. I don't know why I am still struggling to stop myself feeling insecure about the whole venture. And clinging to the belief that, having survived so many… obstacles along the way… that just maybe it is something that is simply meant to be. Something that I must… simply follow through after everything that has happened to me, at this particular stage in my life.

Anne and I have drawn up an agenda for the week ahead and are already being quizzed about it. Some want to schedule time for this, some for that and some… well, they don't seem to want to schedule anything at all. Barry, for instance, judging by the uneasy question he asks – "Where is the nearest pub?"

A small part of me, I must admit, wouldn't mind joining him for a few glasses of wine myself right now but Anne deals with his request rather better. "Yes, we could all go to the pub tonight and get absolutely sloshed, or… or we could make a gentle start and see how we all go from there. The pub isn't going anywhere, is it, Alison?"

I smile rather than tell them all that there isn't, in fact, a pub… well, not one for 10 miles anyway… which may be just as well because one or two of the blotchy faces here (even more than Barry's) suggest they may have difficulties in that direction.

Especially the four old ladies from a homeless community in the city, who somehow survived the long journey in the battered old van they were brought in. Something made me determined to prevent this turning into some kind of… I don't know… middle-class love-in and I was delighted when their community director (who I know – I worked there a couple of years ago) phoned to confirm that they were coming.

Anne begins by asking everyone simply to tell the group of 16 of us our names to introduce ourselves. A couple of women in their late 30s, with clipboards on their knees, seem to grow a little impatient with the incredibly slow progress of even this apparently straightforward task. But then the varying approaches, I quickly discover, speak volumes without folk really saying much.

"Alex! Karen!" the two younger women inform us succinctly enough, both turning immediately to their left for the next person's turn.

Others try to offer more information, on where they're from, their jobs, their marital status (or breakups), their families, their pets and... last of all their history of various addictions and breakdowns, as if they want to get it all out in the open straightaway.

Finally we come to one of the homeless folk, Rosie, who doesn't appear to be quite with us. Her friend Beryl intervenes. "Her name's Rosie. Rosie, they want to know your name! Tell them, for God's sake," she demands of her.

"Hey?" responds Rosie.

"Tell them before we all die of cold in here!" Beryl repeats to my embarrassment, even though it must be 70 degrees in the room, with the central heating on and a log fire ablaze.

Rosie though is still not registering with the question, and instead stands up, before launching into an old musical tune to the general astonishment of everyone. In fact, she sings the whole song, unaccompanied, with the most beautifully expressive voice you could ever imagine anyone having, let alone someone in her 80s, before she simply stops and sits down.

"Well, there you are. That's Rosie. She didn't sing for years, but since she's been in the community nothing'll stop her," Beryl says.

"Hey?" says Rosie. "Where's the tea? Aren't we having a

cupper yet?"

An older man, Mervyn, is so moved by all of this he begins crying, while the rest simply respond by looking awkward, nonplussed or clapping sporadically and uncertainly. As the whole room is filled, indeed even overwhelmed, I suddenly realize, with a sense of... of our deep human frailty...

By the end of the night I find myself absolutely exhausted with the whole buildup and first-evening experience, and just before bed, I pass Elizabeth, a lady in her late 50s, who is one of four staying in the house, in the upstairs corridor. She pauses to ask me about the picture on a small table of a little girl on a coastal path close to home.

I tell her it is my daughter, Ellie, who would have been seven last month. I smile, fully accepting now that my wounds are always evident for everyone to see. Elizabeth, after another pause, smiles back, with unmistakable pain etched on her face, the pain of another story... wrestled with ceaselessly... but finally accepted and borne for life. You get to... recognize them.

But also... to accept, from time to time, I think, just how far you have come. Or more likely, I suppose, just how far you have been brought... almost astonishingly, in truth. Whole new perceptions, possibilities... life... once all the resistance has gone.

After a while I fall asleep having managed to quieten my mind, but I am woken up after just half an hour by the sound of people moving about in the lounge below. Coming downstairs, I peer through to see Beryl, Mervyn and a younger man, Steve, having a cup of tea by the fire, which I had left to go out, but which has been re-ignited. Beryl is even smoking.

OK, I had told them to make themselves at home, but it is half past eleven and I am worried about just what kind of state they might be in come the morning. So I decide to go and break up their little gathering, especially as they may wake up some of the other folk.

But then almost immediately part of me wonders if there just may be something positive about what I am witnessing. That it may actually be... helping them to settle in. Initially I am not sure what to do. Maybe I should ask Anne. But then I sense somehow that... yes... I am confident enough to make this decision myself. So, with a little uncertainty, I leave them to it.

The wildness of the night gives way to a calmer, sunnier spring morning with a warm, gentle southerly breeze. I don't know what possesses Anne, considering what Beryl said about feeling cold the night before, but she asks me to set up breakfast on the patio outside!

I am just getting used to that decision, when she suddenly comes over – while checking the agenda for the day – and shocks the life out of me. "We're going to have to tear all this up," she says.

"What!" I reply.

"It won't work now that I have seen just how diverse the group is, especially with the folk from the homeless community. Don't worry, it'll be fine. It'll all work out. It may even work for the better," Anne tries to reassure me.

I am not reassured. Well, I try to be. Because deep down I know I should just be OK about it... trust that it will work out... but part of me still finds it so hard to... let go.

Whatever, Anne simply turns and smiles, almost as if it is Hanif of old who is smiling reassuringly at me, before she begins to greet everyone coming over from the old cowshed.

They all arrive in dribs and drabs but the setting, at least, appears to have a reasonably calming effect on them and offers topics of conversation, within which everyone can comfortably engage – my garden and, of course, the weather.

I have grown to love my garden and have literally, I have felt at times, put my heart and soul into its... gentle restoration. Together with the wonderful sea views, it seems today to allow nature to... express itself and even, I suddenly feel to... to cloak us in all its glory.

Once everyone is settled (especially with cups of tea in front of them), Anne begins by amplifying on her new approach which tells us that whatever we may have brought with us this week – whatever feelings about ourselves – including any worries or... or guilts or... or old wounds – we should try as much as we can to begin each day by putting them all to one side. So that we can focus solely on who we are right now, on our relationships with God, our spiritual natures, which is far more central to who we are.

Of course, this may seem difficult, strange or even impossible to some of us, Anne persists, but if we can empty our minds by concentrating regularly on something as basic as our breathing... and even connect that to all that is around us, we will, in time, actually be able to experience a silent presence within that even now is waiting for us.

Just as I nervously wonder what kind of reaction we will get to all this, she warmly points to the instinctive outpouring of Rose's singing the night before as an expression of this inner presence, and the joy and love that it offered to each one of us.

"Hey?" says Rosie, aloud, hearing her name.

"She likes your singing, that's all," responds Beryl, equally loud.

"Well, I'm not singing yet, tell her straight. I'm not a bloody gramophone. Anyway, it's too early, I haven't even finished my tea yet," says Rosie.

And there, right there and then, I find myself reflecting on something Hanif spoke to me about just before his sudden death last year: just how each of us, not necessarily Rosie, can sometimes be held back by a... reluctance... a tragic reluctance to let ourselves go... and express a... natural joy and love that stirs within us... very often, I think he said, due to the... yes, due to the "corruption of our true being."

A corruption, he went on to say, that drives us to deny so many genuine feelings, emotions and experiences, even our very... instincts, I think he said. So that we end up struggling with many situations and relationships. As our... fears tighten their mental grip on us, I especially remember him saying. With our love not only denied its full blooming, but sometimes any kind of blooming at all. So that our whole life, he felt, can become far more of a struggle for survival. Instead of... being guided by a vision of hope.

My struggle for survival, as overwhelming as it has been, has, in truth, I know now, been even more than about Ellie. It has been about a life that I only glimpsed up till then and a lack of... understanding, I suppose, that, to a degree, stopped me being anything like fully... aware.

So much so, of course, that I had absolutely no sense of the... eternal when Ellie passed away and, to a degree, I am still wrestling with it. Still wrestling with so, so much. Despite all I have experienced. Despite all that has changed within me. And as hard as I have tried. As hard as I still try.

Why is everything so hard?!

Even though Hanif always told me not to strive so much but to try to approach situations far more gently... and lightly... far more... accepting of who I am right now... so I could always be open to so much more... whatever that really meant.

"In the end," he once said to me, even though again I couldn't fully grasp what he was saying. "In the end, you will surrender enough to accept the great loss you have suffered, so that it becomes the most powerful source of grace that can be given to you."

A grace that since then I've very gradually become to sense a little more in my daily life. Leading me to believe that sometime in the future, who knows, I just may become half as... patient and... understanding... and especially as caring as Hanif always was with me.

But not yet so confident, of course, that I can simply put into practice what Anne has done – by changing everything and throwing it all wide open to what will be!

Even though, as soon as the following evening, her emphasis on creating "an undemanding atmosphere" and responding to the present moment quickly seems to bear fruit. When – out of the silence which continues to unnerve one or two people but is by now helping others to relax – Josie, another from the homeless community, becomes one of the first to react, in her own emotional way, to the plea to speak only when a genuine urge arises.

"The good Lord is with me now. I don't know much but I know that. He is all there is. This is another day when I would not be alive but for Him. He knew what my life was. Until the folk from the community took me in. Giving their time, themselves for nothing. All my screaming and fighting.

"They went through it all with me. Without ever giving up on me. Until, in the end, I yelled it all out. And then I realized something. Realized something about... about love is I suppose what I am saying. And I am not embarrassed to say it anymore. Not just the love they showed me either. But even though I couldn't believe it... some love in myself, would you believe... some love they helped me to feel in myself. The biggest miracle of all."

"What's Josie saying?" Rosie interrupts.

"Agh, just her usual... she loves us all, you know," Beryl responds.

"Well, tell her I love her and all, especially for lending me her rug," Rosie says.

My big, old house, I suddenly began to feel then, might just bear witness to many such outpourings, from so many different people, in so many different ways, at many different stages of their... yes, I suppose, their spiritual awakening, in the days, weeks and, who knows, even in the years ahead.

Anything... yes anything might be possible.

Just so long as all our... worries and... fears can finally be silenced, I guess, so that we can uncover... and then express... previously hidden truths about ourselves. Whether simply amongst a few folk... or... during the increasingly intense and emotional hours when we all start to feel secure enough to... share things together in larger groups. As we have been doing more and more this week.

Sometimes one or two people may not say very much to you personally about themselves, or even appear to care much about you, but their giving in other ways special to them tells you a little of who they really are and I suppose their... journeys and instinctive feelings towards you or people in general.

One such person, this particular week, though old and tired at the end of a life of... apparent struggle, continued to offer in such a way. By singing to us regularly, so much so that the love for her that was so clearly being felt by the other three women from the homeless community spread very quickly to the rest of us as well.

Indeed we felt so close to Rosie yet again as she gave another impromptu performance on the Thursday evening before sitting down and quickly falling asleep as usual.

Falling asleep...

Or so it seemed...

Until we tried to wake her up for a cup of tea.

But found that we couldn't.

The whole experience of someone dying in your company is, of course, extraordinarily... traumatic... whatever the circumstances... but it is especially so when you witness those who have shared so much with her... pouring their hearts out before her now inanimate body. A body but... even more a spirit, of course, which I increasingly sensed at that moment to be alive with us one minute but then... the very next, departing this world. On towards what many of us believe, or at least... desperately hope, is an... eternal... experience that lies behind all our lives.

Very quickly, I too found myself nearly as distressed as everyone, perhaps because of my already emotional reaction to my first week, and who knows what else was happening inside me... so much so I could not, nor did I even seek, to hold it back. Indeed, not many of us did. So much so it became a very easy decision as to what we should do next. Once the doctor and ambulance had been it was never going to be a matter of simply ending the week.

"We have all become very close and now more than anytime we need to stay together and be true to who we all really are and what we are feeling rather than run away from it," Anne said to both myself and Angie, a carer from the community, who had been with Beryl, Josie and Rosie all week and knew Rosie well.

So we gathered everyone together over breakfast the following morning to tell them that although we were all very sad and even in shock, we could not avoid what had happened and simply go home straightaway. So we would try to celebrate Rosie's life later that evening, our last evening, in the best way we could. Because, Anne tentatively tried to remind us, there was so much to celebrate even amidst such sorrow. Everyone was invited to contribute with stories and a few songs, and Angie would tell us a little about Rosie's life as she knew it.

Anne spoke privately to Angie and I in the garden later on. "We cannot share the kind of week we are sharing and then somehow separate this from what has just happened. We must trust in the spiritual presence within each person here, which I believe is alive right now like never before. God will be with us tonight, as will Rosie. I am certain of it."

And so... deep down, increasingly... I realized... was I. Sensing – indeed even at times experiencing – during that extraordinarily emotive and unforgettable evening, the eternal link between life... and death. Knowing that there is a force at work... over and above all that we do... that is an invisible... compassionate force... that I have... returned to calling God that continues... each and every day... to inspire all of us towards a greater... intimacy with regards to just who we are... if we will only let Him.

Helping us even to face up to and in time see beyond the terrible pain of... death, especially of someone... so dear to us. Into getting us beyond our... tragic... perception of it with His love... and understanding. Until, in the end, who knows... we just may come to wonder whether... death really is the opposite of life. Or ever has been...

Perhaps... yes... perhaps life really is... timeless and... unending for each one of us, including, of course, for Rosie and Hanif... and... yes, for Ellie too.

What an extraordinary blessing that is for each one of us.

What an extraordinary blessing to realize it on this earth.

Meditation

I do not seek to underestimate the anguish or torment that any of us suffer when I say that one of the definitive tests of us fully accepting God as the Supreme Being and therefore sole influence within our lives comes when we finally stop demanding of Him:

"Why did such and such a thing happen to me?" or "Why is such and such thing not working out for me?", however challenging or even overwhelming certain events may have been to deal with.

It is all very well praying or even pleading for Him to take absolute control, ultimately to live through us, but if we then persist, beyond, of course, our initial bewilderment and suffering, with years upon years of bemoaning what has or has not occurred, we have hardly been allowing Him to lead us out of whatever desperate situation we have found ourselves in. (That is, of course, presuming we have turned to Him in any way at all.)

We may well, of course, in our protesting and screaming, have even blamed God for these events, which may well have taken place randomly and even tragically outside His will through the way we or society in general has dictated that we should live.

But in the end, however they may have transpired, it is not heartless to say that we must surrender our all to Him, who really is there to comfort us when the fallout comes our way. However difficult this may be to accept amidst this disconnected, frantic culture within which we reside.

Indeed our all-loving God will inevitably try to offer deeper insights and opportunities to help guide us out of our sense of despair and narrower perception of how things really are. Crucially if we can calm ourselves enough to listen and to allow Him to transform our pain beyond its present torment.

All with the aim, at the end of the day, of leading us towards a realization that we really can – ironically especially amidst all that has been overwhelming us – wake up to a genuine experience of His spiritual presence. A presence which leads us forward in this world, through a growing realization of our eternal place beyond this world.

The greatest healing He can offer.

The greatest liberation He can offer.

But still, we may ask, just how is it possible to continue standing up courageously to today's mental conditioning and fearmongering that is always pushing our own beleaguered and misguided egos forward every time we lapse from our surrendered sense of who we really are?

Just how do we let go and remain single-minded enough to ensure that our major shift in awareness becomes embedded in our everyday consciousness and therefore guides our daily actions and indeed expectations?

Certainly by focusing and refocusing our attention, from the instant we stir ourselves in the morning to when we finally lay our heads down at night. But also by our commitment to act upon God's Divine nature within, which inevitably will deepen our relationship to Him.

So that this relationship becomes a living reality.

And a living embodiment of His presence.

With actions that increasingly we feel to be realigning not just our sense of what we do in our lives but primarily our very state of being.

Reflected in the wholesale spiritual transformation of who we are.

And the wholesale spiritual fulfillment of who we are.

Something that I would now like us to experience and maintain amidst a mass of people, the purpose of which is to try to stay focused outside the quiet of our own personal meditation and development.

Let's join some major event, such as a peaceful protest march, a spiritual gathering or some kind of carnival. Something that we will hopefully feel passionate about. Whatever, it will be far more of a celebration or appeal for life rather than any kind of drunken binge.

We may never have been on one before, but let us take a chance and invite some friends or even family members, even children to go with us. Never underestimate the impact on any one of them of connecting to what is so inherent within all of us: a sense of the communal, the radical and the sociable.

Importantly let's meditate at length before we go on just how extraordinary all our unique, earthly lives can become through God, leading ultimately to a wholesale transformation of just what we all might accomplish together. Anything, we may well feel, is suddenly possible.

When we arrive at the event, we may well feel confident enough to introduce ourselves to people outside our particular group. And obviously without launching ourselves at them straightaway and freaking them out (or certainly sounding like some evangelical tradesmen), gradually, gently and subtly tap into what inspires and unifies us all, once we get past the everyday and the various fronts we perhaps put on.

Simply ask them genuine questions about themselves and their lives, listening attentively and sincerely to their responses. Trying to relate to and to empathize with them, becoming aware of what truly makes them tick, and what is gracious and yes, spiritual, within them.

Above all though, let's listen silently to them.

And in that silence tune selflessly into them.

Looking into their eyes and indeed through their eyes.

To the light and energy of God within them, that is within us too.

Something that can reveal itself in moments of profound communication.

That can then lead us all to express ourselves instinctively.

To relate in ways beyond our initial expectations.

To act in ways that are compelling and vital.

That can become so empowering to all our souls.

And when coming together can have such a transforming effect.

Let's meditate and then reflect on this whole experience when we get home, recalling perhaps just how invigorated and excited we felt throughout it, how liberated and intuitive we may have felt.

Let's reflect too on just how increasingly proactive God is becoming in our lives and therefore, it may suddenly dawn on us, in so many lives.

Chapter 8

The Spiritual Life

So by now more and more of us are beginning to realize and indeed experience the ultimate truth about ourselves which we may well have become increasingly cut off from since early childhood:

Not only are we are all united with our spiritual God and Creator.

As well as to our fellow souls throughout this transitory life.

But, in the end, we are essentially manifestations of His eternal consciousness.

With His infinite power expressing itself through each and every one of us.

Our old selves – that is our egotistical selves – are superficial and limited in relation to this. A superficiality many of us bravely faced up to as we began to understand, despairingly at times, that some (or perhaps even a lot) of what we have done up to now has been rooted in self-preservation and therefore fear. Critically, because we were denied access to our higher potential by living apart from God's liberating and empowering presence.

The materialist, survivalist, capitalist world therefore is not only a shadowy deception, we discovered, but it is ultimately a tragic one borne out of faithlessness, in which we became indoctrinated into disavowing ourselves of our right to live harmoniously according to Divine grace.

As very many of us pursued, for the most part, our own desperate efforts to survive within not just a disconnected, but therefore a divisive existence, which some people have labeled "the rat race." What grizzly images we have come up with for the system which we have allowed ourselves or have felt forced to live under: cutthroat, dog-eat-dog, never mind the rats.

A system that has always sought to leave the vast majority of us content with the crumbs that fall off the table of the increasingly rich and powerful and even the mentally unbalanced. Or those running the show.

That is if we were able to find any crumbs, which increasing numbers in our world, of course, can't. An obscenity humankind continues to struggle to face up to on the scale required to overcome it. Despite the valiant efforts of so many courageous and enlightened people.

This relentless pursuit of crumbs, however luxurious, even caused so many of us to put to one side our recognition, in so many different ways, of just how fragmented and fragile life has become on a global scale. And of just how distant we have allowed ourselves to drift from the unifying spiritual vision God always had for us.

A full acknowledgment of which, at the end of the day – at the end, very often, of a turbulent, exhausting and humbling journey – has transformed our outlook forever. When, finally, we have begun to perceive ourselves, each other and our world so differently, at last united within God's overwhelming empathy, compassion and love.

Indeed on God's Higher level of consciousness, with our awareness that God is literally omnipotent and omniscient, we now know we can live, not just fearlessly and urgently for the good of all, but boldly and expectantly. In absolute harmony with our humanitarian instincts.

In fact, our spiritual awakening continues to raise us not just onto a more selfless but indeed a sacrificial level of awareness, now that God has nullified capitalism's insatiable and addictive sense of want. As, vitally, He moves us into whatever situation He requires of us with a vision and a voice that becomes our very own. Acting not just upon our faith but our experience of who we are in Him.

A relationship which spiritual teacher Joel Goldsmith describes in the following wonderful way:

> ... this is God's life which God is living as us. Once we begin to perceive this, we will understand immortality... we lose concern for our own life in the realization that God knows how to maintain and sustain His life, which is ours.[16]

His miracle of life, of which we have always been an integral part, but not fully conscious of, until now.

Indeed, our attention, inspired by God, is now fixed primarily not just on helping each other to flourish on this earth, but on sharing in our eternal truth, now that we see everyone in a whole new unifying light.

A realization that puts us at the forefront of God's ultimate work, which inevitably we feel inspired to carry out wherever we go. For we now know we do not have to be priests, lamas or imams. But now that each one of us is alive to God's presence within, we all feel able to make the most of every unique opportunity that comes our way, making us all potential outlets for His Divine love.

Not that God's presence is trying to establish anything new. For how can it?

It is merely ready and willing to call forth what has always been alive in the hearts of people everywhere, as gradually the shroud is removed from in front of so many eyes that, for so long and so tragically, has led us to act in conflict with our true natures.

Like someone struggling deliriously with heatstroke in the desert but ignoring the cooling, reviving presence of the nearby cave and the instinctive, calling voice at the entrance because, all along, we have become conditioned to follow the setting on the compass.

But now, alert to today's mass manipulation, and with our consciousness fully active, we all go forward confidently and purposefully, yet calmly and humbly, in direct response to the voice within that continues to guide us. At the same time looking to identify with the spirit of God within everyone else. Relating to them gently according to who they really are, not just the state of mind that may possess them at the time. As we make each moment a conscious and therefore a sacred moment being expressed through us.

We who are now expressing the ultimate, liberating truth, which will not allow us merely to judge or to try to control others, but to share God's peace with them.

Indeed, of course, it may well be, we will discover, that it is they who are seeking to share God's peace with us, as each of us reveals His empathy and care. Initially perhaps with regards to the weariness and torment and indeed the schism that has plagued us all for so long. As we offer and receive a concerned smile here, some gentle words there, some positive encouragement whenever, that just could... just could offer renewed hope and insight.

Small, selfless, loving acts being repeated everywhere, making a big, global difference. Inspiring each other in who knows what Divine direction for the betterment of all.

For example, in relation to important choices each of us may make in our lives, in particular with regards to our work, we may well find ourselves in situations where it becomes unbearable for us to enact policies or carry out tasks which we now feel are inherently wrong. Our previous trepidation at taking such bold decisions being gradually alleviated by the very different perspective we now have and the encouragement we receive from others.

For sure, this may lead to difficulties with employers still obsessed, for example, with excess profit rather than concerns about human rights or environmental consequences. But even in the most extreme of circumstances, where, in the end, we feel forced to change jobs, we may well find ourselves engaging in fresh, more creative, even influential campaigning roles we never imagined possible. Perhaps leaving behind seeds of doubt in the hearts of people at our previous employment.

So that eventually just maybe we will all start to witness more and more people making daring, courageous decisions reflective of their deeper selves, even if there are economic effects or a wholesale reevaluation of personal priorities that, in the end, we will all need to make.

As growing numbers of us start to become not just activists and messengers for our world but urgent activists and messengers. Rousing others right now, not in two or even in ten years' time, when our fears of today may well be fanned by even more fragmentation and floods tomorrow.

We through whom God always intended to express His true being, both as guides to humankind as well as protectors of planet earth, which the economic order has long since declared war on. Declared war not only on our increasingly precious resources but on that which sustains and breathes fresh life into us.

Not that, it must be said, those perpetrating this growing blindness and aggression are inherently ruthless at all. Because, as should be clear to increasing numbers of us by now, all these unnecessary acts of greed and belligerence, apparently taken on our behalf, are rooted in the destructive system of fear we relentlessly adhere to, seemingly apart from God. Not the innate sense of what makes people who they really are.

That is why, at all costs, more and more of us must expose it over and over, expose it at its core; and at the same time, expose the tragically blinkered desperation of those who defend it and refuse even to contemplate that it is in any way responsible.

Then, and only then, will we all be able to transform it fundamentally and critically, in time, come up with a more enlightened alternative – reflective of God's selfless and giving nature – that will at long last liberate us to live at one with who we actually are.

Harry's Story

I was staying with my 85-year-old mother for a time, helping her clear out her attic, so she could pass things on or let things go, as many of us do, towards the end of our lives. But also... also so that she might be able to help me with my long-term recovery... with filling in the very many large gaps in my memory that are still there... after what happened to me. Gaps that can't be rushed apparently, despite me trying so hard all the time.

She came across some old letters and writings from my grandfather William and especially my great-uncle Harry, who I was apparently named after. My late father had been interested in them and kept them in an old cardboard box, she told me.

"He used to say that some of the same thoughts and questions that concerned him... probably concerned them too. Even though they were from a different generation," she suggested.

I couldn't remember much that had concerned me at all.

Still, in my present predicament, I was encouraged to try anything.

I had met my grandfather fleetingly, during the six years our lives overlapped on this earth. My life missed overlapping with my great-uncle Harry's by around 40 years.

He died, aged 26, in a battle called Passchendaele.

The two brothers had clearly been avid letter writers, I discovered. Expressing their feelings for each other formally, but with genuine affection and good humor. The perils and therefore urgency of the Great War, which I began to look into in some detail, inspired a release to their emotions, no doubt, during those intense and overwhelming years of life and death.

I discovered from the letters that they said goodbye for the first, or it may have been for the final time for all they knew, in late 1914 when my great-uncle enlisted. My grandfather had been rejected by the army because of his asthma.

A wound and a shame he would carry with him for the rest of his days, my mother said.

Harry obviously still felt compelled to volunteer despite knowing just how much he would miss his brother. My grandfather was apparently left to carry on the family piano tuning and repair business with their father. And to look after his wife, Esther.

Harry was to die unmarried.

It is difficult telling from the letters exactly why the two brothers were so close. Two other brothers were born into this world apparently but did not survive more than a few months, my mother told me.

What emerges from the letters was not just my grandfather's fondness for his brother, but even more the... the light, it seemed, that he brought to his life. Though Harry was the younger by 18 months, he seemed to have an extroverted, almost magnetic personality.

"I can only imagine what you are up to over there. Or what the rest of your battalion is making of you. Esther says you would laugh the Germans into surrendering if you could only speak German!" my grandfather wrote.

But clearly my great-uncle had a depth to him too. A depth and perhaps a... passion that stirred his beliefs and his life. I found pages of quotations among his writings, including this one, copied out twice, from theologian and political economist, Thomas Chalmers, 1780–1847. It read:

Thousands of men breathe, move and live; pass off the stage of life and are heard of no more. Why? They did not a particle of good in the world and none were blest by them, none would point to them as the instrument of their redemption; not a line they wrote, not a word they spoke, could be recalled, so they perished – their light went out in darkness and they were not remembered more than the insects of yesterday.

Will you thus live and die, oh, man immortal?

Live for something, do good and leave behind you a monument of virtue that the storms of time can never destroy. Write your name by kindness, love and mercy on the hearts of the thousands you come in contact with.[17]

I suddenly and strangely felt a kind of connection to my great-uncle reading his fountain pen copy of these words from around 100 years ago now. My only personal link to him, to a past time, another world almost. And even though he was long since dead, a small part of him was still somehow alive. Still alive in this expression of his values for life...

I have no idea whether I have lived up to them up to now.

I am 58 apparently.

I hope to God I have lived up to them.

There is something about what they say...

An inspiration in their message.

But my life is a blank.

Almost as if it has been wiped clean.

What I recognized more than anything about my great-uncle, and clearly my grandfather was enthralled by too, was the confident... strangely fearless way he seemed to approach everything he did. This is as apparent from his writings before the Great War as during it.

He clearly did not seem to fear our ultimate fear, which for most of us must be death... or the uncertainty of what lies beyond death, I suppose...

My grandfather did not appear to be like that. He was far more of a cautious man, judging by his writing. He and my grandmother only had one child, my father. She too had to suffer a child dying, this time in labor, my mother said. He also suffered the agony of his beloved brother dying in a war which he could not fight in.

It's impossible to imagine just what these experiences do to people. Whether what they endure is to do with war, the loss of a child or some other... shocking event, I guess, in our more modern times. That, in my case I was told, it might just be too... difficult... maybe even painful for me to recall in detail. Nature, or whatever, may have blocked it out to spare me. To spare so many of us.

Beyond the bare facts that I know – that I had suffered some kind of... of "grievous assault." Apparently random like so many others today.

The following week, a major breakthrough, I received a visit. Or apparently it is finally deemed OK for me to meet two children, who I'm told are my own grandchildren. One is Daniel, the other Alice. Daniel is aged six. Alice is only four. My daughter, Bethany, apparently lives close to Bordeaux in France. She has flown over after hearing what had happened to me.

I show my grandchildren pictures of their great-great-grandfather, William and their great-great-great-uncle Harry, in their smart suits. Both with the moustaches of the day. That Alice thought was chocolate milk shake.

Suddenly I felt deeply moved by the intensity of the moment.

At the sight of my grandchildren staring at pictures of relatives long since gone.

Almost like they were... spirits reaching across the ages, I suppose...

Something my great-uncle might have said at least...

However strange it sounded to me...

What would they both have made of us at this moment, I wondered?

If they were still alive?

What would they have felt meeting these tiny relatives of theirs?

They would have embraced them for sure.

I knew this from the... compassion expressed in their letters. They would have embraced them if only for one second.

And I knew from his writings that Harry would have demanded that they not let anyone tell them what to do with their lives. But instead should try to live them to the full, and to listen to and to trust their own instincts.

"To trust the... spirit of God inside them," was the way he described it in one particular piece of writing...

My daughter... I was so grateful she has come all this way to see me...

I asked her about her mother, of course... my wife... she is alive apparently. I tried so hard to remember. She stared at my bewildered face. I looked back forlornly... and felt her pained expression.

The pain of some kind of separation, I guessed.

The pain of a turbulent separation, etched across her face.

"Mum's fine right now... she's back home," my daughter said.

Suddenly, I knew why this all had to be done so gradually.

Just what have I done with my life?

It all suddenly seemed so incredibly... traumatic now...

Surrounded by my... grandchildren... my family here... and there.

Trying to piece it all together was beginning to tear me apart.

My great-uncle, I soon discover, was far more than just a religious or spiritual man on Sundays. The more I read, not just letters but quotations, the more I sensed he somehow lived his life in a... boldly spiritual way... every day. Not like me, I was pretty sure.

Some of it to do with his young age and being single, I supposed. But perhaps it was simply the way... he was deep down... and chose to be.

He even seemed to live, to a degree, in this fearless way despite what he was plunged into between 1914 and 1917. However, the tone of his letters did alter noticeably from the time he and his battalion left by train and then arrived into:

"Mud, mud, miles of mud. That is what has greeted us, William. Everything and everyone is glued from head to toe. It's all there is. Someone really should arrange for us all to do a spot of gardening. Fair's fair. I've suggested it to the boys and they're game. In fact, they've delegated me to be head gardener. We could have a competition with the Germans. To tidy the place up a bit. I have absolutely no doubt we would win. I'll speak to the captain tomorrow."

Until three months later, deeper into the winter that bridged his first two years of war, his understanding of his new reality had clearly flattened his mood, if not entirely his sense of humor. This letter, to a cousin John, was written from home. Just as well as I doubt it would have survived the censors' cuts I have read about.

"Have I mentioned to you before, John, the impact of mud on our daily lives? I think I probably have! Well, it seemed that things had taken a turn for the better. When the mud became entirely frozen. The only problem is that it was frozen to us. Or we were frozen to it. As it is clearly the domain of the mud. Even when the boys chipped away at the iced mud, they could not get it off. Which is probably something to do with their hands being similarly frozen and therefore not functioning. A fact which makes the grasping of shovels and picks for various activities somewhat difficult. I led such a duty last week. I felt for them all during it, John. I felt for these boys trying to dig so deeply. I at least am older and increasingly feeling older. How are you and Francis, and your father and mother, by the way? Well, I hope. I trust."

Despite this letter, even in my early readings of what he wrote while on leave, there was little evidence of the extreme anger that I was convinced my great-uncle must have felt at the scale of some of the injustices, which we have become aware of over time. His understanding tone even seemed to extend to the mood back home in Britain.

A family friend, Gordon, wrote to my grandfather, "It was good to see Harry on leave. I felt he was in good spirits in spite of everything. He does not appear to harbor any ill-feelings toward people back here as I have heard other soldiers do. He simply says it is not possible for us to comprehend what is happening."

I wondered... would I have been the same?

Have I shown such understanding...

Have I shown such compassion in my life?

I hope to God I have.

Even in rare moments...

Meanwhile my mother seemed to remain quiet and impassive towards me for a mother. Was it simply a reflection of our relationship? Or of how she viewed me after what I have done or not done?

Occasionally she just stared at me... not glared... just stared... weary, perhaps, I hope, rather than anything to do with who I have been. I told her I was very grateful for her putting up with me... though I was not altogether sure what she was putting up with me about.

Only once, in his early writings, did my great-uncle's mood finally extend to breaking out of what I took to be his surprisingly... restrained tone with regards to what he had actually experienced.

At the top of a single sheet of paper he simply wrote:

Just what has brought us to this? Just what could justify it? How could we possibly allow it to happen? We, human beings, to whom love and mercy are so innate within us.

Finally, I came across his most striking piece of writing. An unusually long piece, clearly written on leave but from the perspective of still being at the front.

It... it had an extraordinary effect on me.

As finally it really struck me that a relative of mine, someone whose blood is my blood, had actually experienced such events firsthand. And even more remarkably had reacted in the way he did. I read it over and over... and I still do.

"I spend most of my time now helping these boys to write letters to their mothers and fathers, which is the greatest gift God has given me. The rifle and the pistol have become almost meaningless. The pen is now our most powerful weapon in expressing the anguish of what we feel and any meaning that is left in these, our physical lives right now. It's all we can leave behind trapped so inescapably here.

"It's far easier, I have learned, and I keep telling these boys, in their bewildered innocence, if we can somehow look differently upon all of this and accept that we do, in reality, have very little time left for this world and to write what we do accordingly. In fact, I demand this of them, almost cruelly.

"Surprisingly quite a few seem to manage it, in some shape or form, aided, of course, by the unyielding urgency of our predicament. But for some of the very young ones, the terror and the desperation to cling to life is so incapacitating amidst all this shattering noise.

"If only I could do more to help them confront their acute sense of helplessness, hanging onto what they feel in it, and to express it, I somehow sense they might also be able to experience a little of the strange peace that I am starting to feel. A peace that does not belong here, I know, and is beyond my full understanding, but there is no doubting its presence.

"So I feel I must badger and badger these boys into keeping their hands moving, at the same time preventing them freezing, so I can help them write and write about what they are feeling to the limits of what the censors will allow. Having been good friends with Jim Bryant, an old censor himself, has been a great help.

"For I sense so deeply that these boys are all God's children, and if only I can help them to glimpse this in what they express, just maybe I can get them to feel a little of His love. A love that I know is within them despite all that they are compelled to do.

"So that as many people back home as is possible will feel the true sacrifice involved in all of this. The true sacrifice of such Divine, yet unfulfilled love in them all – for wives and girlfriends, young children and babies, parents and grandparents, brothers and sisters – at least now partially expressed in such fragmented and tormented words.

"So that some of *them* may feel compelled to ask, why they should have had to suffer and lose so much? Enduring, at the same time, the even greater hell of feeling utterly abandoned and forsaken amidst it all. When no human being should ever have to feel so desolate. No human being should have to feel that their only desperate option while still alive here is to yield to the ultimate savagery that a fear of non-existence instills in them.

"Instead of being awake to the light that is truly in all of our hearts. The light that tells each of us that our experience of life should never simply come down to accepting that we will fall into some kind of oblivion at some point. But, instead, can usher in not just a greater understanding about life itself, but of eternal life no less.

"Expressing themselves in their letters therefore is, I believe, such a vital task both for themselves and indeed, in the end, for all those they leave behind. Through the unuttered feelings now uttered, the unwritten regrets now written, the unexpressed sentiments of love now expressed, through the outpouring of what is in their hearts right now, however muddled their words may be.

"All before they meet their final and inevitable resting place on this physical plane.

"So what God is actually doing through me, it suddenly struck me early one morning, is, in fact, not just helping to prepare them for death, but perhaps asking them to herald a greater awakening for our world too. With these letters that are certainly not mere laments to their parents but instead urgent messages from this front line. Hopefully to rouse everyone.

"Oh my God, may it rouse everyone before it is all too late for each and every one of us.

"For they are messages, dear parents, from your children crying to you, almost from the other side. Do you know what they have gone through to write this to you?

"Their hands the crippled state they are in.

Their minds the shattered state they are in.

Their souls the tormented state they are in.

The very least you can do is to search every word.

Handwritten by your own children.

"Their hearts pleading to you.

To read between the lines they have written.

You know their hearts.

So trust them.

Wake yourselves up!

To at least some of the truth of what they have gone through here.

For these boys tell me what they really feel.

I draw it out of them.

To give meaning to their short lives.

Urgency behind their extraordinary lives.

I demand they tell me.

They sweat blood over it.

And then we record it.

It is their last duty.

Before they confront their inescapable fate.

"It is incredible the energy God gives me for this.

The only purpose to our still being here.

The waiting will soon be over.

Even mine.

I could not go on beyond all this.

Because I must die with these boys.

I now know this.

For they are mine.

I am literally them.

United with them.

Our shared fate.

My sons.

Each and every one of them.

"That is what I feel.

Me, the old man now, aged 26.

"I no longer fear anything one jot.

Because if a bullet should enter my brain,

I will merely pass over entirely into God's realm of peace and love.

I am certain of it.

I silently await it.

As I go about my final days, even minutes.

With the zeal of the bullet that is heading for me.

So alive to my every moment.

My physical body having almost left me.

As I float above our already-dug graves.

Above the mud that still clings.

Invulnerable to all that rages around me.

Seeking out only the hearts of these boys.

While calling ceaselessly upon God.

So that in the end we may all smile upon death for the true liberation it brings."

This writing, it suddenly struck me, even in my empty state, was my great-uncle's final message for his generation and the generations that followed that of 1914–1918. This final recording of his brief life… just before his return to his… eternal God as he saw it.

I must admit that I was almost moved to tears when I first

read it, even though I can't... really grasp, of course, what I now see as his extraordinary... experience of God.

I was close to tears... perhaps because I felt the power of its... authenticity in the middle of my own personal situation... even though mine bears no comparison... and I rather suspect lacked any authenticity at all.

A situation where I felt... utterly helpless and yet strangely... urgent about everything...

Where I felt... very exposed... and yet desperate somehow to make amends...

Especially after reading my great-uncle's words.

Which perhaps told me, I don't know, that just maybe I still had time...

Whatever I have done...

However I have lived...

I could still turn things round.

And yet first I must remember.

What I may have blocked out.

What I am blind to.

I can see the pain... the fear in the eyes around me.

I sense something in the atmosphere that lingers around me.

Something has gone drastically wrong.

I must learn what...

I must be entirely honest about it...

... and try to put it right.

Before it is too late.

I then contemplated just how bizarre it was that once we have gone through some... devastating experience or even some crisis or... even a war in our lives... "simply getting back down to it" was the thing to do, something we were driven to do, something I still feel compelled to do.

But how does that approach really inspire the... new beginning that I sensed I should be seeking...?

That perhaps we should be all be seeking?

Instead of, at long last, pausing and trying to learn from our history up to now...

From the words of relatives who are dead but in so many ways still alive.

From the... spirits... of relatives that strangely go on and on.

The Spiritual Life 2

Increasingly liberated of our fear of death, once our hearts and minds are empowered by our growing realization of God's everlasting spiritual presence, more and more of us not only feel but now know that we have less and less to lose in this life, especially any traces of the faithless and increasingly tiresome egocentric self we have gradually let go of.

So that, at long last, we can live every precious moment of our time on this earth like never before.

Through the God we are alive to each day.

And are inspired by.

And the God we fall asleep with each night.

And are embraced by.

The same God who we now fully expect to guide us all away from the widespread delusions of the capitalist system, into far more selfless and indeed dynamic directions that, deep down, we now know we have been desperate to follow as the only way out of our enslavement. And indeed our world's enslavement, which, in the end, we begin to see is so interlinked.

So now, we feel for sure, is not a time to be anything but unceasing and intrepid in our surrender. As we persevere in offering ourselves over and over in acknowledgment of God as the heartbeat and provider of all. So that we then become filled with a real sense of intent about who we really are and consequently with an unremitting vitality to act upon this in our daily lives for the enlightenment and care of all.

Indeed, why would we not want to give expression to this right now?

The sense of freedom that comes with expressing it.

The depth of surety that comes with expressing it.

The unrestrained meaning that comes with expressing it.

As we live for the most part, on a completely different level from our former existence, sometimes, it appears, with little conscious effort on our part.

As we perform deeds and endeavors, way beyond our previous expectations, sometimes, it seems, in subsequent disbelief at what we have actually done... soon after we have gone and done them.

We, who are at last spiritually alive in God.

Spiritually alive in this life.

Open fully to the grace and power...

And... yes...

The very miracle that is available to each one of us.

For that is what our lives are, and always were, miracles. Something we become more and more aware of the more we live them as God intended them to be lived.

As God intended us to live.

Meditation

So, in the end, having perhaps risen from the depths of feeling there was absolutely no meaning to our lives, we finally begin to experience long-standing questions about who we are, why we are here and where we are going to evaporating into the energizing presence we now feel in unity with our ultimate being in God.

As we appreciate, in very precious moments, just what He meant when He said: "Be still and know that I am God."[18]

We are still right now. Very still. And we know. In this silence, that God is not just close to us. He is intimately with us. As the Highest expression of who we are. Of who we all are.

An experience of which inspires us to resolve that our lives will become not only continuous and conscious meditations in Him, but the focal point for all our revitalizing and harmonious actions, which will flow forth from Him.

So that is our final yet most essential meditation: on our whole lives as ceaseless and liberating sacrifices, entirely devoted to the God who created us and whose loving, fearless nature will forevermore be our very own.

Something we are determined to express and celebrate more and more each blessed day, with every encounter we live through having the potential to be a vital, transforming and unique encounter, especially in these urgent times.

Indeed why should this not now be the case?

For this is our God-given life we're living here.

Every cherished breath of it is.

So let's not seek to get it over and done with.

Nor let any job or person try to rush us out of it.

At the same time agitating us so much.

That we do not respond in the positive way God would respond.

In the way our true nature would respond.

Let's be at peace as God would be at peace.

And listen as God would listen.

To all those we share this life with.

And instinctively want to connect with.

Instinctively want to reach out to.

For there is plenty of time for work.

And the creativity of it will only improve.

The humanity of it will only improve.

The impact of it will only grow.

Through the centeredness of our hearts.

Through the unity of our souls.

Through the boldness of our sacrifice.

All flowing consistently from its Godly Source.

At the culmination of a journey that, for so many of us, has seemed to have taken forever. But in the end rings so wonderfully true, reflecting just what we have been through and finally blossomed into:

A child woken to this world,
Alive to its energy and wonder,
Nurtured by all that nature offers,
Meanders amidst gardens of inspiration.
Suddenly snatched.
No faith, no trust.
A mindset to be implanted,
Fear and consequence installed,
A rigid existence ruled by reason,
Our child is no more.
But search for meaning never deserts her,
Though at war within herself,
The raging torment of separation,
No material rewards will ever quell.
Suddenly surrenders.
Fresh insight, fresh perspective.
Offering an end to this hell,
Her Spirit reawakened,
To the silence that feels like home,
The intimacy that heals her soul.

Let God's spirit finally be roused in us all.
Let God's spirit finally empower us all.
So we can experience our unity with all.
Indeed our love for all.

The End

References

1. J. Vanier, *The Broken Body: Journey to Wholeness*, London: Darton, Longman & Todd, 1988, p 77
2. Albert Schweitzer in E. Fromm, *To Have or To Be*, London: Abacus, 1976, pp 158–159
3. Schweitzer in Fromm, op. cit., pp 158–159
4. *New Internationalist*, March 2012, p 16, quoted from Stewart Lansley, *The Cost of Inequality*, Gibson Square, 2011. Billionaires' figures quoted from *Forbes* magazine in Lansley.
5. George W. Bush quoted in the *Guardian* newspaper, January 2001
6. Fromm, *To Have or To Be*, London: Abacus, 1976, p 16
7. Fromm, op. cit., p 63
8. L. Freeman OSB, *Light Within: The Inner Path of Meditation*, London: Darton, Longman & Todd, 1986, pp 74–75
9. *Holy Bible, New International Version*, 2 Corinthians 12:9, Hodder and Stoughton, 1978, pp 1, 116
10. L. Freeman OSB, op. cit., p 75
11. Her Majesty the Queen, Christmas Message 2000, as reported in *The Times*, December 26, 2000
12. M. Scott Peck, *Meditations from the Road*, London: Rider, 1993, pp 197, 200, 202 13. M. Nainoca, Paper 6, "The Danger of Losing the New Testament Pattern of Simple Life-style," from *South Pacific Theology: Papers from the Consultation on Pacific Theology, Papua New Guinea, 1986*, Oxford: Regnum Books and World Vision International, 1987, pp 61–62
14. L. Freeman OSB, World Community for Christian Meditation *International Newsletter*, June 1999
15. B. Griffiths, *The Golden String*, Glasgow: Fount, 1979, p 117
16. J. Goldsmith, *Realization of Oneness: The Practice of Spiritual Healing*, Secaucus, New Jersey: Citadel Press, 1967, p 144
17. Thomas Chalmers, 1780–1847, Scottish minister, professor

of theology and political economist, found in writings of W. Strother

18. *Holy Bible, New International Version*, Psalm 46:10, Hodder and Stoughton, 1978, p 570

BOOKS

O-BOOKS

SPIRITUALITY

O is a symbol of the world, of oneness and unity; this eye
represents knowledge and insight. We publish titles on general
spirituality and living a spiritual life. We aim to inform and help
you on your own journey in this life.
If you have enjoyed this book, why not tell other readers by
posting a review on your preferred book site? Recent bestsellers
from O-Books are:

Heart of Tantric Sex
Diana Richardson
Revealing Eastern secrets of deep love and intimacy to
Western couples.
Paperback: 978-1-90381-637-0 ebook: 978-1-84694-637-0

Crystal Prescriptions
The A-Z guide to over 1,200 symptoms and their healing crystals
Judy Hall
The first in the popular series of six books, this handy little guide is
packed as tight as a pill-bottle with crystal remedies for ailments.
Paperback: 978-1-90504-740-6 ebook: 978-1-84694-629-5

Take Me To Truth
Undoing the Ego
Nouk Sanchez, Tomas Vieira
The best-selling step-by-step book on shedding the Ego, using the
teachings of A Course In Miracles.
Paperback: 978-1-84694-050-7 ebook: 978-1-84694-654-7

The 7 Myths about Love...Actually!
The journey from your HEAD to the HEART of your SOUL
Mike George
Smashes all the myths about LOVE.
Paperback: 978-1-84694-288-4 ebook: 978-1-84694-682-0

The Holy Spirit's Interpretation of the New Testament
A course in Understanding and Acceptance
Regina Dawn Akers
Following on from the strength of A Course In Miracles, NTI
teaches us how to experience the love and oneness of God.
Paperback: 978-1-84694-085-9 ebook: 978-1-78099-083-5

The Message of A Course In Miracles
A translation of the text in plain language
Elizabeth A. Cronkhite
A translation of A Course in Miracles into plain, everyday l
anguage for anyone seeking inner peace. The companion volume,
Practicing A Course In Miracles, offers practical lessons and
mentoring.
Paperback: 978-1-84694-319-5 ebook: 978-1-84694-642-4

Rising in Love

My Wild and Crazy Ride to Here and Now, with Amma, the
Hugging Saint
Ram Das Batchelder
conveys an author's extraordinary journey of spiritual awakening
with the Guru, Amma.
Paperback: 978-1-78279-687-9 ebook: 978-1-78279-686-2

Thinker's Guide to God

Peter Vardy
An introduction to key issues in the philosophy of religion.
Paperback: 978-1-90381-622-6

Your Simple Path

Find happiness in every step
Ian Tucker
A guide to helping us reconnect with what is really important in
our lives.
Paperback: 978-1-78279-349-6 ebook: 978-1-78279-348-9

365 Days of Wisdom

Daily Messages To Inspire You Through The Year
Dadi Janki
Daily messages which cool the mind, warm the heart and guide
you along your journey.
Paperback: 978-1-84694-863-3 ebook: 978-1-84694-864-0

Body of Wisdom

Women's Spiritual Power and How it Serves
Hilary Hart
Bringing together the dreams and experiences of women across the
world with today's most visionary spiritual teachers.
Paperback: 978-1-78099-696-7 ebook: 978-1-78099-695-0

Dying to Be Free
From Enforced Secrecy to Near Death to True Transformation
Hannah Robinson
After an unexpected accident and near-death experience, Hannah Robinson found herself radically transforming her life, while a remarkable new insight altered her relationship with her father; a practising Catholic priest.
Paperback: 978-1-78535-254-6 ebook: 978-1-78535-255-3

The Ecology of the Soul
A Manual of Peace, Power and Personal Growth for Real People in the Real World
Aidan Walker
Balance your own inner Ecology of the Soul to regain your natural state of peace, power and wellbeing.
Paperback: 978-1-78279-850-7 ebook: 978-1-78279-849-1

Not I, Not other than I
The Life and Teachings of Russel Williams
Steve Taylor, Russel Williams
The miraculous life and inspiring teachings of one of the World's greatest living Sages.
Paperback: 978-1-78279-729-6 ebook: 978-1-78279-728-9

On the Other Side of Love
A Woman's Unconventional Journey Towards Wisdom
Muriel Maufroy
When life has lost all meaning, what do you do?
Paperback: 978-1-78535-281-2 ebook: 978-1-78535-282-9

Practicing A Course In Miracles
A Translation of the Workbook in Plain Language and With
Mentoring Notes
Elizabeth A. Cronkhite
The practical second and third volumes of The Plain-Language A
Course In Miracles.
Paperback: 978-1-84694-403-1 ebook: 978-1-78099-072-9

Quantum Bliss
The Quantum Mechanics of Happiness, Abundance, and Health
George S. Mentz
Quantum Bliss is the breakthrough summary of success and
spirituality secrets that customers have been waiting for.
Paperback: 978-1-78535-203-4 ebook: 978-1-78535-204-1

The Upside Down Mountain
Mags MacKean
A must-read for anyone weary of chasing success and happiness
– one woman's inspirational journey swapping the uphill slog for
the downhill slope.
Paperback: 978-1-78535-171-6 ebook: 978-1-78535-172-3

Your Personal Tuning Fork
The Endocrine System
Deborah Bates
Discover your body's health secret, the endocrine system, and
'twang' your way to sustainable health!
Paperback: 978-1-84694-503-8 ebook: 978-1-78099-697-4

Readers of ebooks can buy or view any of these bestsellers by clicking on the live link in the title. Most titles are published in paperback and as an ebook. Paperbacks are available in traditional bookshops. Both print and ebook formats are available online.

Find more titles and sign up to our readers' newsletter at http://www.johnhuntpublishing.com/mind-body-spirit

Follow us on Facebook at https://www.facebook.com/OBooks/ and Twitter at https://twitter.com/obooks